SETH

— the —

ULTIMATE GUIDE

Discover Your True Self

Discover Your Place
in the World

Discover How We Can
Live in Harmony

PAUL M. HELFRICH

NEWWORLDVIEW
Castaic, California

NewWorldView, LLC
PO Box 604
Castaic, CA 91310
www.newworldview.com

Seth: the Ultimate Guide
Copyright © 2010 by Paul M. Helfrich
www.paulhelfrich.com

Cover Design: Joanne Knapp Helfrich
Cover Image: Tekla Brzoza Helfrich

All Rights Reserved. No part of this book may be reproduced or transmitted in any form or by any means, electronic or mechanical, including photocopying or recording, or by any information storage and retrieval system, without permission in writing from the publisher, except for brief quotations embodied in critical articles and reviews.

Library of Congress Control Number: 2010912627

First Printing: October, 2010
ISBN: 978-0-9828123-0-3

Printed in the United States on acid-free, partially recycled paper.

10 9 8 7 6 5 4 3 2 1

"In *Seth: the Ultimate Guide* . . . Helfrich brings out the humanity embedded in this material; there is no claim of infallibility, no dogma of absolute truth, and no rejection of skepticism and critical thinking. Instead, the Seth material provides a framework by which people can better understand their world and how to interact with it. The vast scope of this material is impressive, and Helfrich's organization of it is a tribute to his dedication to a formidable task, and to his articulation of the transformational potential provided by the exercises and insights that permeate these memorable texts, whatever their source." ~ Stanley Krippner, Ph.D., co-author *Personal Mythology*

"Helfrich's writing is knowledgeable and informative. He presents the exceptional and profound psychological and spiritual teachings of Seth with clarity. Readers who do not know Seth's work will find this an excellent introduction, and those who are familiar with Seth's writings will find the book a useful and guide to go deeper." ~ Arthur Hastings, Ph.D., author of *With the Tongues of Men and Angels: A Study of Channeling*

"Since the disincarnate entity Seth, along with other gifted spiritual teachers, has provided me with deeper insights into the quantum physics of the construction of the ego you may also find deeper insights into your own ego in this book." ~ Fred Alan Wolf, Ph.D., author of many books including *Dr. Quantum's Little Book of Big Ideas*, *Mind into Matter*, and *Matter into Feeling*

"Paul Helfrich has, magnificently, and with perceptive awareness, captured the important socio-psychological philosophy of Jane Roberts/Seth. He has lovingly and skillfully shared a gift of significant ideas, concepts and practices that can make our lives healthy and productive." ~ Gwendoline Y. Fortune, Ed. D., author of *Weaving the Journey Noni and the Great Grands*

"Condensing any body of philosophical work into an effective and meaningful reference is always a challenge (especially with one, like this, that began with 49 volumes of source material). But Paul Helfrich has done just that in *Seth: the Ultimate Guide*. This concise yet comprehensive overview of the revelatory teachings of author Jane Roberts and her channeled entity Seth provides an in-depth look at the most significant lessons and insights of one of the 20th Century's most profound yet underrated visionaries." ~ Brent Marchant, author, *Get the Picture: Conscious Creation Goes to the Movies*

"*Seth: the Ultimate Guide* is a highly intelligent and readable presentation of the Seth material. Helfrich concisely elucidates the often complex Sethian concepts and provides a much needed new doorway into our understanding of the reaches of human consciousness." ~ Elizabeth Cody Kimmel, author of *The Boy on the Lion Throne: The Boyhood of the 14th Dali Lama*

"Paul Helfrich has done a beautiful job of liberating the spiritual and psychological teachings of Seth from an earlier format that often obscured as much as it revealed. At such a critical time in human history we cannot overestimate the value of this gift re-given! Apply these lessons diligently, and expect transformative results." ~ James Bradford Terrell, co-author of *A Coaches Guide to Emotional Intelligence*

"Only a compassionate, sensitive and seasoned practitioner like Paul Helfrich could write *Seth: the Ultimate Guide,* a book for beginners as well as those who have long studied and valued Seth's ideas about Consciousness and the Universe. Thank you Paul, for lighting the way to Transcendence!" ~ Joyce A. Kovelman, Ph.D., Ph.D., author of *Once Upon a Soul*

"I have always found the Seth material helpful for my personal growth and I have always loved the integrity of the Jane and Rob material. I endorse Paul's book for helping create a positive context that one can examine the many ideas that Seth offers for one's growth in this life." ~ Charles Hauck, member of Jane's ESP class and metaphysical teacher

"This book totally rocks! As a long time Seth reader, Paul has boiled down the core Seth concepts into one delicious book that you'll be reading many times to experience the depth and breadth of Seth!" ~ Andy Dooley, Spiritual Comedian/Life Coach

Contents

Dedicated with Love and Appreciation to Jane, Rob, Seth,
And all the Speakers who inspire New Worldviews

Acknowledgments

There are many people whose creative efforts helped to inspire this book. Heart-felt thanks to Alan Aspinall, Sandy Astin, Marie Barton, Don Beck, Augustina Blake, Bill Booth, Ron Bryan, Mark Bukator, Laurel Butts, Winter Calvert, Maude Cardwell, Ron and Cathy Churchman, Hal Cook, Ed and Deejay Condon, Lynda Dahl, Lawrence Davidson, Rodney Davidson, Mary Dillman, Andy Dooley, Mary Ennis, Kaan Erdal, Sean Esbjörn-Hargens, Tom and Judy Ewing, Mary Fahey. James Ferrigno, Sean Foreman, Gwendoline Fortune, Kristen Fox, Norman Friedman, Jim Funk, George Garner, Barrie Gellis, Mark Giese, Jim and Loretta Gilbert, Ellen Gilbert, Lucy Gillis, Serge Grandbois, Arthur Hastings, Andy Hauck, John Hawkins, Judy Hensel, Bobbi Houle, Bill Ingle, Ray Irwin, Donald Johnson, Harry Johnson, Judy Johnson, Richard Kendall, Betty Kielty, Beth Kimmel, Jon Klimo, Frank Kollins, Stanley Krippner, Bruce Lipton, Sheri and Sabrina LoBello, Andy Maleta, Bill Marshall, Randy Martin, Carter Massie, Denise Mazzocco, Dawn and Morgan McKay, John McNally, Nardine Neilson, Masahiro Nishio, Barry Noonan, Ann Marie O'Farrell, Oshara, Andrea Pair, Vicky Pendley, Billie Petty, Erin Plummer, Gregory Polson, Bob Proctor, Jan Ramsey, Mary Rouen, Elisabet Sahtouris, Tom Sherlock, Carmen Silvers, Kerstin Sjoquist, Rick Stack, Rich Stammler, Samantha Standish, Michael and Helen Steffen, Helen Stewart, Emmy van

Swaaij, Linda Symans, David Tate, Clifford Taylor, Robert Tyrka, Stan Ulkowski, Robert Waggoner, Nancy and Helen Walker, Melinda Walsh, Tenzin Wangyal, Susan Watkins, Ken Wilber, Fred Alan Wolf, Maurice Wright, and Gordon Yarber.

Many thanks to the ninety-five folks who responded to my book questionnaire and provided me with invaluable feedback about which questions were the most important to ask (you know who you are!).

Big hugs to the more than five thousand intrepid souls who attended various Seth conferences, gatherings, dos, and passed through the Sethnet e-mail list since 1996. You helped me explore Seth's ideas and challenged me to find ways to explain them.

Special thanks to:

- Bob Friedman who believed in the need for this book.
- George Goodenow who introduced me to Bob Friedman and has supported my work for many years.
- Brad Reynolds, Huston Smith, and Ken Wilber for permission to use a variation of their charts on the Levels of Reality and Levels of Selfhood.
- Carol Funk, Elena de la Peña, Joyce Kovelman, Brent Marchant, and Christopher Johnson who provided critical feedback and supported me during the dark days.
- Nicolas, Frieda, Leon, Mary Ann, Nick, Eric, and the rest of my family for all the love and support these many years.
- My "partner in time"—JoRose—whose extraordinary dedication to the pursuit of excellence, creativity, and endless love made this project possible. She also edited the book and helped me find my voice. "Young love lingers so . . . ."

Foreword

I first read *Seth Speaks* by Jane Roberts in the summer of 1976, and it profoundly changed my life. The depth of wisdom on topics like God, life after death, reincarnation, Christianity, and spiritual transformation blew my mind. As I studied Seth's and other spiritual teachings in the three decades since, I came to realize that the Seth Material was one of the great contributions to Western spiritual literature of the late 20th century, though it is still not well known to the general public.

So when the opportunity to write an introductory book came along, I jumped at it!

The main challenges in writing this book—a distillation of forty-nine books—were to determine what to include, how deep to go, and how to best synthesize Seth's ideas for new and seasoned readers alike. The result is an overview of the central concepts, stories, and exercises in a question-and-answer format designed to reveal the secrets of *how* you create your own reality.

Many of the questions I sought to answer were gathered from the Sethnet e-mail list, which I moderated from 1998-2009. The questions are typically those asked repeatedly about the Seth Material, for example, "What's the best Seth book to start with?" or, "What's the best order to read the Seth books?" (There is no single best way, for people often like to randomly browse or read topics of interest based on personal needs.) I also received almost one hundred responses to a questionnaire about which questions to include.

As a result, this book was designed to help you approach the Seth Material *as a whole*, so you can explore any topic in the Seth books for greater depth and detail. It is organized into three parts in which Seth helps you to *Discover Your True Self*, *Your Place in the World*, and *How We Can Live in Harmony*. Together, these sections introduce Seth's "map of consciousness" and provide powerful exercises to get you started with the basics of reality creation.

The exercises are simple, and that's the key here—simplicity. They have been adapted based upon my own experience over three decades, and they are flexible, too. You can do them at your own pace, and tailor them to your personal needs so as not to take an overly dogmatic approach. The goal is to help you "face up to the abilities of consciousness" (Seth's challenge to us all) and develop your deepest potentials.

Though it has been well over four decades since Seth began to speak through Jane Roberts, we are still, in any collective sense, in the early stages of unpacking and applying the core concepts in the Seth Material. As such, the ideas are still very new, so you have a front row seat in which to explore the mechanics— the "how"—of reality creation, as well as the mysterious "you" who creates *all* your reality. Enjoy the journey!

Paul M Helfrich
February, 2010
Castaic, California

Introduction

What is the Seth Material?

The Seth Material was produced by Jane Roberts (1929-1984) and Robert Butts (1919-2008) from 1963 until 1984 through a process called "channeling" in which Seth, a distinct personality, spoke "through" Jane. She was also a prolific writer who published short stories and books of poetry, visionary fiction, and Aspect Psychology.

Seth, Jane, and Rob's work has been published in over forty books that have been translated into eleven languages and sold over seven million copies worldwide. Among these, the Seth Material—over 1,850 recorded sessions—exists in thirty published books. Their writing artifacts have been donated to the Sterling Memorial Library at Yale University in New Haven, Connecticut. The Jane Roberts Archives have been one of the most popular resources there for over fifteen years. Jane and Rob also held weekly ESP classes from 1967 to 1975 (with a handful of "unclasses" through 1979) that have been published as The Seth Audio Collection and individual ESP Class CDs.

Seth was a distinct personality with unique facial and vocal patterns quite different from Jane's. She and Rob held twice weekly sessions in which she would go into a trance state. Seth would come through and dictate information that Rob transcribed by hand, and then typed up. Jane often sipped beer and smoked cigarettes during sessions. After several years of laying a foundation, Seth announced one day that he was going to dictate his own books. The amazing thing was that Seth went on to *dictate every one of his books from start to finish with only minor edits.* Most of the books were delivered in a period of two work weeks!

Clearly something extraordinary was going on, something that neither traditional nor modern worldviews could adequately explain. Jane rejected the explanations of Christianity ("speaking in tongues" or *glossolalia*, demonic possession) and psychiatry (dissociative personality disorder, infantile dissociation). This led her and Rob to explore the phenomenon independently. The result was Jane's *Aspect Psychology*—a theoretical framework to better explain the Seth phenomenon—which was published in three books (see Chapter 14).

KEY IDEAS: The Seth Material was produced by Jane Roberts and Robert Butts through a process called "channeling" in which Seth, a distinct personality, spoke "through" Jane. While The Seth Material is valuable to millions of readers, the phenomenon that created it is not yet fully understood.

Why is the Seth Material Important?

The Seth Material provides a set of ideas that takes readers on a journey of personal discovery and transformation that radically changes their worldviews. Many of us have never been exposed to the spiritual or scientific ideas beyond those we learned as children or found in popular culture. The Seth books help us understand that what we've been taught is, at best, only half the truth, and at worst, outright lies. This applies equally to religious and scientific worldviews that compete for our souls and minds, while insisting that we never question their authority, and that we deny half of our humanity: our internal, intuitive, feeling selves.

Those drawn to the Seth Material soon discover that something *feels* right, familiar, and stokes our common sense, even in Seth's extraordinary claims such as, "I do not have a physical body, and yet I am writing this book."[1] Seth seems genuinely interested in our well-being, growth, and how we can develop our abilities to their fullest. He challenges us to be all we can be, and to take full responsibility for *everything* we create in our lives. He appeals to our inner knowing and to the eternal validity of our consciousness.

Seth explains that we are not at the mercy of a mythic god who lives in the clouds who, when angry, enjoys hellish retribution, any more than we are the random product of soulless evolution in a meaningless universe. The more Seth tells us, the more it becomes clear that traditional religions and modern sciences not only fail to explain the channeling phenomenon that produced the material, but also the relationship between our nonphysical and physical aspects of self.

It's important to maintain a healthy skepticism about every truth claim, because the Seth Material will challenge most of what you believe to be true about God, life, the universe, and most everything else. In the process, you begin to remember who you really are: a nonphysical being with innate intent and purpose who chose to be born into the physical world of space and time, life and death, joy and suffering.

In spite of constant media hype to the contrary, in Seth's view, you live in a safe and meaningful universe designed to nurture your every need and desire. A nonphysical part of you participates in the creation of the universe in every moment, and is a stakeholder and *ally* in the unfolding of your life and evolution itself. Further, you can learn to tap into a wealth of natural resources that are your birthright—the ancient heritage of your soul—and apply them to any challenge you face: health, relationships, money, creativity, and spiritual remembrance.

KEY IDEAS: The Seth Material provides a detailed system in which to better understand Your Self and Your World.

Are Seth's Ideas New?

Yes and no, according to Seth. The ideas are considerably old, as they have been revealed through inspired states to the founders of the world's religions and spiritual groups since the beginning of time. Unfortunately, as life conditions change and consciousness evolves, the potency of the ideas *always* gets watered down by human agendas, ignorance, and distortions. However, the ideas in the Seth Material are indeed *new* translations of revelatory information, though they have not yet been assimilated and practiced on a global scale. Thus, Jane Roberts considered Seth's ideas "The New Way," because they were unconventional and pushed against mainstream standards, as you will see throughout this book.

In this light, the Seth Material can be considered part of the Perennial Philosophy[2] that is consistent in all authentic spiritual teachings. According to author Aldous Huxley (1894-1963) it is:

> . . . the metaphysic that recognizes a divine Reality substantial to the world of things and lives and minds; the psychology that finds in the soul something similar to, or even identical with, divine Reality; the ethic that places man's final end in the knowledge of the immanent and transcendent Ground of all being—the thing is immemorial and universal.
>
> Rudiments of the Perennial Philosophy may be found among the traditionary lore of primitive people in every region of the world, and in its fully developed forms it has a place in every one of the higher religions.[3]

Today, we have access to all the world's major religions and can better see that perennial wisdom exists *in some form* in *all* of them. In spite of their varying origins, the following ideas consistently appear:

1. The physical field is not the only reality, because there is a nonphysical "source field" which is not usually perceived by the physical senses.
2. As long as we never experience our source, we live in a world of separation, illusion, and impermanence.

3. We can, however, learn to directly experience our source, within *and* without, through the use of deep intuitions (or what Seth called inner senses; see Chapter 1).

KEY IDEAS: The Seth Material is a fresh translation of perennial wisdom into the language and cultural framework of the late 20th century Western world.

Is the Seth Material "The Truth"?

The Seth Material is not offered as dogmatic absolutes, but as a flexible framework to cope with the challenges we face. *Seth never claimed to be an infallible source or hold The Truth or The Way*, and made this point very clear early on. He puts the responsibility of discerning the truth where it really belongs, on each one of us. He knew that in spite of his best efforts, there would always be some distortion in the translation process of his ideas into the mold of language. Moreover, Seth understood that as people read the information, they would interpret his ideas in light of their own stages of development and belief systems, which can dilute the process of understanding. As such, Seth never promoted the notion that Rob and Jane were producing un-diluted truth. Still, he knew that his material had a high degree of validity and low distortion.

The Seth Material's validity is ultimately dependent upon our ability to realize its transformative potentials through direct experience. The original mystical experiences that formed the basis of the world's religions and the Seth books can never be *fully* translated into words. As Norman Friedman, author of *Bridging Science and Spirit* (1990) said, "it is literally impossible to really understand these concepts because the mystics do not have a mystical calculus. In short, when the mystic has an experience, merely by the act of converting it into words or even possibly mathematics, it will fall short."[4]

Thus, translations of mystical experience into written form always calcify and eventually become distorted as centuries pass. The main difference between older perennial translations and Seth's is that his ideas are presented in their original form. The

Seth Material has been directly "translated" into the English language and cultural context. Even though his words have been translated into at least eleven other languages, his ideas still exist in a state of very low distortion.

KEY IDEAS: The Seth Material is not presented as Absolute Truth, but as a current, English translation of perennial wisdom. Seth admits that he's a fallible source of knowledge, and while his material is necessarily distorted to some degree, it remains highly valid.

Is Seth Starting a New Religion?

No. Most major religions, while based in Perennial Philosophy, instead promote unproveable claims that are to be taken on faith. The Seth Material is based on direct experience. For example, we can talk about honey being sweet or lemons being sour, but until you actually taste them for yourself, you won't be able to adequately discern the difference.

A religion also functions as a social framework to help people process major life events like birth, puberty, marriage, death, and communicate deeper meaning through ritual, doctrine, and dogma. Seth was clear that his ideas were not intended to be turned into any sort of official dogma.

In this regard, the Seth Material is "person-centered," meaning it focuses mainly on the individual *in relation* to the collective. While Seth discusses mass events and mass reality creation, he does so in a context that helps *you* explore the mechanics of reality creation. Of the thirty Seth books, only one deals with mass events, though historical material is sprinkled throughout. So Seth doesn't discuss things like modern law, music, sports, or economics, for instance, but instead, how you create your own reality *in relation to* social pursuits. Therefore, it's intended to empower individuals to realize their fullest potentials and contribute to society in their own way.

Because of its depth, it *is* possible to apply the Seth Material in an overly dogmatic way that mimics a religion. As such, there are three main mistakes to avoid:

1. **Seth in a vacuum**—to use "Seth said" as proof of truth. Just because "Seth said" this or that doesn't make it true. Seth provides a roadmap of consciousness that must be verified in the laboratory of your own subjective experience. You are the ultimate expert at being you.
2. **Lack of adequate discernment**—to take Seth's metaphors as literal fact. Much of what Seth talks about is metaphysical in nature. That means "beyond" physics, or our ability to empirically measure and verify his truth claims. As such, he relies heavily on metaphor, symbolism, and paradox to explain many ideas.
3. **Sethism**—to take the attitude that Seth is "the best" to the *exclusion* of all other teachings. This is a kind of fundamentalist thinking found in traditional religions and modern sciences.

The Seth Material does, however, exist within the larger context of the world's great wisdom traditions. As you explore it, you will find similarities, differences, and some completely new ideas. Also, it's easy to distort Seth's ideas if you take them too literally or over-intellectualize them *without doing his exercises to test the waters directly*. In this way, Seth provides an authentic system for personal growth and spiritual transformation.

KEY IDEAS: Seth didn't present a new religious dogma. Instead, he provides a "person-centered" system designed to help you explore the mechanics of reality creation. Beginner's mistakes to avoid are Seth in a vacuum, inadequate discernment, Sethism, and over-intellectualizing.

What is Channeling?

Channeling has been found in every culture throughout recorded history. Transpersonal psychologist Arthur Hastings traces it as far back as the Babylonian oracle of the goddess Astarte in the eleventh century BCE. He noted that ancient channelers who:

. . . spoke in trances and ecstasy were considered prophets or oracles for the gods. Even now, in various mainstream and minority religions, within many cultures, possession by the holy spirit, speaking in ecstasy, or possession by spirits is considered a sign of spiritual development, and is often encouraged and facilitated by ceremony and ritual. Channeling may be the current equivalent of ancient prophecy, bringing spiritual guidance and teachings for this time.[5]

Transpersonal psychologist Jon Klimo stated that:

Throughout history and among various peoples, channels have been named according to what they do. Besides the term "medium" and the more recent "channel," other names have included shaman, witch doctor, healer, and medicine man in native cultures. They have also been called fortune-tellers, oracles, seers, soothsayers, savants, and visionaries. In religious contexts, they have been known as priests, gurus, prophets, saints, mystics, and holy ones. And in the esoteric schools they are called light workers, initiates, teachers, adepts, or masters. The majority of mainstream [modern] psychologists and psychiatrists would probably regard the channels as hallucinating, delusional, suffering from dissociative identity disorder (once called multiple personality disorder), schizophrenic, or simply as persons with runaway imaginations, or even as downright frauds.[6]

The last sentence reflects most poorly on the narrow, incomplete view of human personality found in modern cognitive sciences, which have done little research on channeling. While acknowledging that people make fraudulent claims in *every* discipline, we must learn to adequately discern the veracity and utility of information from *any source*, be it a channeler, scientist, minister, philosopher, economist, or politician.

Klimo offered a useful working definition for channeling as:

. . . the communication of information to or through a physically embodied human being from a source that is said to exist on some other level or dimension of reality than the physical as we know it, and that is not from the normal mind (or self) of the channel.[7]

Sociologist Michael Brown defined channeling as ". . . the use of altered states of consciousness to contact spirits—or, as many of its practitioners say, to experience spiritual energy captured from other times and dimensions."[8] Hastings defined channeling as ". . . a process in which a person transmits information or artistic expression that he or she receives mentally or physically and which appears to come from a personality source outside the conscious mind. The message is directed toward an audience and is purposeful."[9]

Channeling can be traced in the United States to Helen Shucman (1909-1981) of *The Course in Miracles*, Alice Bailey (1880-1949), Edgar Cayce (1877-1945), and Helen Blavatsky (1831-1891), among others. An important feature of channeling is the *transmission of teachings* meant to enhance personal and collective fulfillment. While different than mediumship—the communication with those who are no longer physical—both serve important functions. Hastings cited Jane Roberts's work as marking "the dividing point between classical mediums, who called up spirits of the dead, and contemporary channeling, with its teachers, sages, and guides."[10] While there are various definitions of channeling, and even though Jane and Rob found the term misleading, channeling has become part of our reality and vocabulary. Like all definitions, it's open to continued research, debate, and refinement.

Recent research also suggests that we *all* have the ability to channel to some degree, just as we all have the potential to play a musical instrument, write novels, or play basketball. In this light, channeling may be one of "multiple intelligences" like music, mathematics, language, morals, emotions, interpersonal skills, athletic prowess, and so on.[11] The theory of multiple intelligences helps to explain why an individual may be simultaneously very good at some things (for example, writing), average in others (athletics), and not so good at others (math). As such, there can be endless permutations that reflect each individual's natural leanings.

However, if channeling is one of multiple intelligences, it has become atrophied because of various social stigmas. There are religious taboos (demonic possession, heresy) and scientific taboos (dissociation of any kind is always pathological) that have forced this ability underground for centuries. Since scholars now know that channeling has been with us for thousands of years, the Seth phenomenon also provides important evidence that channeling is finding its way back into the mainstream.

KEY IDEAS: There is a three thousand year old recorded tradition in which people speak in "inspired" states and deliver useful information geared toward cultural needs and real life challenges. However, it has become atrophied in the modern era due to religious and scientific stigmas.

Who, or What, is Seth?

Seth claimed to be an "energy personality essence" who had finished his cycle of physical lifetimes (Seth also used the word *entity* to describe the same thing). Jane soon discovered through her experiences with Seth that she was part of a different non-physical entity. The Seth entity was a unique "Aspect self" and so was Jane. They each retained their own identities while being nested like Russian dolls *within* an even larger psychological structure called "All That Is"—Seth's term for "God" (see Chapter 5).

Jane's ability to analyze and describe the Seth phenomenon required years of determined introspection and experimentation. Its creative aspects were undeniable: Jane wrote books, Seth wrote books, and Rob painted and added detailed notes to supplement the books. To find her own answers, Jane had to reconcile an array of psychic experiences. Jane searched for answers to the nature of personal reality with such intensity that she was able to pierce her own psychological veils, and journey deep into her soul. Spurred on by questions such as, "Who am I?" "Where did I come from?" "Where am I going?" "What is the purpose of life?", Jane opened an inner, psychological gateway in which the Seth persona could communicate. His job was to remind us of our own inner voices that spoke to us in childhood and before we were born.

Jane didn't like to refer to Seth as a "spirit" because of the limited connotations that word had within the occult field of her day. She intuited that the Seth persona was a kind of psychological dramatization into terms she could understand within the limits of her stage of development. She also sensed that there were others just like Seth who did not have physical form, but whose existence was as valid as hers. In this way, she sensed that the universe speaks to each of us through various forms of intuition and insight, and that we can learn to listen to our own inner messages and translate them accurately.

If Seth had a greater reality elsewhere, then what actually happened when Jane went into trance? Seth used the term "bridge personality" to describe the psychological structure that allowed him to merge and communicate through Jane.[12] During a session, both Seth and Jane made psychological adjustments so that Jane could "step aside" and allow Seth to merge with her subconscious mind to form a distinct yet temporary personality. However, his true identity and natural focus of attention existed in a nonphysical domain. Therefore, the bridge personality was neither fully Jane nor fully Seth.

In terms of Aspect Psychology, Jane likened her Seth Aspect to a psychic telegram from her entity (soul), one that came with a complete, though temporary, personality structure called a "personagram." It had its own electromagnetic and psychological characteristics that existed only under certain conditions—a trance state that was like a waking dream. However, she intuited that Seth's native state existed outside of our space-time framework.

So the Seth persona we know in physical terms is really a composite of psychological elements, *a temporary construction* that takes on the form of recognizable human characteristics. These include emotions, facial expressions, gestures, sense of humor, and even an accent in order to communicate in acceptable ways within our cultural framework.

KEY IDEAS: The Seth Material was written by a "bridge personality" who is neither fully Seth, nor Jane, but a hybrid. Seth is not human in any traditional or modern definition, and has an autonomous existence independent of physical reality.

Can Anyone Else Channel Seth?

Seth said that he would speak through Jane Roberts "exclusively" in order to maintain his material's authenticity.[13] However, Seth also said many times that, "There are no closed systems."[14] This means that while it *was* theoretically possible for someone else to channel Seth, he *chose* to limit his relationship to coming through Jane for good reasons, to prevent others from hijacking or distorting his ideas by using his name as proof of validity.

Still, people wrote to Jane over the years claiming to channel *her* Seth. To Jane's credit, she was able to debunk these claims as poorly discerned instances of *contact with their own or different entities*. Jane had a no-nonsense approach to dealing with her readers' inexperience. For instance, a man called her up to say that Seth had come through on his Ouija board the previous night. However, he was confused because he had read Seth's statement that he would *only* come through Jane. So what was going on?

Jane explained to him that a variety Seths had appeared out of the woodwork since the publication of the Seth books. However, they weren't her Seth, but a case of mistaken identity for *some* version of his inner self or *other* nonphysical entities. Thus, her Seth served only as a symbol for something deeper within him— his own wider awareness.

Moreover, just as there are over six billion people alive today, there are billions of entities (souls) who may contact and interact with you. The best advice if you were to contact "Seth" is to *call it anything but Seth*, because you are actually contacting a deeper part of your *own* multidimensional awareness. With time and practice, you will learn to more accurately discern the nonphysical entities you come in contact with.

KEY IDEAS: Seth is on the record clearly stating that he would not come through any other people, in order to maintain the integrity of his material.

Is Seth the Only Channeled Source Available?

Hardly! Channeling has a rich history in the United States that dates back to the Spiritualist and New Thought movements in the mid-18th century. However, many agree that the Seth Material represents a gold standard for high quality, practical application, and low distortion in the postmodern era. As such, it paved the way for new generations of channelers to "go public" and present similar information.

One of the most well known is Abraham, channeled by Ester Hicks. She and husband Jerry Hicks have produced a number of best-selling books in the new millennium. They acknowledge the powerful influence the Seth Material had on them when they were starting out in the 1980s. Other channelers influenced by the Seth Material include J.Z. Knight/Ramtha, Serge Grandbois/Kris, and Daryl Anka/Bashar.

Dozens more channelers have "gone public" and tens of thousands more channel in the privacy of their homes and local spiritual communities.[15] Of note is Mary Ennis who channels Elias and has provided a body of work that expands many of Seth's ideas. There is no claim to be channeling Seth, just expanding on many of his core concepts.[16]

Even though Seth said he would only come through Jane Roberts, his ideas are a translation of inner knowledge that *exists independently* of the Seth entity. This knowledge is known by various names in different cultures such as Akashic Records, Cosmic Memory, Terma, Gongter, Mind Treasure, etc.

As you will see, Seth outlined a way to access this information through what he called *alpha states* (see Chapter 7). With time and practice, *anyone* can learn to directly access the kind of ideas found in the Seth Material. The key to remember is that the ideas will *always* be colored to some degree by the overall stage of development, language, and cultural beliefs of the individual channeler.

As such, it *is* possible for you to learn to channel your own entity or another entity like Seth and access similar inner information. The possibilities and creative potentials are endless, though it's best not to get too hung up on whether you're initially making contact with Christ, Buddha, Seth, or other "enlightened masters." That will get sorted out with time, practice, and peer feedback. The main point is that you have direct access to your own wider, enlightened awareness, and the Seth Material provides an excellent springboard to get you started.

KEY IDEAS: The Seth Material exists in relation to many other excellent bodies of spiritual material. It is best known for its high quality, practical application, and low distortion.

Toward a New Worldview

A worldview is defined as the sum total of all intention, behavior, cultural values, and social systems from which any individual or civilization creates its reality. As you will see, Seth's ideas were intended to nurture an emerging new worldview on a global scale. The exciting part is that you have a front row seat to experience how that unfolds!

Sociologists like Jean Gebser (1905-1973) have shown that *cultural development*, while far from a linear (consecutive) process, consists of cultural worldviews that evolve gradually in hierarchical stages of increased complexity (traditional, modern, and postmodern).[17] Each subsequent stage *is built upon the foundation that preceded it.* As they unfold, each worldview creates new challenges that can only be solved by more sophisticated perspectives, or risk regression and arrest. Einstein intuited this when he said, "The significant challenges we face can never be solved at the level of thinking we were at when we created them."[18]

Seth said this in his own way, namely, that consciousness is in a state of constant expansion, which by *its very nature* will lead humanity beyond its current limits. Thus, we will inevitably create problems that can't be solved within the limits of current worldviews. As such, the challenges created by one stage of development will provide the impetus for human evolution to move into new areas of consciousness to provide solutions.

In this light, we now face the dawn of a new worldview struggling to be born. Old ways no longer provide all of the answers. We need new ways to help us solve our problems and get along on an unprecedented global scale. Change is in the air, and the birth pangs involve a *shift in consciousness* never seen before in human history. Seth also predicted a religious reformation that will feature the return of the "Christ entity" to be completed by 2075. The Christ material is among several controversial subjects that include Atlantis, UFOs, alien technologies, Bigfoot, and more (see Chapters 8, 9, and 10).

Seth also suggested that his material would someday become an accepted part of Western culture, and eventually sweep through the world like wildfire.[19] Was this the beer talking, the grandiose ramblings of an inflated ego, the musings of an authentic "prophet," or something in between? It is still too early to tell. As you will see, Seth's ideas are not designed to diminish or subvert previous knowledge sources, but to become a legitimate contribution to the overall knowledge quest.

The goal of this book, therefore, is to contribute toward the realization of those probable futures. It raises more questions than provides pat answers, for every answer provokes new and better questions that reflect the process of growth and evolution.

The channeling phenomenon that produced the Seth books is part of a larger spectrum of altered states that connect us with our own inner knowing—peak experiences, meditation, lucid dreaming, out-of-body projections, shamanic drug-induced, and so on. These states have been consistently experienced throughout recorded history and yet they're still excluded from mainstream Western scientific understanding. As such, you can learn to use the Seth Material to access these states as shamans, yogis, and spiritual adepts have done for thousands of years. For they provide a natural gateway to directly explore the secrets of reality creation.

A journey of personal discovery awaits you. Strap yourself in for the ride!

KEY IDEAS: You stand at the edge a new worldview, one you create individually and collectively to provide new ways to solve problems and help us all get along on an unprecedented global scale. The Seth Material is a transformative tool to help you on that journey.

—PART 1—

DISCOVER

YOUR TRUE SELF

Chapter 1: You Are More Than Your Body!

Who is the "You" Who Creates Your Reality?

Seth used many different words and ideas to point out the multidimensional nature of being. In the simplest terms, our *personality* is the Aspect that exists in space-time, and our *identity* is the Aspect that exists outside of space-time in what Seth calls the "unknown" reality. Personality lives and dies in a physical body, but identity is a "source self" that is eternal and indestructible. This is Seth's version of the differences between our physical body/mind and immortal soul.

If you're skeptical about having an immortal soul, that's fine. As we saw earlier, healthy skepticism is a trait strongly encouraged by Seth. As such, various exercises are included throughout this book to help you explore the ideas and put theory into practice. The idea is to never take anything "Seth says" as final proof of its validity. We will always come back to our own direct experience for that.

A way to better understand the difference between personality and identity is to imagine yourself as "one made of many." In other words, your physical personality is a distinct "Aspect self" that functions like a nested Russian doll within your nonphysical identity, which in turn functions as a wider "Aspect self."

Your personality has likes and dislikes. You're better at some things than other things. You give yourself a name and others call you by it. Your personality is associated with your body that consists of various physical aspects—organs, bones, nervous systems, immune systems, blood systems, and more. Each consists of smaller aspects called cells—around 55-75 trillion of them. Your cells are made up of molecules like potassium, hydrogen, nitrogen, and oxygen. These molecules consist of quantum fields made of aspects like protons, electrons, neutrons, quarks, bosons, and even smaller "strings" called p-branes.

Each of these parts of your body is a whole that is always greater than the sum of its parts, or aspects. Your personality is similar to this, and it eventually incorporates your identity. So you are like an "infinite onion"—the more layers you peel back or add on, the more "wholes made of parts" you find!

As we said, your identity exists outside of space-time. It can be thought of as an *entity,* which Seth refers to by a name. Throughout the books, he refers to Jane Roberts as *Ruburt* and Rob Butts as *Joseph. Entity names* include all the Aspects within their identities, and are a unique feature of the Seth Material. If you were to talk to Seth, he would address you by an entity name.

This is Seth's way to help you imagine yourself as something much more than your physical personality. It can seem mysterious at first, because for all you know and remember, you appear to exist only as a personality in space-time. Seth says that we intentionally "forget" our deeper identity for a variety of reasons, chief of which is to create new experiences, something highly sought and valued by our entity.

KEY IDEAS: You are a multidimensional being who simultaneously lives in physical reality and an "unknown" nonphysical reality.

What is the Conscious Mind?

Seth also referred the personality/identity system as the *conscious mind*, because there are no isolated parts. Just as a fish doesn't know it's surrounded by water, our personality isn't generally aware that it's nested within a vast multidimensional entity. Once we become aware of our entity, we realize that we are much greater than just our physical self. Your entity can seem god-like, and making first contact is often a mind-blowing, life changing experience. In traditional terms, these experiences are called *satori, revelation, gnosis,* or *enlightenment.*

Seth's point is that *you have direct access to your entity via the conscious mind.* However, most of us have yet to develop this ability. So while direct contact with our entity remains a latent potential realized by few, the potential is in each of us and represents the next great evolutionary leap for humankind. Seth's map of consciousness is clearly intended to help us navigate this transition knowing that what we experience is real, healthy, necessary, and not at all pathological.

Seth described three complementary structures in the conscious mind:

- **Personality** (consists of an *outer ego* or waking identity)
- **Subconscious** (mediating function between outer and inner)
- **Entity** (consists of an *inner ego* or eternal identity)

Put simply, *this is the multidimensional "you" he refers to when he says, "You create your own reality."* This is a very important map to understand, because most of us have been taught from birth that we exist as a single, separated self, isolated from everyone and everything else.

One way to understand this is to think of the conscious mind as an iceberg. The tip of the iceberg represents your personality, the outer ego-self. The air around you represents the space-time framework that you live in. Here time unfolds from past to present to future in fairly predictable fashion.

The water line acts as the subconscious "layer" between the tip and submerged Aspects of the iceberg. Your subconscious manages vast amounts of physical, emotional, and mental data, which frees up your personality to do other things like cooking food, reading books, or inventing warp drives. Your subconscious never rests, and works constantly to track all your experience—feelings, smells, tastes, sights, sounds, etc. It automatically digests your food, grows your nails and hair, and regulates body temperature, blood sugar, and neurochemistry.

As you move beneath the "subconscious" water line, you find a much larger entity that exists in the "unknown" reality—a *spacious present* without space or time. This dimension may seem mysterious or alien since you can't perceive it with your physical senses or intellect alone. To explore it, you need a set of psychological "deep sea diving" tools called the *inner senses* that we'll explore shortly.

From this perspective, deep within the ocean of identity, we can also contact other lifetimes—other selves that exist in other time frameworks. The personality you know is but one of many within your entity. Imagining yourself as a "cell" or "organ" within a multidimensional being takes some getting used to!

But Seth, in his clever way, provided a variety of practices to test this directly. The following is a simple method to familiarize yourself with your own entity.

Exercise 1—Feeling-Tones

Reminder: Seth's exercises should always be done with an open mind, playful heart, and curious spirit. They're intended to reveal aspects of experience that normally escape your attention by manipulating your consciousness in a fun way. The idea is to tailor them to your personality's unique desires and intent over time.

Now, find a place where you can sit quietly and won't be disturbed. Make sure your cell phone is off, and clothing is comfortable. Undo your belt, or take off your shoes, whatever helps you to relax.

Next, slowly take 2-3 deep breaths to release any tension. Then close your eyes, and turn your attention inward. Take time to settle your body, feelings, and thoughts.

Now, sense the feeling-tones of your being. Simply sit in silence, and remind yourself that these feeling-tones exist. You will sense them in your unique way.

Simply *experience* the feeling-tones of your being.

Try to minimize whatever preconceived notions you have of what's supposed to happen.

Whatever happens is exactly what is supposed to happen. The only standards here are found in your own feeling-tones of being.

As you think, "Am I doing this right?", simply allow the thought to come and go. You can't do this wrong. It's very easy. Simply *be* your awareness, your being, your self, and become familiar with how it *feels*.

If you experience *emotions* like peace, gratitude, joy, or bliss, they are *not* feeling-tones. They are states that will result from centering your awareness on the simple feeling-tones of your being. Try to sense *beneath* your emotions to find your own unique feeling-tones.

There is no time limit, keep it enjoyable. This practice will help you get in tune with the deep rhythms of your being. Concentrate on the *being* aspect, not the thinking aspect.[20]

Finally, a lot of people miss the boat by assuming that creating your reality involves mostly the outer ego and its beliefs, thoughts, feelings, memories, etc. According to Seth's "iceberg self," this is only one third of the reality creation story!

KEY IDEAS: The "you" in "you create your own reality" is much more than your outer ego. It includes your subconscious and inner ego. Together these form the conscious mind—the "you" who creates your reality.

Why are the Inner Senses Important?

In the West, we have become culturally conditioned to believe that our five physical senses—sight, hearing, smell, touch, and taste—are the only scientifically valid means of perceiving the truth about reality. On the other hand, traditional religions often promote a limited view of mystical states as being the domain of their founders and leaders. As such, they often discourage others from exploring mystical states by accusing them of being false prophets, heretics, or demonically possessed.

However, both are true but partial perspectives and have something to offer. We now know that there are different yet complementary ways to perceive truth, and they work together to create our reality. For example, the Christian mystic St. Bonaventure (1217-1274 CE) long ago described three "eyes of knowing"[21]:

- **Eye of contemplation** (beyond facts, direct, experiential)
- **Eye of mind** (intellectual, *mediating, interpretive function* between contemplation and physical)
- **Eye of flesh** (five physical senses)

All three provide valid ways of "seeing" the truth about reality. However, when we confuse them or claim that only one is the best or only way, we severely limit our capacity to discern or express truth. Modern science includes *only* the eyes of flesh and mind, and completely rejects the eye of contemplation. Traditional religion over-emphasizes the contemplative visions of their founders and minimizes the importance of the eye of flesh that underlies scientific method.

Seth's inner senses stress the crucial function of the "eye of contemplation" that modern science has marginalized. Like a muscle that doesn't get regular exercise, our inner senses have become atrophied. This situation is made worse by the constant bombardment of mainstream messages that elevate reason and intellect over feelings and deep intuitions. Seth's main point, as some scientists and mystics know, is that *they all work together for a more complete picture of the truth about reality.*

The inner senses still abound in the popular imagination as "the sixth sense." They complement our physical and mental senses (intellects), but Seth says they are used primarily by the inner ego, not the outer ego. The inner senses do not function in the outer ego until they can be handled correctly because they utilize the core energies of reality creation—they are literally used to create worlds!

As we learn to use our inner senses, Seth strongly encourages us to maintain equilibrium between our physical, mental, *and* inner senses. With time and practice, our outer ego widens its awareness as it learns to venture more deeply into its subconscious and inner ego. Seth challenged Rob and Jane early on to develop their inner senses. Later he challenged the students who attended Jane's ESP classes. To get started, you must stop identifying exclusively with your outer ego, and learn to identify with your inner ego. Once you make this conceptual shift, you will begin to activate and control your inner senses. However, you must demand your very best effort as you experiment.

The Seth Material is not for those who want a "dummies guide" to reality creation, though material like that serves a useful, introductory purpose. Seth insists you must *develop* your intellect *and* intuition, since those abilities are central to consciously creating your reality. You must be willing to work hard, but as always, Seth reminds you to keep it fun and be playful, joyous, and spontaneous.

The inner senses can be grouped into three main types that work together, just like our physical senses. These are not hard and fast designations, for they ultimately blur together as understanding and experience deepens:

1. **The empathic senses** are not empathy or compassion as we understand them, but involve a literal mergence with any object, creature, or person. In the case of a person, it means feeling their emotions, bodily sensations, and feeling-tone of identity. A playful example is *Being John Malkovich* (1999), a movie in which people entered a portal inside the actor's body/mind and shared his every experience for a short period.

2. **The conceptual senses** are also a type of mergence, but rather than merging with a "thing" where you experience the qualities of "thingness," you get inside of a *concept pattern* or multidimensional blueprint of an idea. A concept pattern is a potential for action that isn't limited by the boundaries of a "thing." With the conceptual inner senses, you are able to play guitar like Jimi Hendrix or paint a picture like Cézanne. These inner senses are used

in what is called *god-communion* or *mystical union* with All That Is.

3. **The time-based senses** involve experiences with forward, backward, shortened, stretched, and sideways time sequences. An example would be experiencing the richness of a long life in a single day, or an hour that stretches for centuries through the lens of a snail's nervous system. They also serve as the gateway to other time frameworks and dimensions. (For details on the nine inner senses, see Appendix 1.)

Exercise 2—Psy-Time

In the Feeling-Tones practice, you began to experiment with psychological time, or *psy-time*. This is the gateway inner sense that opens the doors of perception and activates the other inner senses. In this practice, we'll go a little deeper.

Once again, find a comfortable place to sit. You can even lie down, but the idea is to remain awake and alert, not to fall asleep.

Now, imagine that your inner world is as real and vivid as the physical one. Gradually turn off your physical senses. Simply turn your attention inward, and imagine that you have a set of inner senses you can activate with your mind. You can mentally flip a set of switches, turn on inner lights of different colors, or imagine taking a dive into an inner ocean.

Another choice is to turn your attention to your "mental screen," a place centered in your forehead, until lights, patterns, or colors appear. If thoughts intrude about daily worries or trivia, simply observe them, and allow them to go away. Then return your attention to your "mental screen."

You are not ready to proceed until your attention settles on only your inner senses, inner ocean, or "mental screen."

After a while, you will feel alert, aware, present, and very light. You may begin to see bright lights, or hear sounds or voices. As you progress, you will begin to feel apart from your physical time sense, because you're essentially turning it off, and turning your inner senses on. Your time sense will begin to stretch, flex, and flow in its own unique way.

Gradually, you will begin to have various kinds of inner experiences. These may include extrasensory episodes, or periods of inspiration and problem solving. They may also lead to out-of-body experiences.[22]

KEY IDEAS: Our inner senses reveal our independence from physical matter and help us become aware of our unique multi-dimensional identity. We can learn to use them to discover our inner source and enrich our physical lives.

What is Your Purpose in Life?

Some of the biggest problems facing people today are feelings of alienation, depression, and lack of purpose. The symptoms are all around us: broken families, crime, wars, drug addiction, sex addiction, food addiction, and on and on. If we live in a meaningless, chance-driven universe, as modern science claims, what's the point of living? Do we really suffer from religion's "original sin," which claims we're flawed from birth because our spiritual parents, Adam and Eve, disobeyed God?

Seth says it's no wonder we've created so many *dis-eases* and social problems, given the conflicting and destructive values we're taught from birth by mainstream worldviews. Not only do we "live in a safe universe"[23] designed to nurture our every need, but we, as multidimensional beings, *each have an innate purpose.* But it has nothing to do with science's selfish genes or God's will. It has to do with our entities. Nice!

Seth introduced what he called *families of consciousness* to show how our entities work directly with us to create our reality. The families of consciousness are a metaphor, symbolic of something deeper within us. They are primordial "psychic races" that provide the "source energy" that fuels our universe, planet, and bodies.

Seth used a family metaphor because it is our most basic and cherished social structure. Culturally speaking, the family concept forms the foundation of our social, religious, economic, political, and legal institutions. Jane regarded Seth's families of consciousness as a thematic framework to help us perceive and better understand aspects of our entities that have been ignored by modern scientific disciplines, particularly psychology.

To better understand this, take a moment to imagine the psychic reality of the 6.5 billion human beings with whom you share the planet. Imagine this collective as a "Rainbow of Consciousness," where each color represents a single family intent. When viewing this Rainbow from afar, you can't find the exact place where red ends and orange begins, yet you can clearly distinguish both colors. As your vision zooms in, each color reveals shades of gradation, and the edges that seemed to separate from a distance disappear. From this perspective, the nine families similarly extend into an *infinite spectrum* of consciousness with lots of room for variations. As such, we aren't limited to nine discrete "colors" or intents, and there is great diversity *within* each family.

Seth stated that he, Rob, Jane, and many of their students belonged to the *Sumari* family (artistic intent). In larger terms, we can slice the "pie of consciousness" any way we like, but as we explore the collective group of entities responsible for the creation and maintenance of our universe, we will come to share an emotional and psychological feeling that *belongs to* one of these nine main groupings.

Ironically, Seth pointed out that those with Sumari intent will tend to have some difficulty with his metaphor. Are there really nine families? Why not seven, or sixteen? How can our entities be expressed in such finite terms? Even Rob and Jane experienced initial skepticism when Seth introduced this idea in such concrete terms. However, Jane quickly intuited that each family could have subdivisions that focused upon endless varieties of specialization depending on the general life conditions in any historical period. So mathematically there could be hundreds of thousands of permutations of these innate or soul intents, and that made more sense.

Jane also cautioned that the names and their characteristics shouldn't be taken too literally. They are not clubs, cults, or a new way to marginalize people. It is a typology of innate intention that exists at the soul level, one that influences and colors *all* reality creation, and gets reflected in our physical lives.

In other words, we don't want to limit our thinking to nine "tribes" and use this as a means to separate or rank people. In fact, this is a beginner's mistake to avoid. Instead, Seth's family metaphor is meant to help us better understand the amazing diversity expressed within *all* human beings. It is a typology that transcends race, color, creed, sexual preference, and other "tribal" associations. Thus, they are complementary expressions of purpose and intentionality within *all* people and entities (see Chapter 6).

The main point is that you are born with an individual purpose in life! You, as an entity, chose a unique predisposition, so that within any social role, job, or situation you *naturally express an interest* in healing, or fine arts, or parenting, athletics, spirituality, teaching, invention, reform, discovering new truths— anything under the sun! Therefore, identifying your intent helps you create your reality more easily, because when your choices are in alignment, things you find fulfilling manifest more easily. Coincidences and seemingly random events *always* occur to support your purpose in life.

KEY IDEAS: The nine families are a metaphor to show that you are born with an innate intent and purpose to your life. The universe exists to nurture and help you live it as fully as possible.

Exercise 3—Nine Families of Consciousness

Before you read the following, take a few minutes to review your own life. Go back as far as you can remember. Notice those activities, interests, or relationships that have always come naturally, effortlessly, and consistently brought you great joy and fulfillment. Those are all expressions of your family of consciousness intent.

The examples and social roles below are very general and intended only to ballpark, as there is great variation. Keep in mind that your personal intent may be a variation or hybrid. In all cases, it will be unique to you.

You can also use psy-time to playfully explore which family of consciousness you belong to. Even though you will find that you have all the traits listed below to some degree, you will gradually keep returning to one grouping that has been constantly emphasized and has dominated your life experiences to date. With time and practice, you will clearly settle on one of the nine areas below.[24]

Sumafi (Su-ma'-fi)
They deal primarily with teaching, managing, and passing on original knowledge with low distortion.
Examples: Emmanuel Kant (philosopher), Elaine Pagels (religious scholar)
Social Roles: Scholars, Scribes, Librarians

Milumet (Mil'-u-met)
They have strong mystical leanings. Most of their energy is directed in an inward fashion. They are deeply involved in nature, and more psychically gifted than most. They provide mystical nourishment for the collective.
Examples: Saint Francis of Assisi (friar), Maya Angelou (poet)
Social Roles: Mystics, Farmers, Gardeners

Gramada (Gra-ma'-da)
They specialize in organization, innovation, and invention. They are vital, active, and creatively aggressive. They initiate social systems and organizations.
Examples: Albert Einstein (physicist), Bill Gates (business founder)
Social Roles: Inventors, Politicians, Statesmen, Business Leaders

Vold
They have excellent precognitive abilities in terms of probabilities and one purpose in mind: to change the status quo in any area of interest.
Examples: Martin Luther (religious reformer), Martin Luther King, Jr. (civil rights leader)
Social Roles: Activists, Revolutionaries, Reformers

Ilda (Il'-da)

They emphasize the interplay and exchange of economic, social, and political ideas. They are travelers who carry ideas from one country to another, mixing cultures, religions, attitudes, and political structures. Seth has great affection for them!

Examples: Gypsy Rose Lee (stripper), George Carlin (comedian)

Social Roles: Merchants, Musicians, Comedians, Salesmen

Sumari (Sum-mar'-i)

They are primarily creative, naturally playful, humorous, and relatively uninhibited. They are impatient, however, and will be found in the arts and in less conventional sciences. They promote our cultural, spiritual, and artistic heritage.

Examples: Jimi Hendrix (musician), Jane Roberts (author)

Social Roles: Arts, Academics, Entertainers

Tumold (Tu-mold')

They are principally devoted to healing, though they don't have to formally practice medicine. They may be psychics, social workers, psychologists, priests/shamans, florists, politicians, and royalty. They promote natural healing no matter what occupation.

Examples: Barack Obama (politician), Deepak Chopra (physician)

Social Roles: Wide Range

Zuli (Zu'-li)

They are mainly involved with the exploration of all bodily activity. They seek to perfect the beautiful, elegant, and performance capacities of the body. They may also explore opposite qualities to extremes, and often appear at the beginnings of civilizations where direct physical bodily manipulation within the environment is of key importance.

Examples: Serena Williams (tennis player), Joseph "the Elephant Man" Merrick (celebrity)

Social Roles: Athletes, Dancers, Movie Stars, Tattoo & Body Piercers

Borledim (Bor-le'-dim)

They focus primarily upon parenthood, often have large families, and excel in nurturing healthy children with brilliant minds, healthy bodies, and strong emotions. Their ideas often spring to prominence before large social changes, and help initiate them. They are closely related to Sumari. They provide a healthy, vibrant Earth stock.

Examples: Mr. Rogers (TV host), Martha Stewart (businesswoman)

Social Roles: Parents, Pediatricians

Chapter 2: You Create Your Own Reality

A New Age Mantra, But What Does it Mean?

The saying "you create your own reality" was coined by Jane Roberts in her most popular book, *The Nature of Personal Reality* (1974). It became a new age mantra, and remains the central and yet most difficult to understand tenet of the Seth Material.

As we just discovered, the "you" who creates your reality is a multidimensional being, one who uses physical, mental, and inner senses, and has an innate intent and purpose. Within the context of your entity, you *always* create your own reality. You cannot *not* create your own reality because your entity and subconscious maintain the physical conditions that allow you—the outer ego—to exist within a stable physical, psychological, and spiritual *system*.

Only after ten years and 609 sessions—which "barely outlined" a conceptual foundation—did Seth dedicate an entire book to explain how you can tap into your subconscious and entity to unleash your own multidimensional power. What follows is an overview of the four main approaches Seth took to explain the mechanics of reality creation:

1. An idealist approach: **metaphysics**
2. A quantum mechanics approach: **physics**
3. A cellular approach: **biology**
4. An introspective approach: **psychology**

The Metaphysics of Reality Creation

Jane Roberts wrote *The Physical Universe As Idea Construction* in September 1963 during a powerful three-hour altered state that preceded Seth's arrival the following December. The forty-plus page manuscript laid the theoretical foundation for what Seth would flesh out over the next decade, and outlined how your entity literally creates the physical matter in your body. It explained that consciousness, which is no-thing, forms the basis of the universe, which is some-thing, using a set of processes in which All That Is manifests into the world we know.[25] Key concepts included:

- All physical reality, all matter in our universe, consists of idea constructions.
- Your entity constructs physical matter through mental transformations of energy.
- Space is simply the absence of any idea constructions.
- Growth is the process in which an idea construction fully manifests within the properties of matter, and space-time.
- Your subconscious functions as a translation zone for any idea's manifestation through your entity into your personality.
- All matter, all idea constructions, are formed by individualized bits of energy.[26]

Seth explained that your entity functions as a powerful "source generator" that constantly translates its infinite potentials into whatever reality it seeks to explore through *primary constructions*. For instance, your physical body/mind is a primary construction projected into the physical universe by your entity. It is an attempt to form a replica of the inner psychic essence of your entity within matter. (It can never completely accomplish this because all systems are open and dynamic, and therefore your entity would be "stuck" here.)

Secondary constructions are your perceptions of other constructions (beings and objects) through your physical, mental, and inner senses. Secondary constructions are composed of atoms and molecules, but don't contain the unifying, integrating personal direction of your entity. When you go about everyday activities like eating a meal or talking to friends, you create *secondary constructions*.

Seth pointed out that each primary construction creates its own unique *space continuum* of secondary constructions. In Seth's example, if five people were present at a Seth session, and Jane put her glass of iced-coffee on the table, there would actually be five glasses, one for each secondary construction created by each person. The notion that an individual glass exists independently of a perceiver, "out there somewhere," is inaccurate.[27]

We can apply this to all objects. Seth says that what we consider inert, dead matter is actually conscious and experiences a kind of generalized interiority. Thus, we have a multi-perspective matrix of individual space continuums occurring all the time, a veritable hall of mirrors in which our joint secondary constructions coexist.

Physical form—as primary and secondary constructions—is *not* an inherent characteristic of matter as we're used to thinking of it. Instead, form is the result of all the entities who jointly create the physical universe. Put another way, matter alone has no means of maintaining duration in space-time. Thus, *matter is not capable of growth by itself*. The matter in seeds does not grow into the matter in grass. That is only the surface level appearance created by our physical and mental senses as secondary constructions. Physical growth is the result of processes within the entire "iceberg-self" that constantly transform "source energy" into matter. Our current sciences have yet to discover these processes.

Seth also pointed out additional secondary constructions that he termed *apparitions, thought-forms, pseudo-forms, personality fragments*, and *projections*. They are used to explain related phenomena such as out-of-body projections, poltergeists, and so on (see Chapter 4).

KEY IDEAS: Your body/mind is a primary construction projected into physical reality by your entity. Your perception consists of secondary constructions in your own unique space continuum generated by your physical, mental, and inner senses.

The Physics of Reality Creation

Seth provided another concept to explain the mechanics of reality creation that he called *CUs,* short for *consciousness units.* All constructions within All That Is—physical, biological, psychological, psychic, or spiritual—consist of CUs. They are non-physical and contain infinite potentials for expansion, development, and organization while maintaining their unique micro-individuality. No matter how they combine with other CUs, their micro-identity remains inviolate. Their freedom from space-time allows them to be clairvoyant and precognitive.

CUs are not personified in terms of feeling-tone like your entity. They are a more basic species of primordial, aware-ized consciousness. They represent the most basic "unit" in which All That Is constantly fragments into "The One within the many" (see Chapter 6). They are the "vitalizing force" in our physical universe, and their potentials for creativity are infinite. Though they transcend space-time, they simultaneously form it. CUs may appear in several places at once, yet paradoxically exist in *all* places at once. Atoms contain "many millions" of CUs. Each CU influences all others, and may move through the past or future as well as dimensions of time that modern science has yet to discover.

To use a quantum mechanics analogy, CUs act as particles when they take on the properties of matter, and act as waves when nested within dimensions that are faster than light. The simultaneous wave and particle aspects of CUs are what make the existence of our inner senses and related psychic phenomena possible. These include "psi" phenomena (telepathy, clairvoyance, precognition, and psychokinesis), near-death and out-of-body experiences, lucid dreaming, channeling and automatic writing/painting/music, the subtle human energy field, spontaneous healing, interdimensional UFOs, stigmata, crop circles, levitation, teleportation, bilocation, remote viewing, and encounters with sentient beings (identified as angels, demons, faeries, leprechauns, etc.).

Seth also described an intermediary form taken by CUs as your entity projects itself into physical form. He called these emanations *EEs*, short for *electromagnetic energy units*. These are the forms taken by CUs once they get earmarked for physical constructions. They are a form of incipient matter, a "slowed down" version of CUs that penetrate the threshold of our physical universe in the form of QFs (short for *quantum fields*[28]).

Your entity, through an intense creative effort on a cosmic scale, cooperates with every other entity to co-create and maintain our physical universe. Physical reality can be considered a by-product of our super-conscious entities as they jointly project EE units into the physical field. Just as your physical form is projected into a primary construction, *all* matter is literally an offshoot of the exuberant creative action of our entities.

Seth added another important physics metaphor called *coordinate points* to show how the physics of your "iceberg self"— CUs to EEs to QFs—scales into the physical field. Coordinate points function like micro-black and -white holes, blinking on and off at incredibly fast rates—so fast that these blinks are invisible to your nervous system, which operates at much slower speeds. For example, it takes several thousandths of a second for the nerve signals in your skin and brain to register hot or cold. Though Seth never specified the exact rate, a coordinate point may blink at what physicists call *the Planck constant*—the shortest known possible pulse within matter—once every 5.3×10^{-44} seconds. That's 5.3 trillion, trillion trillionths of a second!

Coordinate points pulse energy between dimensions and function as invisible conduits for CUs and EEs. They act as energetic transformers that maintain linear time and continuous creation. They permeate all space and are activated by emotions, feelings, and thoughts of sufficient intensity—the more intense the emotions, the quicker the physical materialization. Smaller than any particles known to current science—extremely minute—they activate the behavior of atoms and molecules similar to how the sun helps plants to grow. There are three types[29]:

1. **Absolute**—Only four intersect all realities, contain primal energy, and are mathematically pristine.
2. **Main**—Sources of vast power, they propel what is not yet physical into physical form. Seth cites the Egyptian pyramids of Giza as an example of a lasting structure built on a main coordinate point.
3. **Subordinate**—The most common, they are vast in number, and space is filled with them. They help transform thought and emotion into physical matter.

Understanding the methods in which ideas become physical matter would radically transform our current sciences and technologies. We could create physical matter more effectively and efficiently, and build more permanent buildings, roads, and other infrastructures that would last for centuries. Crops and livestock could have higher yields and feed the entire planet, while maintaining a high quality of life for all involved. There are endless potentials once understood.

EEs of sufficient intensity automatically activate subordinate coordinate points and accelerate the formation of idea constructions. Your thoughts, emotions, and feelings exist *as* EE units, and with the aid of subordinate coordinate points literally create matter. Mental images, supported by strong emotions, form a kind of blueprint upon which an object, condition, or event manifests.

But one caution: this process is *neutral*. You will create idea constructions based on fear or joy, hatred or love, so it's a double-edged sword. Therefore, learning to be fully in touch with your feelings, emotions, and thoughts will help you make important changes in your life more easily.

As we begin to include the "iceberg self"—the "you" who creates your reality—into our physics, we begin to radically reorient our conceptions of the mechanics of reality creation.[30] Seth's physics are still considered meta-physical ("beyond physics" and therefore unproveable) by modern physicists who don't recognize or include their inner senses. This is why Seth introduced the inner senses early on, and why learning to develop them is so important. They are a key to help further unlock the secrets of physical reality.

KEY IDEAS: The physics of reality creation involve the trans-formation of All That Is as CUs into EEs into QFs. Physical space-time is permeated by a variety of coordinate points that enable the process.

The Biology of Reality Creation

Your body system manages an incredible array of functions like healing, blood pressure, hormone levels, digestion and elimi-nation, hair growth, audio, visual, and sensory inputs, sleep cy-cles, and more. Its cellular processes are managed by your sub-conscious, which frees up your outer ego to do its job of access-ing the best life conditions to ensure stability for everyday life.

Cells form building blocks for all multicellular organisms, from plants, insects, fish, to you. They form your body's skin, blood, bones, organs, and immune and nervous systems. While new cells are born and old ones die constantly, every cell-based biological form, including your body, maintains its overall form without skipping a beat.

Your entity and subconscious maintain a type of "gestalt con-sciousness"[31] in and out of time in order to manage cellular proc-esses that have linear (physical) and nonlinear (nonphysical) functions. This means that they can perceive past, present, and future, which are crucial to maintaining your body's health and survival.

Thus, your body's cells have a unique memory system that al-lows them to instantly assess and communicate life conditions to *every* cell in your body. Your body consciousness compares past conditions and predicts necessary changes to maintain equilibrium.

Your cell walls take "pictures" of moment-by-moment status. These are not visual images, but highly coded electromagnetic energy fields. Your body consciousness then constructs "precog-nitive pictures" and compares them with two models:

1. Your body's ideal state of health.
2. The body image held in your conscious mind and belief systems.

Correlations occur, communications buzz back and forth, and your beliefs, thoughts, and emotions affect whatever changes are needed to bring the two into alignment. This process is constant and happens at lightning speed. This is how your body maintains its equilibrium and ensures physical survival.

Each cell is aware of *all* probable pasts and futures, along with those of *all other cells*. If you were burned, cut, or broke a bone, then the memory of those cells is programmed into the cells that replaced them. These memories provide a healthy model that promotes cellular healing when faced with new injuries or diseases. Cellular memories will even seed dreams to help restore your body to good health. For example, you may dream about needing more vitamin C or to stop eating certain foods.

All these functions are made possible by CUs and EEs as they function underneath the threshold of physical reality (QFs). In a sense, each cell is a vast universe initiated and maintained by the power of CUs. The EEs function as the threshold for CUs as they manifest into physical constructions.

As such, your body system has an inner communications network that puts supercomputers to shame. Emerging from the basic CUs/EEs/QFs that form matter, your body is the foundation upon which your outer ego is able to function. This amazing physical and biological system supports your ability to create your own reality at the cellular level.[32]

KEY IDEAS: Your body consciousness employs a microscopic cellular communication and memory system. It processes past and future probabilities at lightning speed to provide the foundation for health and all reality creation.

The Psychology of Reality Creation

Your entity functions like a power station to assist in all aspects of reality creation. Yet here you are in physical reality, perhaps hypnotized by conventional beliefs that you are limited to a body whose existence is extinguished at death. You may believe that you live at the mercy of events, people, and things outside of your control. But nothing could be further from the truth!

As mentioned earlier, Seth dedicated an entire book, *The Nature of Personal Reality*, to introduce you to your real self and provide methods to begin to take control of your life. He provided psychological methods to explore your reality through introspection—the art of self-reflection and self-awakening. However, Seth cautioned not to reflect on your thoughts so much that you begin to mentally short-circuit. It's just that you will continue to run on subconscious automatic responses until you become fully aware of what's in your conscious mind.

Seth's methods and exercises *demand concentration and effort*. In other words, he doesn't offer a quick-fix, but encourages persistent inquiry to *notice*, *recognize*, and *identify* your ingrained habits of mind. Further, his exercises produce altered states that are quite beneficial in expanding your awareness. The three Exercises in the previous chapter are foundational exercises designed to help you become more aware of the contents of your conscious mind. But there is more we need to consider.

Seth's psychology focuses on the role of *thoughts*, *ideas*, *beliefs*, *expectations*, *emotions*, *feelings*, *impulses*, *imagination*, *dreams*, and how they work together. These are all processes within your conscious mind that you can learn to control. The more focused your mind, the quicker the manifestation. Seth points out that many people have lazy mental habits. Therefore, the key is the intensity of your desire.

When done properly, you can bring a single-minded, laser-focused desire in harmony with your intent to bear on any challenge you face—relationships, jobs, finances, health, and so on. Like many things, you get out of it what you put into it. It's one thing to imagine a million dollars in your bank account and take no action towards manifesting it, and another to identify and follow one's intent, become knowledgeable in business beliefs, and create a million dollar company.

One of the biggest mistakes beginners make is to reduce Seth's metaphysics, physics, biology, and psychology of reality creation to simplistic one-liners like "thoughts create reality." There are many examples where Seth says, "Your thoughts create this or that . . . ," but this needs to be understood in the wider context of *all* his ideas, which includes your multidimensional *self*, *senses*, and *intent*. These are the core processes that work *systemically* to create your reality, so it's important to keep your focus on the larger picture as you go.

Besides, if thoughts alone create all your reality, then every thought you have about hurting or imposing your will on others would instantly manifest. The world would be instantly destroyed every time a child had a temper tantrum! Obviously, there are checks and balances in mass reality creation that prevent that (see Chapter 12).

KEY IDEAS: Your multidimensional self, senses, and intent work together as a powerful system. Learning to focus your habits of mind (beliefs, thoughts, emotions, etc.) through intent and desire is the key to creating changes in your reality.

How Do I Get Started With Belief Work?

One of the main practices in Seth's psychology is learning to work with beliefs. They permeate your thoughts, emotions, and expectations, and are constantly mirrored in your behavior. As you change the intensity behind your beliefs, you change their effect on your behavior. You can turn sickness into health, poverty into wealth, loneliness into a loving partner, or vice versa—anything you wish. It depends on what you focus upon.

You have thousands of beliefs, and they cluster around you like planets around the sun. If a solar system represents the sum of all your belief systems, then the sun represents your conscious mind, and each planet represents a core *belief system*. Some planets are bigger than others because you tend to concentrate on certain beliefs more than others. Determining the size and amount of "gravity" in your "belief planets" will help you make successful changes in your life.

Seth outlined important *types* of beliefs:

- **Core**—Foundational *belief systems* such as "morality," "emotions," or "perception" whose "gravity" attracts similar core beliefs. These are the "master codes" expressed in *all* human behaviors. The actual *content* of your core belief systems will be uniquely colored by cultural factors and your stage of development.
- **Limiting**—Beliefs that inhibit growth, widening, and impose artificial constraints on your fulfillment and creativity, such as, "I'm incapable of happiness," "Nobody will ever love me," or "My body's urges are sinful." Learning to free yourself from self-imposed limitations is a key outcome of belief work.
- **Invisible**—Beliefs held as a fact of life instead of a belief *about* life. They are not buried or unconscious. They include unexamined assumptions about the nature of reality that may no longer serve your growth and fulfillment, such as, "God always punishes sinners," "Women are naturally subservient," or "Scientific method is the best way to know Truth."
- **Subsidiary/Corollary**—Offshoots of core beliefs. As core belief systems are identified and addressed, false or distorted subsidiary beliefs simply lose their energetic affect. They still exist as potentials, but are neutralized. For example, if a core belief is "My life has purpose," a false corollary belief may be, "My everyday actions are not important," which would be neutralized as the core belief gains prominence.
- **Directional**—The beliefs that children receive from parents to ensure their safety or promote cultural values, such as, "Don't talk to strangers," "Stay away from people from that ethnic group," or "Say your prayers before you go to sleep." These can remain into adulthood and turn into limiting beliefs if never examined.
- **Conflicting**—Subsidiary beliefs held in simultaneous opposition that manifest physical, emotional, psychological

and spiritual symptoms. For example, holding the beliefs that it's important to write (because I enjoy writing) and it's important to *not* write (because I don't want to write to my parents) may produce confusing signals to the hands, leading to tension, stress, and cramps when writing. However, once fully identified and addressed to, the opposition and symptoms can be neutralized.

- **Joint**—Beliefs shared in relationships, such as, "The best motorcycles are Harley-Davidsons," "Football games are fun to attend," or "We don't vote for Democrats." They attract "birds of a feather."

- **Body**—Beliefs about the body's function and whether those functions are healthy or unhealthy, socially acceptable or not, such as, "It's not okay to pick your nose in public," "Brush your teeth after every meal," or "Wear your scarf or you'll catch a cold."

- **Negative**—Beliefs that generate strong emotional and imaginative connections that produce unhealthy, even pathological symptoms, such as, "My father didn't love me," "I am a failure at everything I do," or "The world is full of viruses and other diseases out to kill me."

- **Active/Passive**—Active beliefs are those used by the conscious mind, passive beliefs lie *latent* as potentials to be activated by the conscious mind.

- **Private**—Personal, individual beliefs. When you change beliefs, you may get mixed messages from others intended to sabotage your new beliefs because you no longer align with theirs.

A beginner's mistake to avoid is thinking that as you change your beliefs, you will eliminate your own belief systems. Belief work *neutralizes* the energy of beliefs, but your core belief *systems* will always remain as potentials. For example, you can address the core issues involved in overeating, and be fine for months or years until life conditions change, the triggers flare up, and you resume overeating as a coping or defense mechanism against a perceived threat.

The process of lasting change involves many factors and takes time to master. As you proceed with Seth's psychology, your worldview will undergo a radical reorientation. You will begin to understand that if you create *all* your reality, then nothing simply *happens* to you. Your life is the result of your choices, and you can choose to make changes whenever you're sufficiently motivated.

When you begin to work with your beliefs, you'll start to see them reflected everywhere—in your place of worship, school, home, and business—all reinforced by family, friends, and media. With time and practice, you will hone your ability to notice, recognize, and identify beliefs and make the changes your heart desires.[33]

KEY IDEAS: Learning to work with beliefs can be a fulfilling, life-changing process. There are many types of beliefs and belief systems, all of which can be changed or neutralized to suit your own purposes and needs.

How Do I Change My Beliefs?

In this section, we'll explore the tools Seth provided for effective belief work.

- **Use natural hypnosis,** the process in which your subconscious acquiesces to conscious belief. If you use it to create difficult circumstances like illness, broken relationships, lost jobs, and so on, then you can also use it to turn those situations around![34]

Recall that intensely focused desire accelerates physical manifestation, so natural hypnosis helps to focus your desire for change. Hypnosis is a state of highly concentrated attention on specific data to the exclusion of everything else. When there are no mixed messages or conflicting inputs, your conscious mind shuts out extraneous data and narrows its focus with laser-like precision. This tool can be used to activate new beliefs and neutralize old ones.

In this way, you naturally hypnotize yourself through your beliefs *about* reality. You simply accept them and ignore everything else that conflicts with or contradicts them to instantly manifest those beliefs into your everyday life.

- **Use the present as your point of power.**[35] This has to do with the way your conscious mind experiences the past, present, and future. The present is where the nonphysical meets the physical. It is where you choose from a vast pool of probabilities *according to your beliefs*, which in turn act as a set of directions given to your conscious mind to help organize and reorganize past experience. The past and future exist as an infinite set of potentials until you make a choice and take action in the present, or what Seth calls the *moment point*.[36]

Therefore, *the present is the point of power*. It is where your focused desire sparks action, manifests change, and promotes growth, healing, joy, health, creativity, and vitality. Once this tool is activated, it establishes an important foundation to build upon.

Exercise 4—The Point of Power

Find a comfortable place to sit and relax, feet on the floor, hands at your side, and back straight. Take several deep, lingering breaths to detach from the concerns of your day. Once you are comfortable, repeat the following mantra:

"The present is the point of power where I create *all* of my reality."

As you repeat these words out loud or silently in your mind, *focus upon the certainty that your physical, emotional, and psychic abilities exist in every fiber of your being.*

Use all your energy and attention. If your mind drifts into anything else, instantly bring your full attention, desire, and concentration back to your mantra and the certainty of your abilities.

Do this for no more than five minutes each day, and then simply forget about it. Try not to look for instant results, or if it's working or not working. *Try it every day for three weeks.* (That's an average time for belief and behavioral changes to begin to take hold.)

Extra Credit: Write the mantra on a piece of paper and put it somewhere you're sure to see it every day, like your bathroom mirror, computer monitor, or phone.[37]

- **Focus on the half-filled cup.** You never know exactly what you're going to create. Life consists of good times and bad times. Hopefully the good far outweigh the bad. But as you work to neutralize undesired situations, another trap to avoid is to get stuck on the negative parts of your past. When you focus *only* on the half-empty cup of your past, you tend to ignore the positive aspects that are always present.

The half-filled cup is always present in the moment point.

Many problems occur when your conscious mind blocks out anything positive, and instead settles on a constant stream of negative beliefs. As mentioned earlier, your entity is neutral in terms of providing you the "source energy" (CUs/EEs/QFs) in which to create your reality. The key is to focus your intense desire on the half-filled cup and learn to recognize the positive aspects that *always accompany* painful, even traumatic experiences. It's normal to focus on pain and suffering during difficult times, but taken to extremes it can effectively block out your natural healing impulses.

- **Be honest.** Regularly check to see if you are sabotaging your attempts at change by not being completely honest with yourself. As you will learn, your outer ego has various defense mechanisms that can seriously impact your ability to honestly self-report. As they say, denial isn't just a river in Egypt!

Denial and repression are what prevent you from mining down into the specifics of your core belief systems. They allow you to lie to yourself and to others. They keep you spinning on a hamster wheel of satellite and conflicting beliefs as you send mixed messages to your entity who, in turn, is designed to help you manifest "what you concentrate on."[38] Again, reality creation is a double-edged sword. If you find yourself surrounded by difficulties, you must begin to realize that your own choices and beliefs have led to your present circumstances, and must honestly begin to notice and identify them if you wish to make permanent changes.

- **Use bridge beliefs.** Conflicting core beliefs generate conflicting thoughts and emotions. You can bridge the gap and unite them with a bridge belief that finds similarities between them. For instance, Jane Roberts held conflicting core beliefs between her writing self (fiction only) and psychic self (spiritual only). Only when she recognized that they *both* enjoyed writing could she allow them both to flourish. Bridge beliefs also operate in the dream state as your subconscious mind processes conflicting beliefs. You may dream of crossing a bridge, river, ocean, or abyss safely. Whatever dream symbols you use, you will wake up feeling energized and rejuvenated.
- **Don't play the blame game.** As you begin to address your challenges, it's normal to look for causes and place blame this or that person, event, or even lifetime, if you believe in reincarnation (see Chapter 5). As long as you continue to place blame on outside causes, you are not taking full responsibility for your life's circumstances. *You must take full responsibility for everything in your life and stop blaming others for your problems.*

With time and practice, you can begin to identify how you got yourself into your present circumstances, but in all cases, Seth reinforces that you *can make significant, permanent changes at any time*. You are *never* a victim of past circumstances or lives.

KEY IDEAS: The toolbox to changing beliefs includes natural hypnosis, the present as the point of power, the half-filled cup, honest self-reporting, bridge beliefs, and taking full responsibility for your life's circumstances to eliminate victimhood.

What Are Some Obstacles to Changing My Beliefs?

We've explored ideas that challenge much of what you've been taught. Conceptualizing yourself as an Aspect nested within a larger multidimensional being takes some getting used to!

Learning to turn on and properly utilize your inner senses to produce transformative states requires you to expand your self-concept. Connecting with your innate intent helps you better understand your purpose in life. Beginning to work with core belief systems in the point of power requires introspection focused through intense desire. *It all takes time and practice.* Here are some typical obstacles to avoid and suggestions on how to work through them.

- **Realize that change takes time.** It *is* possible to effect quick change sometimes, but more often than not, change takes time. We live in a quick-fix society. Instant "cures" abound. Have a headache? Take this pill. Need to lose weight fast? Use this diet. Don't like your nose, boobs, or butt? A simple operation can fix that. You can create killer abs by wearing an electro-stimulating belt while watching TV! Many of these claims are exaggerated or untrue. There is value to slowing down to take a more nurturing path, in spite of cultural messages that say otherwise.

- **Become aware of victimhood beliefs.** You live in a culture of engrained victimhood that constantly bombards you with the belief that you're a victim of accidents, economic downturns, disease, wars, natural disasters, criminals, terrorists, and on and on. The list of excuses for your problems reads like the side effects of an unnecessary drug for yet another disease concocted by a pharmaceutical company. Conventional thinking constantly reinforces just how bad things are by constantly trumping up the half-empty cup in its many guises. It's all about scarcity over abundance, fear over joy, and the "demonized other" monitored by a "terror alert" rather than cooperating to solve mutual challenges.

- **Be kind to yourself.** Another challenge in doing belief work is when you do your very best and nothing changes or *things get even worse*. You may feel that Seth is wrong or you are a failure at learning this "reality creation stuff." Feelings of failure can trigger beliefs of guilt, inadequacy, and low self-esteem, which only perpetuate the half-empty cup. Again, it takes time, persistence, understanding, and a deep desire to make changes. Keep doing the practices over time, and positive change *will* occur.

- **Be kind to others.** There's nothing worse than telling someone with a serious illness that "Seth said, 'you create your own reality'" if they are not ready or able to understand it. You simply lay a new age guilt trip on them for not being able to create an instant cure. It's more complicated than that! People experience difficult situations for a wide variety of reasons, and each situation is unique (see Chapter 12).

- **Trust in your entity, follow your intent.** You create your reality 100%, with constant help from your invisible power house, your entity. Seth talks about situations where your entity exercises a kind of "veto power" over your egoic choices through impulses and seemingly random coincidences that align more with your innate intent. Conflict always arises when you stray from your intent. Your entity always does its best to get your attention and guide you toward fulfillment. Consider your own death. If you create your own reality, then you create your own death. Yet how many people consciously, joyously participate in their death? Most people are in denial of their own deaths. So what happens when it's time to die? Your entity always provides the best circumstances to guide you through the process (see Chapters 5, 12).

At some point, you—the outer ego—must learn to *cooperate* with rather than blame what you can't fully control, and that includes your entity. Only then can you open the channels, expand your conscious mind to work more fully with your entity, and proactively change your life.

KEY IDEAS: Strategies for overcoming obstacles to changing your beliefs include: realize that change takes time, become aware of the many guises of victimhood beliefs, be kind to yourself, be kind to others, trust your entity, and follow your intent. Here's a toast to keeping your cup half-full!

What is the Relationship between Beliefs, Thoughts, and Emotions?

Western society elevates reason and logic (masculine) above feelings and emotion (feminine) and assigns these to male and female gender roles. Generally, men are taught *not* to be overly sensitive, and to *not* express their feelings and emotions. Women are taught *not* to be overly intellectual, and to *not* assert themselves or dominate. When feelings, instincts, and actions remain bottled up with no socially acceptable outlet, what results is often unhappiness, dissatisfaction, depression, increased aggression and even violence.

However, intellect and emotions are meant to *complement* each other and be used to your advantage, regardless of gender. Intellect is a function of your thought process, and feeling is a function of your emotions. Thoughts are like clouds in the sky, they come and go. Emotions are like waves on the ocean, they ebb and flow. Together, they create calm, sunny days and tremendous storms, even floods and hurricanes! Just as the weather changes, so do your thoughts and emotions.

Your outer ego uses both to accurately assess your physical environment, which in turn activates your body's mechanisms to bring about a proper response to any situation. If you hold a lot of fearful beliefs, then your thoughts and emotions will create turbulent conditions. If you hold a lot of joyful beliefs, then your ocean and sky will be sunny.

Together, they form a dynamic system that reflects your core belief systems. As such, *your beliefs always generate thoughts and emotions*, not the other way around. Change or neutralize your beliefs, and you'll change your thoughts and emotions. Therefore, if you learn to notice and identify which beliefs trigger your thoughts and emotional responses, you can reduce stressful situations by recognizing and addressing them. Most beliefs are not intellectually based, however. As you pursue belief work you must begin to reconcile how your emotions and imagination also relate to any particular belief.

While you may feel one way or another without any discernable cause, with practice you'll begin to see that you create all events through thoughts and emotions based on your beliefs. Your thoughts rely on association and attract similar thoughts like a magnet. They also reject any thoughts they *think* are threatening to your well-being.

As the saying goes, "Belief-birds of a feather flock together." Your thoughts and emotions always follow suit, and will always lead to your core beliefs. As such, you can't fully understand your thoughts and emotions until you fully understand your beliefs.

It's also very important to regularly affirm that your beliefs, thoughts, and emotions are unique, blessed, and natural expressions of All That Is *within you*. They form an essential communication system in which you express yourself and get feedback from others. As you progress with belief work, you will reinforce your personal power, ability to act in the now and live a more fulfilling life.

However, affirmation isn't some kind of naïve acceptance of everything that you encounter in life. It doesn't mean that nothing matters, and everything is just fine all the time! Affirmation doesn't imply that you should sit back and do nothing, or that your life is in the hands of Fate or your entity.

If you always give in to someone else's demands to live your life a certain way, you deny your own natural being and freedom. Instead, you have the power of free will to act and choose in the moment point. As such, you may affirm your uniqueness by saying, "No thank you!" to any person or situation that doesn't promote your growth and fulfillment.

This kind of blessed, freeing affirmation always promotes new connections and inner discoveries. It pulls from the deepest aspects of your being the exact information and insights needed to solve any problem. As you learn to lovingly affirm yourself, it will become easier to identify, recognize, and address your beliefs. The more any belief inspires you to develop your abilities, the greater it affirms your true being.

In summary, your conscious mind is a multidimensional feedback system that works with a complex array of factors to seamlessly create your reality. Learning to unlock the secrets of this system, with time and practice, is what the Seth Material provides. You can manifest your heart's desires in alignment with your intent, overcome any obstacles once you understand you put them there, heal dis-ease, mend relationships, create love and abundance—you *can* have it all!

KEY IDEAS: Your beliefs always generate thoughts and emotions. Change your beliefs, and you'll change your thoughts and emotions. Affirm the power of your being by honoring yourself as a unique, blessed, and natural expression of All That Is.

Exercise 5—Changing Beliefs: Rearrange the Furniture of Your Mind

The next time you create disturbing thoughts and emotions, take some time to trace them to their source beliefs. (You can also do this using psy-time.) With practice, you will learn to trace the unimpeded flow of your emotions back to particular beliefs that you may then change.

1. *Notice* the thoughts and feelings. You may have normalized the process of repressing them, so for starters, just acknowledge their existence and don't push them away. Don't try to substitute what you think are more appropriate or positive ones. That's only more of the same repression mechanism at work.

2. *Identify* which beliefs trigger specific thoughts and feelings. For example, you may *notice* a knot in your stomach, or a feeling of dread. Then ask yourself, "What was I just thinking about?" Try to trace your thought process backwards. You may have had a phone call, an e-mail, or conversation that set you off without knowing it. Someone may have said something that triggered a response that made you feel inadequate, worthless, stupid, poor, ugly, the wrong gender, race, social group, etc. Identify

these as *your* beliefs. Once identified, you can consciously change them.

3. *Rearrange* your beliefs by imagining that they are pieces of mental furniture. Picture a familiar room in your mental screen. Take a moment to open the drawers, cabinets, etc. and explore them. Then associate the belief you've identified ("I don't have enough money") with any piece of furniture, say a couch. Take a couple minutes to playfully rearrange, discard, or replace it with another piece of furniture that you associate with your desired new belief ("I always have enough money").

Then let it go. During your day, when you notice and identify the old belief arising again ("I don't have enough money"), playfully remind yourself of your new piece of mental furniture ("I always have enough money"). Concentrate fully on this new belief each time you need to. In time, you will find the old belief changes into the new one.

Note: Practicing these three steps every day for at least *three weeks* will set your intent to your subconscious mind that you are ready to become more fully aware of invisible beliefs. Remember that belief work is a process and a habit that will allow you to identify and change specific beliefs that no longer suit you.[39]

Chapter 3: Love, Gender & Sex

What is Love?

Love has inspired countless generations of poets, composers, and artists throughout history. It's universal to the human experience, and yet can be hard to define. As we will see, love has many different expressions, meanings, and contexts. There is the emotion of love. We may express feelings of love for our self, others, or All That Is. There is also the love of art, or of knowledge.

Then there is "God's love"—the divine, loving, creative subjectivity of All That Is—which Seth often refers to as *value fulfillment* that promotes the maximum development for each individual in relation to All That Is.[40] It provides the impetus toward all creative action in physical and nonphysical terms. In this way, individual growth, creativity, and happiness are innately nurtured by every Aspect of All That Is in a joint cooperative effort for the maximum benefit of one and all. This is one way that Seth expresses *divine love*, one that transcends yet includes human love.

When it comes to expressions of human love, most are natural acts of altruism and compassion for others based on mutual well-being. Random acts of kindness by strangers—good Samaritans—are a fine example. But underneath that lies a divine love that serves as the *foundation* for them all. Therefore, value fulfillment cannot be limited to only human expressions of love. All That Is by definition seeks to lovingly promote all variations of *all* forms of consciousness, no matter how minute or grand, so that they have the best chance to manifest, create, and develop. Each and every Aspect is innately loved and blessed.

It's this gift of creativity, of consciousness, of divine love that nurtures your life each and every day. You don't need to search for It since It *permeates your being.* The love of God as value fulfillment constantly propels every fiber of your being. Every CU/EE/QF is saturated with it as well. As you learn that your "iceberg self" is *always* connected to every other self, there is nowhere else you need to search for God's love, for it is always within you. In this light, your very existence is proof that God exists!

Finally, no human being can own, sell, or regulate divine love. No institution has the power to excommunicate you from Your Self! Any philosophy or dogma that claims to do so is highly limited. The Bible says, "The truth will set you free," and that Truth is manifest each and every moment as divine love *in you*!

KEY IDEAS: Value fulfillment promotes the cooperative pursuit of maximum development for each individual in relation to All That Is. This is the divine love that permeates your being, and can never be lost.

What is the Difference between Gender and Sexual Preference?

Your entity, which expresses divine love for and through you, isn't male or female but the *source* of those characteristics. Even though Seth used a male entity name, he never said that his identity was solely male. Because he had lived so many lives as female and male, *"he"* would be considered genderless, as well nameless. He used Seth for *our* benefit, because we're used to associating names and characteristics with gender.[41]

Recall that Seth referred to Jane as *Ruburt* and *he*. Again, this is a convention (entity name) that Seth used to introduce and acclimate students to their "iceberg self." Even though your entity is transgendered—beyond gender—it serves as a "source self" for all expressions of gender and sexuality.

Western culture has artificially exaggerated the division of male and female characteristics. Daytime, the sun, and outer ego (waking self) are associated with the masculine. Nighttime, the moon, and subconscious (dreaming self) are connected with the feminine. Males are taught to be rough, aggressive, and violent, and females soft, nurturing, and passive.

However, there are no innate sexual preferences hardwired to your genitalia (sex organs). These come from the innate leanings of your entity expressed in your personality. Gender is primarily a biological function designed to promote the survival of the species. Gender roles are mostly the result of cultural conditioning.

According to Seth, early humans were far more democratic and less specialized in terms of gender roles than current scientists realize. Men and women worked together, and children learned to hunt with *both* parents, though mothers would stop and nurse along the way. The qualities of inventiveness, ingenuity, intuition were never delegated to one gender over the other. Social roles were much more homogenized then, and not as specialized as today.

While we have normalized certain male-female functions for practical purposes in Western culture, they are *not* innate to the design of the species. Due to our exaggerated separation of male-female qualities, we have become somewhat limited in regard to aspects of gender and sexual preference in favor of social norms that may no longer serve a useful purpose.

KEY IDEAS: Gender is primarily a biological function designed to promote the survival of the species. Your sexual preferences are not hardwired, but are the result of the innate leanings of your entity expressed in your personality. Gender roles are the results of cultural conditioning.

What Do You Mean, I'm Bisexual?

As you begin to explore deeper Aspects your "iceberg self," expect to encounter events that may not fit into your preconceived notions of gender roles and sexual preference. Because your entity, or primary identity, is male *and* female, both genders influence your current gender.[42] For example, you may dream of yourself as a member of the opposite sex, but that doesn't mean that you're gay or lesbian! It simply means there's great flexibility to your subconscious dreaming self and entity ("you are more than your body!").

As you begin to explore, you will encounter other variations of gender roles and sexual preference that may initially confuse you. As always, the idea is to keep an open and curious mind. Your entity is a "psychic bank" of potentials driven to explore as many variations as possible. So psychologically speaking, there is a "male" within each female and a "female" within every male.

Austrian psychiatrist Sigmund Freud (1856-1939) believed that humans were innately bisexual and that heterosexual behaviors were learned from parents and other social influences.[43] Swiss psychiatrist Carl G. Jung (1875-1961) discovered what he called *archetypes* in the human subconscious—types of innate, universal blueprints for male and female expressions of psychic energies.

Two of these archetypes are called the *anima* (female qualities) and *animus* (male qualities). Jung noted that all males have an *anima* and females an *animus*. The male anima consists mainly of subconscious elements of his mother, sisters, aunts, and other influential female role models from childhood. The female animus likewise reflects subconscious influences of father, brothers, uncles, and so on.

Seth noted that Jung only scratched the surface of the subconscious, and that the role of the anima and animus extend far deeper that he supposed. As such, your anima (female) also embodies the essential interiority, intuitive, and inward characteristics of the creative impulse within all consciousness. Your animus (male) also embodies the naturally aggressive, outbound creative impulses that create all physical constructions.[44]

American biologist Alfred Kinsey (1894-1956) crafted a seven point scale of sexual preference in the 1950s that ranged from exclusively heterosexual (male/female) to exclusively homosexual (gay/lesbian), with five categories in between reflecting a *bisexual* preference. His research revealed that many people held bisexual preferences in private while paying lip service to socially accepted heterosexual conventions.[45]

Seth is unequivocal that gay and lesbian activity is a *perfectly natural sexual expression*—biologically, emotionally, psychologically, and spiritually. Additionally, all sexual activity was never meant to result in childbirth alone. That would result in overpopulation. Therefore, the variety of sexual expressions available to you is a *blessing* and natural means of fulfillment.

Seth pointed out with irony that while people fear expressions of bisexuality—because they think it promotes the destruction of the family, low morals, and confused sexual identity—in reality that more accurately describes the present state of the Western world! That is, just the opposite results when we repress and deny elements of our innate bisexual nature. Again, your entity contains both genders, and explores *both* elements in every lifetime. Therefore, a deeper understanding and acceptance of how these energies work *together* would solve many of our current social problems, including acts of violence, murder, and those just mentioned.[46]

Traditionalists insist that the Bible admonishes gay and lesbian sexuality, and that's the final say on the matter. However, the modern view is not so black and white. The Bible's Old and New Testaments were written over a period of six thousand years to guide an agrarian (farming) culture during times when human populations were much smaller than they are today. Human evolution continues, and we now live in a post-industrial Information Age whose complexity and global population dwarfs those premodern times.

Seth and others' claims that our species is innately bisexual provide a basis for the social cohesion and cooperation necessary to promote well-being and civilization building. How this plays out in the future will have an important impact on the emerging new worldview (see Chapter 14).

Learning to acknowledge your bisexual nature will help you come to terms with the innate male *and* female within you. Again, *it doesn't mean you have to become gay, lesbian, heterosexual, or even "bisexual."* That's always a sexual preference. But there *are* gender roles and behaviors you can begin to explore.

It can be as simple as a man becoming comfortable with expressing emotions (crying in a movie theater, saying "I love you"), helping with "woman's work" (dishes, laundry, the kids), pursuing the arts (play the flute, paint), or exploring dreams. For a woman, it can be as simple as becoming comfortable showing interest in a sporting event, science and mathematics, joining the workforce, or taking charge in the bedroom.

The bottom line is that your gender roles and sexual preferences are influenced by your entity's innate bisexuality. What works best is entirely up to you! Your gender and sexuality are healthy expressions of your Spirit-in-flesh. They were never intended to be denied or debased. Any dogma or philosophy that does so is highly limited.

KEY IDEAS: Your entity is the source of gender and sexual preference. It is innately bisexual. Therefore, gender is not hardwired toward an exclusive sexual preference. It doesn't mean you have to become gay, lesbian, or heterosexual. It means that when you come to terms with the innate male <u>and</u> female qualities within you, the more you will know your deepest self.

What is the Relationship between Love, Devotion, and Sexuality?

Love is a powerful, emotional energy that promotes devotion to self and others. *It naturally seeks expression in everything you do.* It is innately creative and also promotes exploration and curiosity through your sexuality.

Your "iceberg self" is a dynamic, spiritual system that always seeks your greatest joy and fulfillment. However, it exists beyond such distinctions, and while its native language usually escapes you, it's based upon a "language of love" whose human expression includes gender, emotions, and sexual preferences. Together, these expressions of divine love reflect your deepest connection to All That Is.

Love always seeks to promote dedication and commitment. Therefore, you must learn to love yourself before you can truly love anyone else. By self-love, Seth doesn't mean the narcissistic kind that's self-absorbed and entranced by its own surfaces, but rather a sense of corporeal integrity and dignity that nurtures empathy, compassion, and creativity. In the process, you learn to embrace your being and expand your awareness. Only then are you able to *truly* love others and maintain fulfilling long-term relationships.

In their healthiest forms, sex and love merge with emotional expressions of love and devotion to others. Therefore, sexuality and sexual freedom need to occur for individuals to thrive, which doesn't necessarily imply promiscuity, but often does imply passion.

However, in the same way we often confuse gender with sexual preference, and gender roles with masculine and feminine energies, we also confuse love and sex. This has led to all sorts of problems and artificial limits, because it's possible to have sex *without* love, love *without* sex, and sex *with* love.

In the first case, sex serves as a biological function of gender to enable reproduction and perpetuation of the species. Corporeal love is always present, but the emotion of love may not be present or even possible.

In the second, all forms of affection, love, and passion do not have to include the sex act. Your intentionality, or purpose in life, seeks multiple means of expression. When you feel a sense of purpose, you bring a deep passion to those activities, causes, and vocations that fuel your deepest love and devotion. In other words, your sexuality doesn't always have to include the sex act, because there at times when it's inappropriate or not even desired.

In the third, you *naturally* merge your sexuality with the emotion love. As you learn to fully love self *and* others, you realize that sexual activities are designed to be loving and satisfying. They will always promote dedication, commitment, and growth.

They are perfectly natural as long as they don't involve forms of violation (see Chapter 11).

As such, sexual repression, abuse, and domination and submission have no part in the natural life of our species, or that of animals. These can be traced to religious beliefs where love and devotion were artificially separated from the physical act. They became permissible only through religious visions or altered states, for only "God's love" was considered good enough to justify an ecstasy otherwise considered debased by the flesh, and our animal heritage.

In this light, healthy expressions of love, devotion, and sexuality will *always* provide a deep sense of meaning in your life. Together, they constantly reinforce all expressions of intent and purpose to promote your deepest fulfillment.

KEY IDEAS: Sex is first and foremost a biological function of gender to enable reproduction and perpetuation of the species. Love and devotion are emotional expressions that don't always include the sex act. However, when sexuality is merged with love and devotion, it brings you closer to understanding your divine nature as a beloved expression of All That Is.

What is the Relationship between Love and Hate?

Love and hate are intimately intertwined. They serve as bookends for a spectrum of emotions naturally designed to initiate change and action.

As we've said, love is a powerful, emotional energy that promotes devotion, dedication, and commitment to self and others. *It naturally seeks expression in everything you do.* It is naturally creative and promotes exploration and curiosity.

If love is a beacon for expressions of fulfillment, then hatred is its absence—the shadows and darkness. It's a natural mechanism designed to express our feelings and deeper sense of love, often when people we love, including ourselves, fail to meet our expectations.

Many people experience emotional problems or physical symptom (dis-ease) because they are afraid to acknowledge and properly vent their anger, which then builds into hatred. If you believe that hatred is bad or evil, then you may try to inhibit its expression, and eventually turn it on yourself. You end up hating yourself because you're afraid to express anger at someone else. You may try to dam up or pretend hateful feelings out of existence. You may try to ignore them, and repress negative feelings whenever they arise.

Those who commit violent crimes often have a history of conventional behaviors on the surface level, but underneath is a cauldron of unexpressed anger and rage that seeks expression. When they have no socially accepted means to express their growing anger, their sense of powerlessness grows until it erupts like a volcano. Often people learn to equate power with a kind of *artificial aggression* that leads to violent, unsatisfying behaviors, and a vicious, self-perpetuating cycle of powerlessness results.

Anger, rage, or hatred, when expressed as innate aggression, won't explode into seriously violent behaviors. Hatred creates a sense of power that initiates action. It communicates a need, purpose, and intention. In the animal world, there are normative rituals of behavior that communicate growing natural aggression during mating season or over territorial disputes. One animal eventually backs down. Power gets expressed, steam is blown off, and things settle down.

Therefore, it's healthy to express anger and even hatred because it's a distorted version of love propelled by what Seth calls *natural aggression*. It's a mechanism designed to blow off steam and communicate to others that a personal boundary has been crossed. Those boundaries may include your beliefs, personal space, belongings, home, work, parents, siblings, or children. Once expressed, things usually settle down. It's only after repeated instances where proper venting has been blocked or circumvented that serious violence erupts.[47]

Seth pointed out that when Christ taught, "Turn the other cheek," it was intended to diffuse violence, not to condone it. It was a symbolic representation of submission, like a wolf or dog displaying its belly to an aggressor. The baring of teeth, growling, and other body postures are designed to express natural aggression and limit violence. These gestures are designed for communal survival and cohesion. However, they are *not* intended to say, "It is okay to hit me again, or continue to abuse me."

Moreover, there is never a single, final version of mutual love between people, for love is always dynamic. It can quickly change to anger or hatred, and back again. Because a loved one attracts your best qualities, you see yourself in their eyes and something even greater is mirrored back. But in that reflection you may also see an idealized form.

Parents and children, and life partners, share a particular kind of intimate relationship in which they often perceive the difference between the real and such an ideal. As a result, there is often annoyance when those differences occur. For instance, when a child screams, "I hate you!" it really means, "Why are you treating me so badly when I love you so much!" In other words, the child's anger is a distorted expression of its love for their parent or sibling.

Further, they may be taught to not only inhibit vocal expressions of hatred, but thoughts of it as well, for hateful thoughts are considered as bad as hateful behaviors. They then become conditioned to feel an unnatural guilt when they imagine hating another. As they repress such thoughts, they no longer recognize those feelings on a conscious level. They become split off as *shadow* elements into their subconscious, which become invisible to their outer ego. Feelings of anger, resentment, and hatred *still* exist, but they remain repressed because they are afraid to even notice or acknowledge them.

Thus, they play a game of hide and seek with themselves to become *dissociated* from their own naturally aggressive feelings of hate. These repressed resentments then get projected outward onto others—a parent, a neighbor, a member of another race, or an enemy in wartime. In all cases, however, they find themselves simultaneously attracted to "the other," because their true repressed feelings *include* love, but are now expressed on the surface as projections of hatred.

They also become bonded with the object of their hate, which was originally based on unexpressed love in the form of natural aggression. In this way, they exaggerate all those differences from the ideal, and focus upon them to the exclusion of everything else. Love remains buried, and hatred rules the day.

In any given case, all of this is consciously available each individual. It requires only an honest and determined attempt to become aware of your own beliefs, thoughts, and emotions. Even your hateful fantasies, left alone, will return you to a reconciliation that releases love.

In this light, emotions form a very important feedback mechanism within your "iceberg self." You can't live without emotions any more than you can live without belief systems. To repress them is to deny them. Only when you learn to *trust* your naturally aggressive emotions will you open the door to experience altered states of psychic knowledge like channeling, dreaming, meditation, and out-of-body projections in a safe and healthy way.

KEY IDEAS: Love and hate are two sides of the same coin. Hatred, when expressed as natural aggression, doesn't explode into seriously violent behaviors. It's a natural function meant to communicate need, purpose, and intention by blowing off steam. When you repress feelings of anger and rage, it often leads to physical, emotional, and psychological problems.

What About Loving Self & Others?

While Christ taught that you should "Love thy neighbor as you love thyself," Seth suggests you turn that around to "Love yourself as you love your neighbor,"[48] because we often acknowledge the goodness in others, but don't afford ourselves the same courtesy. Again, you must learn to love and accept yourself, your own strengths and weaknesses, before you can adequately love another. This opens the door for you to further develop your abilities and realize as much of your entity's potential in physical form as possible. This, in turn, contributes to the collective development of your culture and planet.

When you truly love another, you learn to accept *their* strengths and weaknesses because you have consciously come to terms with your own. You are better able to give them the benefit of the doubt so they can develop into their authentic self. Thus, when you allow another the freedom to express themselves in

ways that may deviate from your own ideals, rather than con-
demn, you will allow their best selves to flourish. That is, you
will no longer confuse your own ideals with the reality of their
expressions, and both can happily coexist *without any
contradiction.*

Some version of this has always been expressed in the
perennial wisdom traditions and world's great religions.
For example, the Bible says[49]:

> Love is patient, love is kind. It does not envy, it does not
> boast, it is not proud. It is not rude, it is not self-seeking, it is
> not easily angered, it keeps no record of wrongs. Love does
> not delight in evil but rejoices with the truth. It always pro-
> tects, always trusts, always hopes, always perseveres. Love
> never fails.

In the long run, you come to realize that value fulfillment (divine love) always conquers all because it reconciles *every* expression of human love, compassion, and respect. As you learn to allow value fulfillment to guide your every action, you promote
your best interests along with those of others. In this way, you
add to the overall quality of your own life *and* the world.

While you may find yourself immersed in the shadow side of
love at times, divine love is *always* available to help find your
way in any relationship, whether it's with your self or with others. As we will explore more fully in Part 2 (Discover Your Place
in the World), reality creation also has a collective dimension that
must be taken into careful consideration. And in Part 3 (Discover
How We Can Live in Harmony), we'll explore its ethical dimension as well.

*KEY IDEAS: The most important relationship we have is first
with our self. It is only through self-love, self-compassion, and
self-respect that we learn a deep affection for the integrity and
worth of our human nature. Only then are we able to truly love
and respect others.*

Chapter 4: The Unlimited Power of Dreams

Why are Dreams Important?

Every twenty-four hours, you cycle through a series of states—waking, dreaming, and deep dreamless sleep. These states occur throughout every stage of development—as a fetus, baby, child, teenager, adult, or senior. You have dreams every night, even if you don't remember them.

We tend to consider the waking state as "normal" reality and all others as secondary, paranormal, or abnormal. Seth points out repeatedly that *all* states are valid and necessary. As such, dreaming is only one "altered state" among others, such as channeling, alpha, meditation, drug-induced, and shamanic.

Dream states were very important in traditional cultures. They were used to divine the future, heal sickness, and find food and water. In the West, the outer ego became so dominant that its waking reality came to be considered the only real one, so while physical and mental senses were considered real and encouraged, inner senses were repressed and atrophied.

Dreams were considered by early 20th century science to be nothing more than chaotic ramblings of subconscious material, a nocturnal period of insanity. It was only in the 1950s, when the first brain measurements were made, that scientists "discovered" that rapid eye movement (REM) coincided with intense dreaming activity. Only then—when scientists could match dreams with physical evidence—did dreams become "real."

However, *everything* dreams and all matter and energy have some kind of generalized awareness and interiority. Dreams have no beginning or end, just as there is no beginning or end to your subconscious or entity. Only our awareness of the dream begins and ends as we change back to the waking state. Here, we believe in beginnings and endings because they are so evident in our physical experience—movies, dinners, mornings, even lifetimes begin and end—so we've imposed this view on dreams and the "unknown" reality, too.

The dream world is a permanent construction that allows your entity to experience physical life. It is a natural by-product of the primal CUs/EEs/QFs used by your entity in reality creation. Dreams have their own electromagnetic properties as they get translated into your brain, but they also exist independently because of the multidimensional nature of your entity. The dream state is like your waking state because both are *camouflage* realities.

Seth often refers to idea constructions in physical and dream reality as camouflage. Your camouflage reality consists of primary and secondary constructions (as we explored in Chapter 2), but there are many other kinds of camouflage. Each camouflage reality has its own *root assumptions,* or local laws.[50] In our physical reality, they are the conventional scientific laws. Things like the speed of sound and light, time and space, gravity, strong and weak nuclear forces are all root assumptions we learn to manipulate as physical beings. We become so habituated to them that we take them for granted.

As we turn our attention to explore the dream world, however, we need to learn new sets of root assumptions. For in dreams, you can walk through walls, fly, turn into an eagle, breathe underwater, and much more!

KEY IDEAS: You dream every night, even if you don't remember it. Dreams are an important function of your subconscious mind. As you begin to explore the dream world, you will need to learn new sets of root assumptions.

Why Should I Explore My Dreams?

All true knowledge comes from our own direct experience. You can learn only so much from a book, which at best provides an accurate map. But *the map is never the territory*, and Seth's practices are designed to help you directly explore the subjective territory of your inner self. Seth encourages you to trust the evidence of your own physical, mental, and inner senses first and foremost.

Dream work helps to gradually widen your outer ego and create familiarity with your inner self. Dreams provide an excellent laboratory because they reflect your own personal imagery, symbols, and feeling-tone. They work in concert with belief work because your beliefs operate in the dream state, to a large extent, and the more you familiarize yourself with your beliefs, the better you are able to adequately interpret and utilize your dreams. The goal is to make your subconscious conscious, expand your sense of waking identity to include your dreaming self, and gain familiarity with your unique dream symbols and the root assumptions you'll encounter in various dream dimensions.

The first step is to get a journal to record your dreams. It can be a notebook or a computer document. You can also use a voice recorder (there are many inexpensive ones now available), and transcribe them into your journal at a later time. Keep these tools within easy reach by your bed.

Exercise 6—Dream Recall

The key to dream recall is a highly focused desire to remember, capture, and interpret your dreams. Before you to go to sleep, give yourself the following suggestions:

1. *My dreams are very important to me.*
2. *I wish to remember my dreams.*

3. *I will record my dreams when I wake up.*

Concentrate on those three ideas fully for no more than a couple of minutes. The more intense your desire and focus, the quicker you will manifest the ability to recall your dreams.

Next, when you first wake up—*don't move*. Engaging your body's motor functions can obscure the details of dream recall. Mentally review your dreams and identify the core elements— feelings, colors, locations, emotions, people, animals, activities, and time setting. If you have trouble remembering, ask yourself, "What was I just doing?" to prompt your subconscious mind to respond.

Then, get up and record your dreams in your notebook or voice recorder. Taking time to boot up your computer is not rec- ommended in the beginning stages. Add a date and time to each entry. Even if you don't recall a thing, add that as an entry. The idea is to establish the routine of the practice.

In time, you will find that recording your dreams helps you to recall other parts that you didn't initially remember when you woke up. As your waking mind processes the dream imagery, you will also begin to make connections to previous dreams with similar themes.

If you have problems with dream recall, there may be certain beliefs that are blocking them. Even Jane Roberts was caught off guard by Seth's initial emphasis on dreams, because she could recall only nightmares, which she believed were the "the self gone mad." If you recall only unpleasant dreams, you likely have some limiting beliefs to unblock. This is how regular belief work complements dream work. You have to get to the bottom of the limiting belief, identify it, and neutralize its blocking energies.

Many of us have been raised on a cultural stew of orthodox religion and psychology. The Church's "sinful self" and Freud's "unsavory subconscious" are two deeply ingrained belief systems that promote fearful conceptions of the subconscious that can block dream recall. As you identify limiting beliefs, remind your- self that your subconscious is *not* a hotbed of unsavory, dark, embarrassing urges. It's a *natural*, helpful Aspect of your "ice- berg self" designed to promote your greatest fulfillment.

Exercise 7—Identify Limiting Beliefs That Block Dream Recall

Remind yourself that your subconscious is a crucial Aspect of your "iceberg self" that makes physical life possible. Honor it, be curious, and keep an open mind in your desire to explore your dreaming self.

Now, give yourself a suggestion before going to sleep to have a dream about what's blocking you. Tell yourself that it will be the last dream you have right before you wake up. Spend no more than a minute concentrating on this, and then forget about it.

When you wake up, don't judge the initial dream response, just do your best to recall as much as possible, and add it to your journal. The deeper meaning and revelation of specific limiting beliefs may suddenly dawn on you later in the day, or over the next few days.

The key, again, is to focus your desire on the *importance* of your dreams, and your *desire* to connect directly with your dreaming self.

Try not to over-worry, that will only reinforce the limiting beliefs! Relax, stay playful, and let your subconscious mind do the work.

If you still are blocked after several attempts, ask your subconscious mind to give you an important clue during the day, one that will help identify what's blocking you. Spend no more than a minute concentrating, and then forget about it.

You may be talking to a friend, doing work, taking a shower, or watching a movie when you'll get a sudden knowing—the light bulb will go on!

When done properly, Seth's method for dream recall will allow you to remember more dreams in a month than in your entire life. Jane and her students verified this. However, Jane noted that there are natural cycles of better and worse recall. This is the effect of seasonal solar and lunar cycles, exercise, food, dis-ease, and other life conditions. So dream recall is ultimately unique to each individual. Be persistent, playful, and constantly reinforce your desire to remember, record, and interpret your dreams.

KEY IDEAS: Dreams are a gateway to the contents of your sub-conscious mind for reflection and expansion of consciousness. Learning to remember and record your dreams as a daily practice is a crucial tool. Belief work complements dream work because you will learn to recognize the effects of core belief systems in both areas.

Which Sleep and Dietary Habits Promote the Best Dream Recall?

Seth's suggested sleep and eating habits promote the best conditions for overall health, which directly impact dream recall. For instance, it's detrimental to have the body inactive for eight to ten hours every night because some of your consciousness actually leaves your body during sleep. Even though body consciousness remains, you can be away too long. Oversleeping also reinforces the separation between waking and dreaming selves.

Seth suggests you place your bed so your head aligns to the north, which takes advantage of the Earth's magnetic fields. Further, he suggests six to eight hours of sleep per day, including naps[51]:

- Two periods of three hours with *proper suggestions* given to insure the body's full restoration. ("I will wake up refreshed and alert.")
- The longest period should be at night.
- Five hours as the maximum period, plus a two hour nap if needed,
- OR a four hour period with two naps.

Poor eating habits promote needless stress and aging in the body. Dietary changes to support Seth's sleep regimen include:

- An equivalent of light snacks throughout the day instead of three large meals.
- Snacks begin immediately upon arising, and are interspersed throughout your day.

- The goal is to reduce habits of overstuffing and starving bodily tissues.

Benefits of making sleep and diet changes include:

- Improved dream recall.
- Higher peaks and greater flexibility of conscious focus.
- More steady renewal of physical and psychic activity.
- Creative abilities quickened.
- Increased concentration, problems seen more clearly, learning capacities improved.
- Reduced fatigue.
- Eliminated insomnia.
- Reduced depression, mental instability, senility, even schizophrenia.
- Aid the development of spiritual and psychic abilities.
- Increased enjoyment of the natural world.

Seth also cautioned that in order to maintain a clear and powerful focus you should engage frequent periods of rest and eating in-between physical activity. Otherwise, there is a danger that you will misinterpret and distort your perception of dream reality if your body/mind is overly stressed and unbalanced.

The changes suggested here will promote new beliefs and changes in behavior. Take your time, experiment, and learn what works best for your lifestyle. You will encounter natural resistances to making changes as your body, emotions, and habits of mind adjust. As we discussed in relation to changing beliefs, you may also encounter resistances from family or friends who notice your new habits and pressure you to conform to old ones.

Gradually rebalance your daily routine, and allow your new sleep and eating habits time to get established. Remember, it usually takes three full weeks to adopt new beliefs and behavioral changes. You will be impressed with the results!

KEY IDEAS: Seth's sleep and dietary framework is designed to blur the barrier between the waking and dreaming selves. It promotes greater flexibility of consciousness, better dream recall, and improved physical, emotional, and mental health.

What are Therapeutic Dreams?

You can use your dreams to heal the physical, emotional, and mental aspects of any dis-ease. The process of *dream incubation* involves targeted suggestions and strongly desired outcomes using natural hypnosis. Jane used the example of her close friend Sue Watkins, whose chronically sore shoulder bothered her for several years, flaring up and receding time and time again.

One night, Sue had a dream in which Seth appeared and explained methods directly to her subconscious mind on how to handle aggression and anger in acceptable ways. When she woke up, she no longer remembered the details of Seth's methods, but noticed her symptoms were greatly reduced, though not completely gone. Upon reflection, Sue realized that she had been taught as a child (directional beliefs) to repress her emotions. The denied expression of her anger began to affect her arm and shoulder as symptoms of bursitis.

Several weeks later, Sue had another experience, one that involved waking and dream states, in which she heard a voice instruct her to place wet tea bags on a particular area of her shoulder for a half hour a day for six days. The voice instructed her to relax her body, allow circulation, and use her breath to inhale "life" and exhale "poison."

Two weeks later, in the middle of the night, Sue heard the voice again say that the exercises were healing her body. As she learned to channel her aggressions away from her shoulder, her soreness was greatly reduced. This is an excellent example of how working through limiting beliefs and using the subconscious mind (the voice) can promote the healing process over time.

Health issues are most often caused by negative beliefs in the form of habitual destructive feelings that directly affect the body. Dis-ease does not happen first and then create unhealthy beliefs, thoughts, and emotions—*it's the exact opposite*. Learning to focus suggestion and desire through the dream state allows your subconscious mind and other Aspects of your entity to activate healing energies within your physical body. In all cases, you must come to terms with the emotional, mental, and psychic beliefs that relate to your symptoms if you wish to permanently heal them.

KEY IDEAS: You can learn to use dreams to activate the healing powers of your subconscious mind through targeted suggestion and focused desire. Belief work is a complementary part of the process.

What are True Dreams from the Gates of Horn?

In May 1974, Seth challenged ESP class students to give themselves the suggestion before going to sleep to have a "true dream from the Gates of Horn." Seth was clear that even though this technique was traceable to the Egyptians (and Greeks and Romans, too), his definition was slightly different.

While the ancients believed that dreams from the Gates of Horn were authentic subconscious messages, Seth suggested they also had further value in *helping to recognize beliefs, and harmonize and energize our being.* This is another type of therapeutic dreaming that's not targeted to a specific dis-ease, but is used to mine helpful information from your subconscious.

As class members explored their dreamscapes in the ensuing weeks, they reported ecstatic, joyful, and profound dream imagery. They labeled these dreams as "completely different" in terms of their emotional feeling tones. One person reported feeling more in tune with his environment (weather, animals, people), and his body. Seth pointed out that "true dreams" probe deeply into the beliefs *beneath* your everyday reality to help your subconscious mind better understand its role in reality creation, hence the vivid dream imagery and energizing effects on your body/mind.[52]

As you gain familiarity with the dream state and subconscious imagery, you will also become aware of other realities, and begin to notice *unofficial information* bleeding through into your waking state. In the midst of mundane activities, you may begin to experience "waking dream states." This is not unnatural, as you daydream on a daily basis. You are simply used to blocking these deeper waking states because the imagery may initially seem intrusive, odd, and out of the blue. But as you train yourself to have mental leeway, remain curious, and go with the flow, your inner senses will become increasingly active.

You may begin to experience clairvoyant imagery, clairaudient sounds, and even telepathic communications. Seth cautions that fearing a loss of identity in such experiences is the main obstacle to overcome. Widening your self-conception through dream work helps you neutralize such fears, because you learn that your subconscious mind and dreams are sources of important communications from your entity.

In this way, you come full circle. In addition to exploring your dreaming self, dream work also allows you to become more aware of subtle nuances in waking states and their dream-like qualities. You can obtain important insights into personal issues, solve problems, and promote healing.

KEY IDEAS: True dreams from the Gates of Horn help you explore the beliefs behind everyday reality, and the mechanics of reality creation through dream imagery. They help to harmonize and energize your being.

What are Out-of-Body Projections?

Out-of-body projections and their cousins, lucid dreams, are exhilarating types of dream states. If you want direct evidence that you are more than your physical body, there is nothing like the first time you consciously exit your sleeping body, look back in amazement, and explore the dream world in your dream body!

In out-of-body projections and lucid dreams, your outer ego becomes conscious *within* the dream state. The focus can vary from semi-lucid to extremely lucid. The more you can activate your critical faculties and maintain the state, the more lucidity is generally present. The main difference between projections and lucid dreams is that in lucid dreams, you may simply come awake and drift back into dream consciousness. With projections, there is always a sense of leaving and returning to the physical body.

Your exit from your physical body may be accompanied by the sensation of a strong electrical current running up and down your spine into the back of your head. There may be initial resistance to projecting because your physical body experiences sleep paralysis—no matter how hard you try to move, you can't. This may cause fear initially, but it's nothing to worry about. In time, you learn *not* to move your physical body, and instead, to focus on changing state and projecting out.[53]

Seth identifies three dream bodies that work together that you may utilize during a projection or lucid dream. Each subsequent body moves further "inward"—away from physical constructions—and uses more of your inner senses. Seth calls them the first, second, and third form. As you begin, you will usually project from your sleeping body into the first form, used for your regular (non-lucid) dreams. You can project from the first to the second or third forms, but you will return to your body in reverse direction, consecutively from third to second to first.

In all cases, as you return towards your physical body, you may experience *false awakenings*, meaning you actually "wake up" in another form's dream bed that's so real you become momentarily confused and think you're back in waking state. Only when you wake up in your physical body do you realize the difference. This is a normal occurrence and nothing to be concerned about.

It takes time and practice to acclimate to the change of forms and perceptions that accompany each dream body. As you expand your self-conception, these become *much* easier. As you familiarize yourself with your own dream forms, you'll learn to identify the different root assumptions that govern each, because they characterize the limits of what you can and can't do in the dream state.[54]

- The **first form** is what you use for regular dreams, lucid dreams and projections. You can levitate, and perceive past, present, and future of physical reality, on a limited basis. You may encounter subconscious fears materialized in the form of "phantoms"—secondary dream constructions—but *once recognized* you can simply order them to, "Go away!" You will be able to look back on the bed and see your body, though this isn't recommended in the early stages, as it may end the projection prematurely by attracting you back in.
- In the **second form**, perception expands and consciousness widens. You use this form to participate in group

dreams where you share dream experiences that you can corroborate when you wake up (see Chapter 7). As a rule, you won't encounter subconscious materializations. Ordinary dream elements are lessened, longer durations of projection occur, and there is extraordinary vividness or clarity of focus. You will encounter a variety of primary constructions that you can't order to disappear. Some may exist in your past or future, and it takes experience to discern the difference. For example, you could find yourself projected within the body of a soldier in battle and experience his pain, until you learn to project back into your own second form. You will not be able to see your sleeping physical body in this form, though you may be able to sense it.

- The **third form** is an authentic projection form, meaning that you can perceive past, present, and future in *other* dimensions as well as this one. You can also experience formlessness—a type of nondual consciousness—in this "form." You may attempt to use all your inner senses, though this is rare because you have defense mechanisms to automatically shield you against overly strong inputs, as full-bore inner senses are the purview of your entity. You will no longer have any awareness of your physical body. This is the most difficult form to maintain, because it allows entrance into other dream dimensions far removed from your physical body.

- The **third form** is also the vehicle of the inner self and what you use when you leave your body at the moment of death. So there's a natural disorientation that, once acclimated to, makes the transition to the afterdeath environment smoother (see Chapter 5). Any construction you meet will be a primary construction, which you can't will away, so they can be dangerous, like any primary construction in waking reality (cars, fires, sharp objects, etc.). Seth cautioned to approach these constructions with respect and care, but to freely explore them.[55]

Again, when you successfully project to other dream dimensions, you will experience unusual imagery and new root assumptions. In all cases, you will wake up and translate your experiences through your physical brain and belief systems, which are based upon waking root assumptions. Therefore, try not to be too literal as you explore. Keep an open, skeptical attitude about what you encounter, and continually stoke your sense of fun and adventure.[56]

KEY IDEAS: Lucid dreams and out-of-body projections provide direct evidence that you are more than your physical body. There are three projection forms, each one moves further "inward" and uses more of your inner senses.

Probable Selves and Your Dreaming Self

Seth outlined a variety of Aspects within your entity, some of which sound exotic at first. But as you progress with dream work, you'll discover more and more of these submerged parts of your "iceberg self".

Every day, you make minor and major choices. You decide what clothes to wear, what to eat, and when to go to sleep. You may also decide to take a new job, get married, buy a home, or travel to a foreign land. There are different amounts of emotional and psychic energy behind each of your choices. What would it be like if your entity had the ability to explore every possible choice?

In every decision you make, you choose from an infinite set of probabilities. The process is so automatic that you generally don't even notice it. But with a little introspection, you can begin to notice and explore probable roads not taken. For instance, what if you didn't take that job, or marry that spouse, or go to that city for vacation? According to Seth, some Aspect of you, called a *probable self,* traveled down the road you didn't.

Since your waking self is so focused in physical reality, you don't usually tune into your probable selves. However, your entity has a multidimensional communication system that constantly goes on beneath the surface and is managed by your subconscious, which includes your dreaming self. You have learned to tune out these communications based on ingrained cultural habits and limited self conceptions.

Therefore, from your entity's perspective, there are actually multiple "tips" to your "iceberg self." They exist in probable dimensions. Their sense of time runs parallel to ours, so there are bifurcation (splits) and intersection points between all of them.

A modern physicist named Hugh Everett (1930-1982) intuited this in his "many worlds interpretation" of quantum mechanics published in 1956. He stated that all probable events exist as infinite wave potentials in QFs until *you choose one* and collapse the QF's "wave function" into particle-based perception. Therefore, physical reality exists as an infinite set of probable worlds, people, objects, decisions, and so on.

Everett's theory comes closest to a scientific explanation for the physical aspects of Seth's probable selves. According to Seth, not only do the QFs that make up your body consist of massively parallel information processes, so too do the CUs and EEs that make up your entity and subconscious. *Therefore, you can use the dream state to communicate with a probable self.*

Seth introduced probable selves early on to help expand your self-conceptions to include submerged Aspects of your "iceberg self." Even though your outer ego is unfamiliar with its probable counterparts, portions of your subconscious manage them *all* and react to inner data that would otherwise overwhelm you. These stimuli are often expressed within dreams to inform you of potential dangers or successful outcomes to challenges you face. In this way, there is a constant give and take between all your probable selves and your dreaming self.

Your dreaming self, like your subconscious, is free of space and time as you know it. Even further inward, your entity has access to many millions of probable conditions, situations, and Aspects. Together, they conspire to provide you with helpful information whenever you face difficult situations and life changing choices.

KEY IDEAS: You can learn to use the dream state to communicate with probable selves and explore probable choices to help you make important decisions, solve problems, and promote healing.

What are Some Other Cool Dream Experiments?

With time and practice, you'll discover what works best for you. You'll begin to identify various patterns of beliefs and imagery in your dreamscapes. Seth suggests that you:

- Check dream events against daily events in order to identify any clairvoyant (telepathic) or precognitive (future) elements—evidence of your inner senses at work. Identify past, present, or future locations, which may suggest interest in clearing up old business, or considering current choices and how they will play out.
- Notice the roles being played by dream characters such as parents, siblings, students, and teachers. Are they strangers or familiar? Strangers may be familiar individuals to your probable selves, nested within your entity.

In noticing these elements, you may begin to gain unique insights about other people, locations, or events. As you continue to experiment, over the years you will provide important evidence for how the different aspects of the subconscious and entity function. If enough people were to combine their insights and experience, we could map entire new areas and functions of human consciousness.

For example, in noticing that some dreams occur in an unfamiliar place, you may find that they portend future events beginning to bleed through into your subconscious mind. Jane Roberts discovered that most of her precognitive dreams took place in unfamiliar locations, and therefore was able to more accurately interpret them as such. Dreams may also serve as warnings of events to avoid, like taking a jet, driving somewhere, or eating certain foods.

Dream work provides an important method to prove the validity of Seth's map of your "iceberg self." Unfortunately, many people *believe* that they don't have the time or energy to pursue it. Since you dream every night, doing a little bit every day—just fifteen to thirty minutes—can lead to important insights in your waking life.

KEY IDEAS: Dream work and belief work go hand in hand. As you learn dream recall and journaling, begin to note patterns in locations, characters, times, emotions, and connections to waking life situations.

Chapter 5: Birth, Death, & Reincarnation

What Happens Before Birth?

When you first read Seth, you may begin to feel like Dorothy in the *Wizard of Oz* (1939) who said famously, "Toto, I have a feeling we're not in Kansas anymore!" It's an apt metaphor for entering the strange and intuitive domain of your "iceberg self."

When Jane Roberts began the Seth sessions, she considered reincarnation only an intellectual concept with no validity. However, she felt very close to Rob when they first met, and they romantically entertained the idea that they could have known each other in previous lives. That was the extent of it until Seth introduced new material to challenge their beliefs.

Like Shakespeare, Seth compares each life to an actor entering a play. "All the world's a stage," the situation, props, circumstances, and challenges are *chosen prebirth*. Each "play" involves unique creative challenges like exploring science, art, or religion, or learning to use intellect, emotions, or explore relationships.

We each write our own scripts and play out the drama. Not only do we choose our parents, but our entity also plays a vital role in the creation and maintenance of each physical environment in cooperation with all other entities.

Why would anyone choose to be born severely handicapped, to a mother with HIV, to live in poverty, starvation, plague, or genocidal warfare? On the other hand, why would anyone choose to be born a queen, billionaire, genius, or movie star? Seth offers no one-size-fits-all explanation except to say that each individual situation is unique to that person's innate intent (see Chapter 1).

It's a beginner's mistake to blame your life's challenges on your entity, or to assume that your entity forces you to suffer, or belongs to a cabal of entities fallen from God's grace, or takes part in some grand conspiracy to oppress you. Those are all variations of "sinful self" dogmas, because they claim you're predestined to a life of suffering. They promote a blame game that puts the responsibility for your situation on someone or something "outside" of you. Seth encourages you to avoid those teachings, well, like the plague!

Instead, he points out that your entity IS YOU. Your entity *always* has your best interests and fulfillment at heart because it is not separate from you. Your entity is your innermost, indestructible self. You are a physically manifest Aspect who is always connected through your subconscious and inner senses. Seth speaks of separate Aspects only to point out the different structures that are accessible *within* your conscious mind, but in the end they all work together as a magnificent reality creation *system*.

Seth points out that birth is by far the most traumatic physical event in relation to death. Obviously, some die by violence and painful dis-ease, but the physical birth pressures on the fetus and mother are *always* intense, and there can also be complications. But once you make it safely into the world of space-time, you're on your way!

KEY IDEAS: Birth is more traumatic than death for most people. You choose your parents and life conditions <u>before</u> each life, which is like a play, and you are the actor. People choose all *sorts of life conditions which may include seemingly difficult challenges, but all lives have their own challenges and rewards.*

Is Reincarnation Real?

Yes and no. Yes in the sense that we *do* live more than one lifetime, but no in the sense that we *do not* experience linear (consecutive) lives. Conventional notions from Eastern religions contain "true but partial" understandings of the way your entity functions. The idea that you're born, live and die, have an interim or "Bardo" period, and then reincarnate is partially true, but *only* from the perspective of your outer ego, which experiences linear time. Again, your entity exists in a spacious present that experiences nonlinear time. Therefore, from this perspective, *all your lifetimes exist simultaneously.*

We live as many lives as necessary to develop our creative potentials and prepare ourselves to enter other dimensions of experience. There is a minimum set of requirements for any entity who wishes to experience our physical universe. First, there is a minimum of three basic roles: mother, father, and child. Seth makes the adult/child distinction because adulthood is necessary to gain a deep understanding of the human condition.[57]

These three roles provide a baseline to ensure these essential types of experience are included. However, there is an additional requirement: *you must develop the fullest use of your potentials.* This requirement is what causes most entities to be born many more than three times.

Together, these form the minimum "commitment" any entity agrees to experience when entering our physical reality. Seth never gave a maximum limit to the number of lives, but it's enough to provide adequate experience to prepare your entity to manifest in more complex dimensions.

In terms of reincarnation, your entity doesn't simply send out an old version of itself time and again. Each life is "freshly minted" and develops along its own individual lines. So "you" exist in many variations and timeframes simultaneously.

Moreover, each incarnation has probable selves. As such, your entity must learn to manage a large cluster of personalities spread across past, present, and future time dimensions. In this context, *reincarnation simply deals with probabilities within multiple space-time frameworks.* When your entity originally manifest, it was like a huge firework that exploded different Aspects into a vast probability framework. Each physical self was then free to explore its own unique probable framework.

Overall, each reincarnational and probable self perceives itself to be the center of the universe, and exists *as* the center of the universe. Each life is a physical expression of your entity, who manages all these Aspects. But your entity is not a quantifiable "unit" solely defined by physical measurements. In those terms, "you" remain unquantifiable.

KEY IDEAS: From any incarnation's perspective, there may be the appearance that one life follows another in consecutive fashion. But from your entity's perspective, all your lifetimes are simultaneous. Your entity agrees to explore the roles of mother, father, and child—and to develop your abilities to the fullest— when it manifests in physical reality.

What Happens When We Die?

There are no accidental deaths—each death is chosen within the context of your entity's overall fulfillment. However, there's no rule that says you have to die from dis-ease or a severely reduced function of your body/mind. These creations are the result of culturally ingrained beliefs. You can choose to leave your body when it's your time, and you can live to be much older than the current average mortality age.

In response to modern cultural beliefs, the outer ego has become *extremely* separated from nature and its inner source to the point that many people don't believe in God or a soul, much less life after death. People who hold these beliefs tend to be in denial of their deaths and rage at the "existential meaninglessness of it all" as death approaches. Dylan Thomas (1914-1953) famously expressed this modern ethos as, "Rage, rage against the dying of the light."

However, death is a process, just like life. You live in the midst of small deaths every day. You "die" every night when you go to sleep and your outer ego relaxes its grip and acquiesces to the dreaming self. You wake up "reborn" every morning. Your body replaces dead cells constantly, and every ten years you completely replace *every* cell. In terms of the blinking CUs/EEs/QFs, you "die" infinitesimal deaths trillions upon trillions of times every second, but it's so fast you don't even notice it! In this context, Seth humorously opines we are as dead now as we will ever be. So death is not the end, but a new beginning.

There is no specific moment of death. It is unique for everyone. While your consciousness leaves your body, it takes time for your body to decay and morph back into base elements, all of which are *still* conscious and contain interiority. But your "iceberg self" no longer needs your body, nor is it ever limited to physical constructions.

Further, it's possible to *consciously* participate in your own death. This is a well-known practice in the Eastern mystical traditions in which a yogi or yogini consciously wills themselves out of their bodies at the moment of death. In the Hindu tradition, this is called *mahasamadhi* (see Chapter 8).

Again, no matter how peaceful or traumatic, no death occurs by "accident." A car collision may be involved, or plane crash, or shipwreck, but in all cases your entity "has your back," so to speak. It's really up to you how involved you wish to be in creating your own death. For those who don't believe in life after death, or in a soul, they will tend to choose a method to disengage from physical life *at the entity or subconscious level.*

Seth discussed the case of a man killed by a seemingly random brick that fell during a 1970s earthquake in Los Angeles. A student wondered why this individual would walk out at the very moment a piece of fatal debris was falling? Seth said that even though he was *subconsciously* aware of all probable events at his entity layer, his death was not predestined. Thus, it was a probable death based upon free will and choice—an inner nudging acted upon in the moment point.

In other words, he was ready to move onto other dimensions of reality, and was subconsciously seeking a means to disengage from physical reality. Therefore, based upon his outer ego's beliefs, needs, and intent, he was ready to move on and the earthquake spontaneously provided an acceptable means to do so.[58]

After death, then, you exist in the third form of your dream body, as mentioned earlier (see Chapter 4). If you're not overly familiar with it, you'll have to adjust to the new root assumptions you encounter. Your body may appear exactly the same as it did at the time of death, or it may be adjusted to any age you choose. In all cases, there is a transitional experience so that you become aware of your new situation. These are not somber experiences, and tend to be more pleasant and vibrant than most experiences in physical reality. Therefore, familiarity with lucid dreaming and projections of consciousness are very helpful ways to prepare for your own death.

Moreover, you will create your own reality after death, based upon the cultural roadmap you subscribe to. Your immediate experience will be based on ingrained expectations and belief systems. In premodern cultures, the river Styx had to be crossed in a boat, replete with a boatman. If you believe in heaven and hell, you may initially experience St. Peter's Gate or Satan's hell fires. If you believe in nothing, then you'll experience a period of nothingness. However, these are all self-generated secondary constructions and *not* permanent.

There will be guides to assist as necessary. If you pass away after a long and stressful illness, you may initially experience your hospital bed, but there will be new "nurses" to help you understand what has taken place. If you have strong connections with family and friends, they may be there to greet you. If you are interested in other lives, you may meet acquaintances from those times. Telepathy operates so that your true beliefs and feelings are available to anyone you encounter, and vice versa.

Seth shared a story in which he acted as a guide for an Arab man in his initial after-death experience. The man had died horribly during the Crusades—suffocated by hot coals. He was a Muslim who believed in Allah, but harbored a secret belief that the Jewish Prophet Moses was even more powerful. So Seth played the role of Moses, and another entity played the role of Allah. Because of this man's beliefs in force and violence, they had to wage the battle he expected for his soul.

The man cowered in fear at the mighty sky battle as these god-like figures exchanged claims on his soul. Each had hosts of followers behind them. Allah wielded a sword, Moses set it aflame, and Allah dropped it to the ground. Eventually Moses produced a tablet inscribed with "Thou Shalt Not Kill" and exchanged it with Allah, who in turn gave Moses his mighty sword. Their followers blended into a sun and they both said, "We are one."[59] Only when his conflicting beliefs were resolved—the opposing elements united—could his situation then be explained to him.

Finally, after-death environments don't exist on another physical planet or anywhere in the physical universe. They exist *within* nonphysical fields inside CUs/EEs. Because they're cleverly nested "underneath" the physical field, they don't take up any space at all. In this way, the dead literally exist side by side with the living, separated only by different perceptive mechanisms.

KEY IDEAS: Your initial afterdeath experience will be based on whatever cultural roadmap you believe in. You will learn to deal with new root assumptions in a new environment, which exists "underneath" matter. Experience with your three dream bodies in this life makes the transition much easier.

What are the Mechanics of Transition?

Once you understand that you are "dead," you enter into a deeper transition experience. Seth discusses this in paradoxical terms. While all lives are simultaneous from your entity's perspective, from *your* after-death perspective, you still exist as a primary construction creating your own reality via secondary constructions.

You may experience a wide range of new things that include *thought-forms*—projections of your own fears or joys objectified as a "demon" or "goddess," for example—or *pseudo-images* that you send to others every time you think of them. These are all secondary constructions, and are not imbued with the full force of a primary construction. Once you recognize them as such, you perceive them as the harmless secondary constructions that they are.

At some point, you enter an in-between period—a "midplane of existence" similar to the Buddhist Bardo state—in which many issues are considered. But Seth's version of reincarnation involves a lot more than just deciding to engage another life or achieving some kind of final enlightened state. A wide variety of decisions are available according to your overall development. In general terms, he outlines three main choices:

1. Plan another life.
2. Deeply explore your previous life.
3. Enter another probable system. This is beyond any "reincarnational cycle."

The first choice is used to seek balance from your preceding life that may have focused excessively on, say, intellect over emotions. Another life may be chosen in which the emotions are ramped up and the intellect made secondary. In this way, your entity learns the value of something it has never experienced. Some will work out problems in easier ways, others in more explosive ways. Some will reincarnate before they are ready, for a variety of reasons. Though the necessary planning has not occurred, there are no mistakes, and the entity learns from each experience in the long run.

There are also group dramas that may attract you to your next life, and you will rejoin people you have known in past lives. Or you may be more of a loner, or without deep interest in any specific historical chapter. Some may choose to experience every possible racial type, though this is not a requirement.

The second choice is used to explore probable variations within your past life and make changes. Given the nature of probabilities and probable selves, there is great potential to experience the roads not taken, or to create new ones. In all cases, this option generates new experiences for your entity.

The third choice is for those who've developed their abilities as far as possible through a reincarnational cycle within a particular system. Some may choose to reenter the cycle acting as teachers. This is similar to the Buddhist notion of the *Bodhisattva*, an "enlightened" being who is finished with reincarnations, but chooses to return to help others awaken and fulfill their potentials. Though Seth never refers to the entity's condition as enlightened in that particular sense, the similarity is of interest.

Therefore, at the moment of death, in all cases, you don't experience instant enlightenment where all the answers are known, or become all-wise. You may or may not have access to all your other lives. As stated earlier, there is no room for the lazy. Your entity is imbued with the need to create, experience, and develop its potentials. In all cases, afterdeath mechanics are designed to promote new experiences.

An important question arises: since there is no absolute heaven or hell, in terms of traditional religions, "What about good and evil?" Without the motivation to do good deeds for fear of eternal punishment, what's the point of being good or developing at all? Seth said that conventional beliefs in right/wrong and better/worse can sometimes be misleading (see Chapter 11).We are simply exploring vast probability fields to learn the mechanics of reality creation and develop our abilities.

The reincarnational cycle helps our entities to develop within a physical system in very human terms. Because ours is an exceedingly complex framework, there is much to be learned. As such, many of our notions of good/evil simply don't apply to the afterdeath environment, because they are based upon distorted beliefs and ignorance.

Overall, the period of transition is not a time of confusion, but of tremendous insight and exciting challenges. Those who understand that "you create your own reality," have some facility with their dream bodies, and can interpret dream symbols will have an easier time.

Seth pointed out that both Ruburt [Jane] and Joseph [Rob] were completing their reincarnational cycles. He said that the time of choosing is complicated for people in their situation, because they finally realize that their "iceberg self"—their basic identity—is more than the sum of *all* their reincarnational selves. At this stage, they become conscious of all their other personalities, past and future. The third choice, entering another probable system beyond reincarnational cycles, now becomes possible. Entities may also choose to become multidimensional teachers and remain behind to help others, though this requires intensive training.

A fictional version of this kind of teacher is Cyprus, a character in the *Oversoul Seven Trilogy* (1995) by Jane Roberts. This highly recommended series explores many of Seth's multidimensional concepts in a playful way. Cyprus teaches an entity—Oversoul Seven, who is trying to earn his Oversoul Eight "stripes"—to learn how reality creation works in the spacious present. Seven goes through various highs and lows as four of his personalities get into all sorts of jams.

One dies and reincarnates. There is a poignant scene in *The Further Education of Oversoul Seven*[60], in which Lydia, who dies in the late 20th century USA, chooses to be reborn as Tweety in 17th century Denmark (a "new" reincarnation occurs *before* the previous one). Tweety is an infant just beginning to walk, and still in diapers.

When the time arrives for Lydia to fully manifest *as* Tweety, she hovers around the parents and baby in her dream body, worried that she won't remember her old self. She can feel herself being drawn more fully into the baby with each passing moment! Seven assures her that the forgetting is only temporary and she will eventually remember her true identity. Like an actor taking on a new role, Lydia finally merges with Tweety, and "forgets" she was ever Lydia.

Lastly, you will *not* come back as an animal. Animal consciousness is very different than human consciousness (see Chapter 10). However, your entity does have the ability to project an Aspect of itself into an animal to experience physical reality *within* those limits. But animals don't have self-reflexive awareness ("I think therefore I am"), belief systems, or experience emotions the same way.[61]

Still, this doesn't mean that all animals have fragments of Uncle Bob or Mother Teresa in them. Nor are animals limited to the same species in every life. There are many different kinds of groupings that consciousness can take, and it requires a certain kind of knowledge to manifest as a complex physical organism, whether animal or a human being.

KEY IDEAS: You will create your own reality after death as well, based upon the cultural roadmap you subscribe to. Once you realize you have died, you experience a period of transition in which you face three main choices: 1. Plan another lifetime, 2. Explore probabilities from your previous life, or 3. Enter another probable system. You will not reincarnate as an animal, but your entity has the ability to project an Aspect of itself into an animal to experience physical reality within those limits.

What are Counterparts?

An interesting part of the Seth phenomenon was that he used Rob and Jane's psychic experiences and development to introduce new material. For example, Rob had visions of himself as a Roman soldier aboard a slave ship, and as a 19th century Jamaican woman. He had also seen himself as a Roman teacher named Nebene. These could have been explained by more conventional notions of reincarnation, but Rob sensed that Nebene and his Roman soldier *shared the same time period*. How could that be?

Seth called them *counterparts—multiple lives within the same time period*. In other words, counterparts may overlap in any period of history to explore various themes, challenges, and abilities. Not only are you biologically related to your family, race, and species in each life, you may also be psychically related to several of your contemporaries *because you share the same entity*.

As such, a black woman may be a white man or child at the same time. The victim may also be a perpetrator. The wealthy woman may exist somewhere as a beggar man. You can be a child on the cusp of one period and an old man or woman on the other. Or there may be only one life that experiences a long, rich, and highly focused creative life, for example, the artist Michelangelo (1475-1564) whose life spanned eighty-nine years in Renaissance Italy.

Rob's Roman teacher was intellectual, cautious, focused on teaching wealthy Roman children, cowed by creativity and his sexual drives, and very demanding and authoritative. On the other hand, his Roman soldier was aggressive, sought adventure, was somewhat insensitive, and blindly followed orders. Rob worked on his writing and painting skills, openly challenged authority, and rebelled against limited social and political structures. In this way, Rob's entity (Joseph) expressed different themes and characteristics in two Roman counterpart lives, in Rob's life, and in many other lives spread across multiple time periods.

The implications of Seth's "counterpart thesis," as Rob called it, and reincarnational and probable selves are staggering. Though they will likely take centuries to fully explore, the most immediate conclusions are these:

- We are related to every human through biology, psychology, and even richer psychic affiliations as counterparts.
- The theory of single, consecutive reincarnations is highly simplistic. Overall, the reincarnational cycle includes as yet unknown nonlinear principles (as illustrated with 20th century Lydia reincarnating as 17th century Tweety).
- Like many war stories where brothers, fathers and sons fought on opposite sides, if you factor in Seth's counterparts, the matrix of relationships at odds during those conflagrations is vast. As counterparts, we literally kill *ourselves* in wars (see Chapter 13).

Together, these Aspects function like the different instruments in an orchestra that play the "symphony of your soul." In this light, a working knowledge of counterparts, and reincarnational and probable selves would radically redefine physics, biology, psychology, and spirituality to promote a deeper sense of connection and purpose among all people.

KEY IDEAS: Counterparts are multiple lives that overlap within the same time period. They cover periods of history from a wide range of perspectives, face unique challenges, and develop unique abilities, all of which fuel your entity's development.

What about Karma?

Conventional beliefs in reincarnation based on karma—the "cosmic law of cause and effect"—are highly limited. Seth points out that from your entity's perspective, all your counterpart, reincarnational and probable selves exist within the spacious present. While bad deeds may serve as a baseline to choose a new life or explore probable variations in a previous one, they *never* serve as grounds for punishment in your next life.

For instance, traditional Eastern religious beliefs in karma hold that people are born into poor families called "Untouchables" as punishment for past sins or crimes. Seth refutes this. Instead, he shows how your "iceberg self" seeks its greatest fulfillment in every life by simultaneously exploring poor and rich lifetimes.

If you're born with a handicap, poor, or into other difficult circumstances, it is *always* a prebirth choice for the personality's fulfillment, not as a punishment for bad deeds. The punishment theory is the traditional Eastern religious version of the "sinful self"—bad circumstances in your next life as punishment. *All* deeds are reviewed during the transition period, and may serve as the basis to plan a new life or explore variations of a past one. But the "truth" of good and evil exists only in the context of culturally accepted beliefs and norms.

As such, they are relative and not absolute. They *are* real, there *are* repercussions, but there is never any *eternal* punishment *or* reward, because that implies a static, finished state, and there is no such thing. Consciousness—All That Is—is in a constant state of becoming. This also means there's no such thing as predetermination. That's too limiting and denies the innate vitality and creativity of your entity and All That Is. You simultaneously exist inside and outside of space-time, and within that larger framework there is an exuberant exchange between all your Aspects.

Therefore, it's a mistake to believe your life's circumstances were *forced* upon you as some kind of cosmic punishment for being evil in a past *or* future life, for that matter. *There are no closed systems*—physical, emotional, psychological, psychic, or spiritual. There is great creative give and take between all Aspects of your entity and All That Is.

On the other hand, if you find yourself in difficult circumstances, you may begin to feel inadequate and wonder why you can't create your reality "better." That's a form of new age guilt to avoid. As we saw, your core belief systems are complex and deep. There are many ways you may sabotage your best interests and health. With time and practice, you *can* turn any situation around.

Seth said that suffering is a natural offshoot of the growth process, but it is *never* thrust upon you by some outside agency, entity, or God. Dis-ease, pain, and turmoil are the effects of misguided energy. As such, they are inherent within the primal vitality of All That Is as potentials for experience, but are never intrinsically "good for the soul." Their purpose, therefore, is to help you *learn to how to stop your own suffering.*

You are also here to learn that other forms of suffering like violence, shame, and guilt are the result of personal and collective ignorance, so when you hurt others, you ultimately hurt *yourself.* When the majority of people understand this, our world will be radically transformed (see Part 3).

KEY IDEAS: Seth refutes the conventional notion of karma as a "cosmic law of cause and effect." Since all Aspects of your entity form an open psychological and spiritual system, they affect each other in various ways. No single set of deeds is ever the basis of punishment in any reincarnation or beyond.

What is Simultaneous Time?

So how does your entity exist in a spacious present that includes simultaneous lives?

One way to imagine this is to consider the design of a fly's compound eye. It consists of dozens of individual lenses, and yet provides a unified visual field that covers a full 360 degrees. In the same way, your entity is a compound self who manages an array of lives nested within different times, and yet maintains a unified identity within a spacious present.

Seth uses the metaphor of simultaneous time to further explain this. It shows how reality creation works in linear (consecutive) ways from your perspective and nonlinear (simultaneous) ways from your entity's perspective. So there's a basic paradox to resolve from your outer egoic perspective: how to reconcile the time and "no-time" functions of the primal CUs/EEs/QFs (see Chapter 2).

Your entity emanates QFs to manifest multiple lives (counterparts, reincarnational and probable selves) across history, but simultaneously uses the nested CUs/EEs to create nonlinear effects that unify them (entity in the spacious present).Your past, present, and future *remain malleable* because of the innate unpredictability of CUs/EEs/QFs. As such, the past is never finished or static, and therefore *fresh action can emerge.*

Therefore, linear time is relative and *not absolute.* Einstein proved this in his general theory of relativity (1916). He showed that gravity affected the speed of light—it "bent" or slightly shifted it. So space and time are "curved" and light never travels in a straight line. Of course, Einstein's theory doesn't account for Consciousness or your entity like Seth does, but then Seth never directly discussed quantum gravity either. Both theories complement each other.

Ironically, the best explanation of simultaneous time isn't found in any Seth book, but in Jane Roberts's *The Education of Oversoul Seven.* The story unfolds in four concurrent time periods as Seven's personalities interact through dreams, projections, and channeling states. Seven eventually learns how they relate to each other—in a nested matrix of past, present, and future time dimensions.

The following chart is viewed from Lydia's 20th century perspective. It reveals how Seven's three other personalities relate to Lydia and each other *when perceived by Seven in the spacious present.*

Century/Character	Past	Present	Future
300th Cen. BC Maah	Past/PAST	**Present/PAST**	Future/PAST
17th Cen. CE Joseph	Past/PAST	**Present/PAST**	Future/PAST
20th Cen. CE Lydia	Past/PRESENT	**Present/PRESENT**	Future/PRESENT
24th Cen. CE Proteus	Past/FUTURE	**Present/FUTURE**	Future/FUTURE

These *nine basic dimensions of time* are also available to you, the outer ego. Your **Present/PRESENT** is always your point of power—the moment point in which *you* choose and interact. Therefore, it's the dimension from which you may communicate with any of your counterparts, reincarnational selves, and probable selves.

Put another way, *your* present serves as a portal—a kind of "wormhole"—in which to communicate with other Aspects of your entity in waking, dream, or other altered states. Their **present/PAST** or **present/FUTURE** is *always* relative to your **present/PRESENT** and vice versa.

Additionally, even though Jane Roberts was a "final focus" in Ruburt's reincarnational cycle, there could be dozens of lifetimes occurring *in her future*! So the time period in which the designated final lifetime ends doesn't preclude the existence of future lives *because of the nature of simultaneous time*. It's simply a designated function in which to end the cycle, nothing more.

Taken as a whole, Seth's simultaneous time (entity, counterparts, reincarnational and probable selves) is a radically different explanation of the "reincarnational cycle" than the traditional Eastern systems that emphasize versions of consecutive, "one-at-a-time-until-enlightenment," reincarnation.

KEY IDEAS: There are nine basic dimensions of time that you can learn to perceive using your inner senses, dream and other states. The present is __always__ your point of power. Your entity uses these dimension-perspectives to keep track of __all__ its Aspects and maintain a unified identity.

What Exists Beyond My Entity?

Thus far, we've explored key concepts introduced by Seth that relate to the nature of personal reality. But there are other Aspects that exist "beyond" your entity, even further inward. They also contribute to reality creation and play important—if normally unseen—roles that need to be considered.

During early ESP classes, Seth allowed a wider personality called *Seth II* to come through Jane. It was asexual, existing beyond our definitions of male and female, and yet providing the "blueprints for reality" that make genders possible (see Chapter 9). Seth II spoke slower and had a more distant vocal tone because "it" didn't use emotions or belief systems in its native dimension. Seth II functions as a kind of future Seth made of multitudinous selves, many of which have *never* been physical. As such, Seth II functions as a kind of intermediary layer of consciousness *between* All That Is and your entity.[62]

Years later, Seth introduced a similar concept called *Life Clouds*[63]—psychic gestalts of *immense* creative power that contain vast probability fields and seed every universe. They function like inner, psychic galaxies of consciousness. Though Seth didn't make a direct correlation between Life Clouds and Seth II, they are very similar in function.

Ultimately, all of these Aspects form a Whole which is *greater* than the sum of its parts. Seth sometimes refers to All That Is as a *Primary Pyramid Gestalt*. Again, a gestalt is a unified whole that is more than the sum of its component parts.

Seth's "god concept" thus goes well beyond traditional notions of a Bearded Patriarch who lives in the sky and throws lightning bolts at people who misbehave. Instead, All That Is expresses the most inward, pure form of Primal Consciousness, the basic Isness or Suchness that *permeates* all people, places, and things. It is the source of all vitality and creative action.

Even the quantum vacuum of "outer space" isn't empty, but is permeated with the infinite potentials of All That Is' emanations of CUs/EEs. Therefore, space is literally pregnant with the potential to manifest QFs under the proper conditions. In this context, physical reality—QFs—functions as the thin "outer crust" of a vast subjective Universe that is truly One Song.

All That Is is radically ineffable, indefinable, and inexpressible, and yet, *It Is What You Are*. Other religions use different words to express the same idea—Tao, Gnosis, God, Brahman, Atman, Shunyata, Allah, Yahweh, Great Spirit, and Great Chain of Being are but a few. Words inevitably fail to convey All That Is' vitality, creativity, and diversity, and yet, in the end it's poetry that comes closest:

The world is an illusion.
All That Is alone is real.
All That Is is the world.[64]

KEY IDEAS: Seth's teachings, for practical reasons, concentrated mostly on the Aspects that make up your entity, but also included Seth II and Life Clouds to show that your entity is nested within even larger psychic gestalts, the sum total of which he calls All That Is. Together these Aspects form The Ultimate You who creates 100% of your reality.

What is the Point of Such a Detailed Map?

In Chapter 1, we began with the notion that "you are more than your body!" Since then we've introduced various Aspects and functions of your "iceberg self." It's normal to initially feel like a small self that's dwarfed by the vastness of your entity and All That Is. However, instead of feeling "less than" your entity, as you explore your own counterparts, reincarnational and probable selves, you'll gradually become aware of the unlimited bank of multidimensional potentials available to you. You *are* the Aspect self that makes choices, and expresses free will in *this* life and *this* now. Your other Aspect selves are there to provide you with helpful insights and healing information to promote your fulfillment.

The key, then, is to learn *how* your outer ego creates your reality *in conjunction* with your entity and All That Is. Therefore, the goal of putting Seth's ideas into practice is *not* to "transcend" or annihilate your ego, or to get lost in other Aspects and deny the flesh, but to begin to recognize their presence and subtle influences *within* you. In this way, you *widen your ego into a completely new structure* that transcends previous limiting beliefs, emotions, and behaviors. This is why Seth provided such a detailed roadmap of All That Is and various practices, so you can begin to explore yourself!

What, then, is the best way to apply this in practical terms?

First and foremost, the Seth Material is designed to help you understand that you have direct access to an army of invisible

Aspects that help "you" create *all* your reality. As you experiment, you will become more familiar with these "subtle energies."

Second, human evolution is entering a collective stage in which we are gaining more direct access to our inner senses in dream and other altered states like channeling (see Chapter 9). Recall the movie *Ghostbusters* (1984) where all the ghosts escape near the end and create mass panic. Imagine the kind of trauma that could result from opening the floodgates of "simultaneous time perception," especially if people don't understand what's happening. They may believe they're going mad when in fact they are only using inner senses to access previously hidden Aspect selves. Talking to dead relatives, experiencing visions of past or future lives, out of body projections, the effects of telepathy, take getting used to!

So take your time, and keep a curious, playful, yet skeptical attitude as you begin to explore the "unknown" reality of your entity. It serves as your direct, personal connection to All That Is—literally a "stairway to heaven."

In closing, the "you" who creates *all* your reality can now be expanded to include:

- **Outer ego** (physical personality: *waking self*).
- **Subconscious** ("collective unconscious": *dreaming self*).
- **Entity** (reincarnational, probable, counterpart selves; families of consciousness: *inner self*).
- **Life Cloud** ("galaxy" of consciousness: *progenitor self*).
- **All That Is** (*The-One-within-the-many*).

KEY IDEAS: Seth's intent is to provide the most accurate map possible of All That Is to help you explore <u>how</u> you create your own reality. He also provides a rich set of practices in which to test the waters through your own direct experience.

—PART 2—

DISCOVER
YOUR PLACE
IN THE WORLD

Chapter 6: "Before the Beginning"

An Emerging Postmodern Creation Myth

Religious and scientific belief systems currently dominate our worldviews in the West. They contain officially accepted belief systems about your self, your world, and how we all get along. They provide a set of beliefs called "creation myths" that explain the origins of our universe, planet, and all life, including the morals and laws that "govern" each. Religion and science's creation myths have competed for prominence over the past one hundred and fifty years.

The biblical creation myth—Creationism—is provided in the Book of Genesis. In it, our universe was created in seven days by a Causal Consciousness, conventionally termed God, who placed humans as the caretakers of all living things, along with a moral code to govern our behavior. The first man—a fully formed adult—"poofed" into existence in a Paradise called the Garden of Eden. He served as a progenitor for the first woman, and thus had dominion over her.

However, a demon in the guise of a serpent tricked the woman to eat from the forbidden Tree of Knowledge, thus committing the first sin. Ever since, humanity as been cursed as the descendents of these original sinners, but can be redeemed by following the rules set forth by God.

In the scientific creation myth, our universe was created by a random Big Bang, followed by a process called evolution that is guided by the principles of natural selection and "selfish" genetic mutation. Evolution, and thus our universe, cannot be proven to be anything but meaningless and amoral because science deals only in objective, "five senses" based facts and processes. Humanity is neither cursed nor blessed, just challenged to adapt as best it can to overall life conditions. There is only physical life, and death is the end. As such, there are no spiritual domains or beings.

When asked during a mid-1980's interview what the world needed, Joseph Campbell (1904-1987) a postmodern mythologist replied, "A new myth." He didn't know the specifics, but he knew it had to be holistic and world-centric: to encompass the entire planet and *all* people, and not be limited to any single race, creed, religion, or knowledge domain.

In the early 21st century, then, we have *three* main cultural worldviews vying for dominance: traditional religious, modern scientific, and emerging postmodern. Each has its own creation myths, though the postmodern myth remains in its infancy.

KEY IDEAS: There are three main cultural worldviews: traditional, modern, and postmodern. The first two have creation myths as seen in the Bible's creationism and science's evolutionism. The postmodern creation myth is still in its infancy.

The Power of Myth

Traditionally, we consider myth to mean something empirically false, as in "The belief that the earth is the center of the universe is a myth." And yet, once upon a time, the majority of people *believed* that to be true. Sometimes there's a thin line between myth and truth based on consensus "facts."

Seth suggested that myth-making is a natural, vital part of human life. He acknowledged its cultural importance, and challenges us to consider those aspects of myth that intuitively express deeper truths than those limited to empirical facts alone. In this context, myth literally gives birth to fact when it reveals inner knowledge through the guise of story-telling by casting deep, *psychic dramas* into imaginative terms. These become the core cultural filters through which we create meaning and purpose in our lives.

Therefore, myth, as Seth defines it, is not a distortion of fact, but the psychological bridge through which certain facts become physical. Myths are more truthful than facts because they embody aspects of inner reality that can never be fully translated into intellectual terms alone. When enough people believe in a myth, it is called a fact since it appears to be self-evident. In this light, myths serve as useful explanations *about* the nature of reality based upon the overall stage of collective consciousness.

As we will see, Seth's creation myth figuratively describes processes that are inherently *non*linear—Causal Consciousness *dreaming* Itself into physical form. To communicate this creation myth, he uses paradox to stoke the imagination and soften the intellect's linear bias. Seth also uses seemingly contradictory statements to make us think about what he really *means* "beneath" his words.

Is it possible that our universe was created by a Causal Consciousness? Yes. Could some kind of Big Bang have occurred? Yes. Was it random or intentional? If intentional, then what was the origin of the Consciousness that "preceded" the Big Bang? On this, modern science remains mute. Yet, understanding this paradox is crucial. Seth said that the best way to reconcile surface level contradictions is to expand our awareness through the wider lens of our inner senses (see Chapter 1).

Seth presented his creation myth in *Dreams, "Evolution," and Value Fulfillment, Vol. 1* (1986). Many of the central concepts outlined in the previous 880 sessions (many of which are presented in Part 1) set the stage for what Seth called his "most ambitious project thus far."[65] The title foreshadows key themes he weaves throughout. Note that "evolution" is in quotes. Seth acknowledges linear evolution in terms of an "order of play" of increasing complexity in the physical field or what he calls *Framework 1* (see Chapter 7). But he also factors in the nonlinear processes of CUs/EEs that remain outside of modern evolutionary theory.

Further, Seth cautions us not to take his myth too literally, because the intellect tends to constrain the associative and imaginative elements that lie underneath. At some point, old myths inevitably calcify to the point where they no longer express the original psychic dramas that birthed them. Therefore, myths need to be understood *metaphorically*—as symbols of something deeper that can never be fully expressed in words or equations alone.

Traditional worldviews tend to interpret myth in literal, concrete terms. If a Holy Book says we're descended from star brothers, then it's *assumed* to be literally true, and no further evidence is accepted. Modern worldviews tend to include only the proof of five senses and intellectual facts, which constrains the deeper meanings of metaphor. Thus, in order to get the most from Seth's creation myth, it's important to use your intellect, imagination, *and* inner senses.

KEY IDEAS: While myth is conventionally defined as something untrue or false, Seth's definition of myth includes deeper truths that can never be expressed in words or equations alone. Seth's myth requires a blend of intellect <u>and</u> intuition to fully understand.

Seth's Paradox of "Before the Beginning"

"Before the beginning," All That Is contained the infinite thrust of all possible creations. In physical terms, the *potentials* for galaxies, solar systems, planets, ecosystems, species, genders—all *things*, all *processes*—have ALWAYS existed in latent form within some kind of nonphysical field.

"Before the beginning," All That Is created nonphysical "generations" of thoughts and dreams. They had such creative vitality that they manifest *their own* ability to think and dream. As such, they yearned for other states of being. Thus, "*before the* beginning," there was an intermediary field—a "dreamtime"—that "preceded" manifestation within Framework 1.[66]

Seth refers to our progenitor entities in the dreamtime as *Sleepwalkers*. They were created "before the beginning" by the thoughts and dreams of All That Is, and functioned as the "designers" of Framework 1. In other words, the design for our universe was and is *implicit* within All That Is, who manifested Itself as Sleepwalkers to do the hard work of constructing our universe *and* us.

Therefore, there *are* designers (note the plural) and a flexible, dynamic design that are inseparably intertwined within all of creation. As such, All That Is is permeated within all of Its creations, which in turn are innately imbued with a primal drive toward creative action.

The key paradox, then, is that All That Is had to solve a *Primordial Birth Dilemma* so that The One could become The-One-Made-Of-Many. It had to reconcile its desire to be both Itself *and* Other-as-Self. When All That Is conceived a way to release the building tension of Its Divine Creativity, the Sleepwalkers *and* our physical universe simultaneously manifest in a divine explosion of unimaginable proportions.

Thus, some kind of "Big Bang" did occur *in physical terms* as newly formed QFs initially manifest. However, the modern myth holds that all QFs emerged from a singularity of infinite density, as a single microscopic point that continues to expand outward from its original point, forming space-time. Seth refutes this, and instead hints that the whole of Framework 1 was *impregnated simultaneously* with early forms of QFs.

In other words, the modern myth is limited to the effects of QFs (energy/waves and matter/particles), but there has always been an eternal, nonphysical field (CUs/EEs) from which the physical emerges. Since this nonphysical field is impregnated with Causal Consciousness, the physical field simultaneously emerged *at all points* as CUs/EEs reached a systemic tipping point. As such, All That Is—as Causal Consciousness—simultaneously birthed our entire universe and yet continues to create it within every moment point, so "the creation" of our universe is an ongoing process.

In this context, "before the beginning" is the story of All That Is' birth paradox—the primordial riddle solved in which no-thing created some-thing, and from which our dream and physical universes were, are, and will be simultaneously born.

KEY IDEAS: Seth uses the paradoxical metaphor of "before the beginning" to show that there is no beginning or ending to All That Is. And yet, the instant that All That Is conceived a way to make the Nonphysical physical, a primordial "explosion" gave birth to the dream and physical universes.

In the Beginning

The traditional biblical story and modern science's Big Bang myth suggest that when the origin of our universe was completed, things were left to run on their own. In other words, All That Is remained "outside" of Framework 1 as God, or as a yet-unexplained scientific phenomenon. In Seth's view, however, Causal Consciousness remains immanent in the physical world, *and is never separate.* Thus in Seth's cosmology, creative action spontaneously thrives everywhere and every-when in the form of simultaneous time frameworks and probability fields.

In the beginning, then, all QFs contained Consciousness. As such, QFs are infinitely creative, innovative, original, and imaginative, though our modern sciences consider all forms of matter to be inert or "dead." Seth does *not* assign human traits to QFs, but asserts that human traits are made possible by their fundamental characteristics.

In the beginning, physical atoms and molecules built from QFs used their inner senses to dream of more complex structures—cells—and explored myriad probabilities in which to best create them. Thus, *consciousness preceded matter* in the emergence of simple cellular life, which in turn would also dream of ways to create even more complex biological forms.

Value fulfillment (divine love) guided the early experimentation of atoms and molecules. Again, value fulfillment is an innate quality of Consciousness that promotes the cooperative development of all potentials within all probability fields so that every aspect furthers the growth of every other aspect.

During the early dreamtime, CUs operated most often as waves using the dream state as connective tissue between emerging particles of matter. The Sleepwalkers were not focused within physical bodies at that stage, but worked out great creative variations in dream bodies in the dream state (see Chapter 4). They searched for the best conditions to create a viable ecosystem that would support multiple species of life.

As progenitor atoms and molecules dreamt about all of the myriad forms they could manifest, the dreamtime was still more familiar, and physical matter, space, and time were initially very unstable. There were formless images that slowly blinked in and out as they began take on stable forms, most of which were still nonphysical. Gradually, these forms stabilized into the kind of physical matter we know today.

During the dreamtime, a spasmodic universe blinked in and out, appearing and disappearing, gradually manifesting for longer periods of time. The Sleepwalkers, likewise, blinked in and out, gradually manifesting for longer periods, as space-time began to stabilize. As such, the dream universe remained the primary focus of all activity.

KEY IDEAS: In the beginning, the dream universe was the primary center of reality creation. Guided by value fulfillment, early forms of matter dreamt of all possible variations that would lead to a stable physical environment so that biological life could emerge.

Sleepwalkers—Our Dream Ancestors

In the beginning, our planet and everything in it—valleys, mountains, oceans, sky, and every species of organic life—were guided by the cooperative group dreams of every type of consciousness involved. Endless probabilities were explored and a mental framework created that began to include probable pasts, presents, and futures. This stage of development lasted for "eons."

As the Sleepwalkers dreamt our planet into existence, they gradually experimented with the ecosystem and all species, including body consciousness. There was another period lasting for eons in which the dream and physical fields were not yet stable enough for mating to be required for physical reproduction. Once the first cellular life became physically manifest, physical mating was enabled. The Sleepwalkers dreamt of everything that we now take for granted—how we'd grow our hair, digest our food, and heal a cut. All of these matters had to be figured out in order to create the most efficient and fulfilling universe.

As our dream ancestors eventually manifest in physical form, they came to rely more and more on their physical senses. All of the amazing calculations and manipulations of energy needed to maintain a physical body gradually receded into the background of the subconscious. Eventually, we no longer needed to be consciously aware of growing our hair, digesting our food, or healing a cut. These activities became "automatic."

Our body consciousness, which became part of the subconscious, then, represents the knowledge and decisions of our dream ancestors "translated" into physical form. There were three main functions designed by the Sleepwalkers that enabled early humans to emerge and function as a seamless *system*.

1. **Entity** (inner ego)
2. **Body consciousness** (subconscious mediating layer)
3. **Mind** (outer ego)

The first people, our "dawn ancestors," were Aspects of the Sleepwalkers who existed in the dream world "before" they were physical. There they worked out the maximum potentials for Framework 1 so it could follow its own ingenuous course. Stabilizing the body consciousness was a preliminary task before the outer ego could fully emerge. In terms of linear time, early peoples' first forays onto the planet were in dream bodies, not physical ones.

KEY IDEAS: As physical space-time stabilized, eons would pass before the conditions became right for our planet to support biological life. This prepared the way for human life to emerge.

The Order of Play in Framework 1

Seth outlined basic stages of physical development in sequential terms. For example, All That Is (as CUs/EEs/QFs) lovingly formed atoms *first* that evolved into cells, which in turn evolved into more complex organs, bodies, and nascent outer egos. However, QFs functioned only as the tip of our collective "iceberg selves" to form all the physical matter in Framework 1. Underneath, there were also simultaneous processes within CUs/EEs that involved probabilities on a massive scale in the dreamtime. The result was a spontaneous, natural "awakening" of various aspects of Framework 1 that began with simpler forms dreaming their bodies into physical form so that more complex forms could gradually do the same. This unfolding of increased physical complexity occurred over eons *after* the Big Bang. Therefore, people and all species didn't magically "poof in" during a six-day period, although, like the biblical creation myth, there was an order of play.

According to Seth, *all* the dreamers in the dreamtime inevitably awakened and emerged into the physical field through a spontaneous process that followed this order of play. After the galaxies, solar systems, and planets dreamed their "bodies" into physical form, the plants followed suit. This, in turn, allowed the animals to manifest so they could feed off the plants and each other. Only then did humans emerge, though our dawn ancestors lingered in the dreamtime as massive probabilities continued to be worked out.

Additionally, there were vast psychic relationships that drove this order of play that involved the nine families of consciousness[67] (see Chapter 1). Recall that they express a typology of nine innate intentions. In this light, the Sleepwalkers functioned as the progenitor entities whose foundational intents cooperatively formed the universe we know today. In other words, once they settled into nine "families" of innate intention during the dreamtime, the Sleepwalkers were better able develop *all* the life forms on our planet, including our entities, which continue to be expressed to this day *through each of us.*

Moreover, there was no single line of development for human beings. There were parallel developments that included the effects of probable selves, pasts, *and* futures that purposefully "mutated" the genes needed to suit overall life conditions. So there's no single common ancestor in that regard, nor did we linearly evolve from fish to reptile to animal to mammal to ape to human. All of those forms exist *simultaneously* nested within the dreamtime, but needed to gradually "awaken over time" in Framework 1 terms.

So there were different species of man-animal and animal-man living side by side at times. Our dawn ancestors lived alongside creatures considered to be our ancestors by current science. There were varying degrees of competition and cooperation among them in different eras. However, none of this was possible until there was a stable planet, and then a stable ecosystem to provide the raw materials for food, clothing, medicine, and shelter for our human ancestors.

While there's a definite order of play over eons, Charles Darwin's (1802-1882) theory of evolution paints a very limited view because it's based upon the belief that form (QFs) evolves consciousness, instead of the other way around. Thus, the theory that consciousness first emerged from random combinations of inert matter (proteins) and electricity in a primordial pool is a modern myth. Seth humorously called this "the myth of the great Chance Encounter"[68] because again, Causal Consciousness (Sleepwalkers) and value fulfillment (divine love) drove the original development of all species.

Seen in this light, Darwin's theory of evolution holds about as much accuracy as the biblical creation story. The notion of single line development is highly limited because it includes only the physical tips (QFs) of our "iceberg selves." However, once we factor in the submerged functions (CUs/EEs) of the Sleepwalkers and value fulfillment, we have a plausible theory for life to *spontaneously and lovingly develop in all times and places at once.* (We'll further explore the nonlinear functions within CUs/EEs shortly in Chapter 7).

Finally, the idea that all species are innately murderous and must battle for the "survival of the fittest" is also highly distorted. It's based upon erroneous assumptions taken from limited observations and incomplete models of our self and world. It unfairly emphasizes competition and underplays the constant *cooperation* within the physical and nonphysical fields. Again, Seth's "evolution" is driven by the inner law of value fulfillment that by design seeks the greatest fulfillment for all species who share the ecosystem.

KEY IDEAS: In Framework 1 terms, there was an "order of play" that "awakened" <u>first</u> as energy-matter (planet), <u>then</u> plants, <u>then</u> animals, and <u>then</u> human beings. The whole process was driven by the Sleepwalkers' nine families of intention in the dreamtime and the law of value fulfillment. As such, Consciousness evolved physical form, not the other way around.

The Garden of Eden: The Awakening of the Outer Ego

Seth pointed out other inadequacies in the traditional and modern creation myths. In the biblical version, the universe was considered perfect in the beginning, but once people got involved, things steadily got worse. There was a fall from grace in the Garden of Eden that was a woman's fault (convenient for societies bent on keeping women subservient to men). In the angelic (dreamtime) realm, things didn't fare much better. The archangel Lucifer, originally a "good guy," was cursed to become a representative of evil who tempts humankind to sin.

The modern scientific universe is even bleaker because it denies Causal Consciousness altogether. Once set into motion, the universe simply runs in its own chaotic manner, with no guiding principles beyond the laws of physics or what Seth considered the "smaller laws of cause and effect."[69] Galaxies, sunsets, and symphonies are all "accidents" of the laws of physics and inert energy-matter. The universe itself will eventually run down through the process of entropy and destroy all life. With the absence of Causal Consciousness, or *any* kind of consciousness, we're stuck with theories about how cosmic dust somehow became self-aware—sentient—with no larger purpose than its pleasure, survival, and propagation.

The Garden of Eden myths found in traditional religious scripture are actually metaphors for the "awakening" of the self-aware outer ego in the physical body *from the dreamtime*. As mentioned earlier, plants and animals preceded humans in this "awakening" process. While Seth didn't specify many details, and of necessity his story is very general, he describes this as a stark process, where our dawn ancestors suddenly felt separate and alone from their dreamtime bodies.

As this awakening occurred, the dream body that served as the primary focal point "before the beginning" faded into a deeper, more subconscious area as the dazzling array of physical sense data began to dominate the waking state. Our physical senses were designed to be so alluring and compelling that we'd use them as our primary form of perception, and push our inner senses into subconscious neurological background activity.

But this development had a double edge to it. The physical body now had to be fed, clothed, and protected from the elements. It was now subject to the basic root assumptions that govern physical reality, like the law of gravity and the speed of light. We, as outer egos, now suddenly saw ourselves as being separate from the environment, earth's creatures, and each other. This initial awakening—the sense of individuality and "separation" from our dreamtime bodies—was terrifying. It formed a collective "birth agony" that we had to adapt to.

With the manifestation of the outer ego more or less completed, we began to hone our intellects and intuitions. Intellectually, we were now able to discern differences and were amazed to perceive a world of objects, qualities, and processes. But we were still deeply connected to the dreamtime and relied heavily on dreams and subjective knowing as we settled into a precise type of linear neurological focus.

As our physical senses fully blossomed, we began to lock into the narrow spectrum of sequential perception we use today. We thus ignored other spectrums—for example, our inner senses—that gradually faded into ghostly, subtle traces that still remain. Today, we refer to the affects of this ghost spectrum as paranormal, psychic, non-ordinary, and altered states.

As we more fully immersed ourselves within outer egoic consciousness, we created a belief system of good and evil based upon our perception of pleasant and unpleasant sensations and experiences. However, this led to all sorts of inaccurate translations and religious belief systems of right and wrong that still exist today (see Chapter 11).

With the stable emergence of the outer ego, our classical sense of duality was created. There was now me and you, us and them, subjects and objects, inner and outer. We had an outer physical body and senses, but also an inner body and senses. As we became more fully reliant on our physical senses, activities like channeling, precognition, and sleepwalking remained as evidence of our inner knowing and heritage. Sleepwalking is a legacy of the Sleepwalkers. It is how we taught our early bodies to walk.

As dawn ancestors, we dreamed our languages and further honed our intellects and intuitions. Our ability to use language initially appeared so magical that words were perceived by our newly "separated" outer egos as coming directly from God. This may be one reason why there are so many references in the Old Testament to God and angels "speaking" to various people.

The transition from the dreamtime to the physical "waking time," terrifying as it was, has been safely tucked away in our collective subconscious (there is no UNconscious) as a means to cope. This repression was a necessary side effect of the "forgetting" of All That Is and the Sleepwalkers by the emerging outer ego. This forgetting—this sense of separation—is where the Garden of Eden myth of being cast out of God's domain originated.

The concept of Satan represents our humanized projection of this deep-seated archetypal fear of separation from All That Is and the Sleepwalkers. Satan *is* "real" in this sense, but in psychological terms, it's an effect of the early repression of our physical birth agony from the dreamtime into the collective subconscious.

Once we "left" the Garden of Eden—the dreamtime—and transferred our primary focus from dream bodies into physical bodies, we were at last ready to explore our unique type of consciousness and intents. We were now free to experiment with the probable courses of action we had set into motion in terms of civilization-building based upon the families of innate intention.

The Sleepwalkers slowly faded into subconscious memory. They left fragments of themselves as entranced entities in the form of mountains, air, and water—all the elements of the earth. As such, they are still with us today, though in physical forms we no longer recognize. And the rest, as they say, is history, or really a set of probable histories that we've only just begun to explore![70]

In summary, All That Is essentially plays a Cosmic game of hide and seek as It *eternally* "forgets" and "remembers" ItSelf through infinite variations while all Its parts innately yearn to "reunite" with the Whole. As such, whenever the "remembrance" is achieved by any part, All That Is spontaneously generates new probabilities in order to temporarily forget Itself, yet again. This primordial paradox is *lovingly intentional* and fuels the endless "dance of consciousness" in which we all play our parts "before the beginning," in the beginning, now, and always.

English humorist Douglas Adams (1952-2001) also intuited this paradox:

> There is a theory which states that if ever anyone discovers exactly what the Universe is for and why it is here, it will instantly disappear and be replaced by something even more bizarre and inexplicable. There is another theory which states that this has already happened.[71]

In closing, a Zen riddle asks, "Show me your Original Face before your mother and father were born." Do you remember *your* Original Face "before the beginning?"

KEY IDEAS: The Garden of Eden myth is based upon our collective birth agony as we emerged from dream bodies into physical bodies. Beliefs in good and evil originated with our experiences with physical pleasure and pain. The personification of evil is based upon our fear of separation from All That Is and the Sleepwalkers.

Chapter 7: Frameworks of Consciousness

What are Frameworks?

In reviewing Seth's creation myth, we explored some of the general functions used by submerged portions of your "iceberg self" to create your physical reality. Now we're going to look at Seth's concept of *Frameworks* to provide further details about the "unknown" reality from which all the events in physical reality originate.

Seth used the term "Frameworks" only for purposes of explanation, as their functions are seamlessly nested *within* your entity. Therefore, they don't function like a hierarchy but as the "spheres of action" required to support and maintain physical reality creation. Any entity that chooses to experience physical life manifests within the following four Frameworks simultaneously[72]:

- **Framework 1**—The physical world, home of your body/mind, space, consecutive time, and the tip of your "iceberg self." Every object and all processes are idea constructions made of QFs, which form the thin outer physical "crust" of our reality. Local laws of cause and effect operate here in full force.

- **Framework 2**—"Source energy" as CUs/EEs originates here and gets earmarked for transformation into QFs by your entity. It operates as a spacious present in which space and time are simultaneous (see Chapter 5). Your entity's *inner ego* operates here to maintain physical life. The dream state and altered states serve as the "connective tissue" between Frameworks 1 and 2. Framework 2 is traditionally thought of as "heaven" and Plato's "world of ideals." The physically dead "awaken" here first. Some laws of cause and effect operate here to help them transition according to their belief systems.

- **Framework 3**—The main period of afterdeath transition occurs here (see Chapter 5). The dead move into this area to access all of their reincarnational selves and counterparts. They can explore probable realities by moving through Framework 2 to access earth-related probability fields. This is where Seth and Ruburt [Jane's entity] initially "met," which was translated through Framework 2 into the Framework 1 Seth sessions.

- **Framework 4**—The source for other nonphysical realities that have little to do with space, time, or anything familiar within Framework 1. Your entity makes the decision to engage a "reincarnational cycle" here. This is also a "gateway" to Seth II, Life Clouds and other more "inward" Aspects of All That Is that "seed" all four Frameworks.

Frameworks 2-4 form what Seth calls the "unknown" reality—the submerged portions of your "iceberg self" in which all physical constructions and events originate. Seth gave little material on Frameworks 3 and 4, as his main intent is to help us learn to take advantage of Framework 2 and practically apply our knowledge to everyday situations in terms of health, relationships, money, creativity, and spiritual remembrance. As we'll see in this chapter, with practice, anyone can learn to consciously access these Frameworks of Consciousness, because you *already* exist there in some form.

Seth's Frameworks generally correspond to what physicist David Bohm (1917-1992) called the Implicate and Explicate Orders. The Explicate Order is the same as Framework 1. The Implicate Order represents Frameworks 2-4. Bohm didn't include functions of consciousness the way Seth did, so it remains beyond the purview of modern physics. Bohm's Implicate Order intuited that physical events are somehow "enfolded" in a potential or probable state before they "unfold" into space-time. As such, Bohm understood that physics can't be broken down into only QFs and the laws governing them, but that there must be something else analogous to Seth's CUs/EEs at work. However, understanding this requires a deeper knowledge of subjective states, inner senses, and Casual Consciousness.

Again, our civilization has chosen a probable course that has developed powerful cognitive, intellectual and scientific abilities, and holds them above all others. But we're now at a crossroads in our evolutionary development, as our commonly-held knowledge cannot solve our problems at the same level they were created. If we relearn how to engage these source fields—a natural part of our species' genetic and spiritual heritage—then we can mine their riches to provide new solutions to our challenges.

KEY IDEAS: There are four Frameworks of Consciousness that make our physical universe (Framework 1) possible. They don't function as a hierarchy, but as a seamless, nested reality creation system.

What is the Difference between Frameworks 1 & 2?

Framework 1 represents all the elements in our physical universe, the world of space-time, life and death, sunrises and sunsets. Framework 2 functions like a powerful supercomputer to instantly calculate the best probable outcomes and guide the manifestation of *all* physical events on personal and global levels. However, you can't use Framework 2 for your own gain at someone else's expense. Certain conditions must be met first, and only when a person or group acquiesces through their innate intents and beliefs will a tipping point be achieved for physical events to occur (see Chapter 12). So there are checks and balances that prevent anyone from just thinking or wishing an event into physical existence.

Framework 2 also functions like a vast telecommunications network in which hidden portions of your entity are in instant contact with *all* others. Every thought, action, and desire ripples instantaneously throughout, seeking the best outcomes for all involved. They function like "strands of consciousness" to send out filaments of intent and desire that seek out similar strands based on inner "laws of attraction and repulsion" to manifest mutually beneficial events. In this way, everything and everyone are interconnected.

Just as there are hidden, multitudinous steps behind every web page download, Framework 2 works behind the scenes to provide the "source energy" for all physical constructions as CUs/EEs. Just as a web browser brings the Internet to your fingertips, your inner ego mediates with all other entities to "browse" Framework 2 for the best outcomes. Your body and all its functions—like breathing, blood circulation, and digestion—wouldn't exist for a moment without its vast support network to probe, calculate, and seek its best outcomes faster than the blink of an eye. Frameworks 1 and 2 thus form a magnificent cooperative venture.

Moreover, what appears in Framework 1 as coincidence is the result of Framework 2's "vast mental studio" that operates behind the scenes to arrange seemingly chance encounters. The decision to change an airline ticket, visit a relative, or read a particular book is prodded by your inner ego's awareness of the best outcomes for you. This gets expressed as inspiration, impulses, and powerful dreams to get your attention. As such, the *multiverse*—these nested Frameworks of Consciousness—is innately designed to provide you with the most fulfilling outcomes based on your intent, desire, beliefs, and value fulfillment.

All the actors on the stage of any period of history are instantly aware of each other in Framework 2. In your dreams, you explore the probable plays in which your life is involved. If enough people become interested in a certain play, and enough strands of consciousness accumulate, then that play will occur. Whether these turn out to be horror films, love stories, or madcap adventures is determined only when they reach a tipping point and manifest as physical events.[73]

In this context, there are no accidents, and no chance meetings or events. Each birth and death occurs within a larger set of intentional choices made by you *and* your entity. Thus, there are no secrets in Framework 2. Everything is public and available, especially in the dream state, which provides you with glimpses of probable outcomes for upcoming events.

Seth added that in the story of Cinderella, the role of the Fairy Godmother—who turns a pumpkin into a carriage, mice into coachmen, and dresses our heroine in a beautiful gown and glass slippers—is an archetypal expression of the human elements within Framework 2. In other words, she's a mythic expression of *your* inner ego, symbolic of the way it tries to grant your every wish and desire, though conditions are attached.[74] In this sense, we all have the innate knowledge of the existence of our inner ego and its abilities in Framework 2. The next step, then, is to learn how to make that knowledge more conscious.

KEY IDEAS: Framework 2 functions like a vast telecommunications network to instantly connect your intent, desires, and beliefs with those of others to manifest all physical events in Framework 1.

What are the Mechanics of Frameworks 1 & 2?

Seth never encourages the use of intuitions and emotions at the expense of the intellect. Again, they work together in complementary fashion. We've learned to use reason to divide up and categorize the universe, and map out various "laws" of cause and effect based on temporal experience in Framework 1. But intuition and imagination have a different kind of organization based on *associations* that transcends the limits of cause and effect. In that regard, Framework 2 employs associative functions that organize probable events in infinite combinations in order to propel them into physical manifestation *based upon our own mental associations.*

As we have seen, our associations in Framework 1 are based upon our beliefs, thoughts, and emotions—the key elements that direct our inner ego to invisibly assist us to create all of our reality (see Chapter 2). Our thoughts and feelings instantly ripple throughout Framework 2 to mix and merge with others to propel events toward manifestation.

If we look at an object like a desk, we know it's made up of atoms (QFs) that are full of space and motion as invisible electrons move around a nucleus. In similar fashion, when we experience an event like a wedding, it appears just as psychologically solid, even though it's made up invisible processes in Framework 2. That is, all events consist of invisible faster-than-light functions as CUs/EEs get transformed from Framework 2 into Framework 1 processes.

Our thoughts have electromagnetic properties that interact, merge, and attract others in Framework 2 to create the collective tapestry and psychological foundations that underlie all the world's events. Since Framework 2 is guided by the law of value fulfillment, it constantly seeks the "best" expressions for one and all, even when the results are natural disasters, epidemics, or wars. In other words, there's *always* a silver lining that meaningfully emerges from even the "worst" events (see Chapter 12).

As such, Framework 2 is innately designed to produce constructive events over destructive events. By definition, *constructive* means to foster growth and development, and *destructive* means to annihilate, marginalize, and inhibit growth. Therefore, constructive or "healthy" thoughts and feelings are prioritized over destructive or "negative" ones.

Since your inner ego functions primarily in Framework 2, it relies on your outer ego's assessment of life conditions in Framework 1 based on your cognitive, emotional, and intuitive abilities. In this way, your core beliefs play a crucial role in your perception of, and participation in, any event. Because you constantly barrage your inner ego with your thoughts and emotional assessments, it is only too happy to provide you with source energy to create the experiences to reinforce your perceptions.

Again, your inner ego is *neutral* in this regard. Whether you concentrate on negative, destructive, and unhealthy thoughts, or positive, constructive, life affirming thoughts, your inner ego constantly helps you physically manifest your beliefs. This is how you create your own reality using Framework 2.

Also, your pre-birth intent based upon your family of consciousness has a big influence on your life (see Chapter 1). Things like heredity and environment, while important, play a much less significant role than we've been led to believe. For instance, as infants we explore all sorts of probable and reincarnational information in the dream state in Framework 2 that suits our intents and has little to do with genetic influences or environmental factors.

Moreover, the personal "life plan" that you set up before you were born—your parents, abilities, race, gender, location—fits within a pool of probabilities with those of your contemporaries. Yet probable calculations occur in Framework 2 so that you may "plan" to meet someone at a shoe store twenty years later as long as it matches the intent of all parties. There are certain "destiny meetings" set up this way as strong probabilities. Again, nothing is set in stone. The future is *always* a matter of choice, not chance.

No matter what kind of mass event you experience—from a national election to a hurricane—your inner ego is aware of all the collective actions that led to your specific participation. Just like walls are made of bricks, mass events are created by a variety of small, invisible actions that join together to form a type of "psychological masonry" based on your intent, free will, beliefs, thoughts, and emotions.

Again, you *always* have free will to make the choices that create your own reality. Your individual consciousness is utterly unique and plays its part in the co-creation of group events. You can learn to how to use your intent, beliefs, thoughts, and emotions to transform probabilities into specific outcomes in Framework 1, in conjunction with your inner ego in Framework 2.

KEY IDEAS: Your entity's inner ego operates in Framework 2 to provide the source energy to manifest any event you experience in Framework 1 based upon your intent, free will, beliefs, thoughts, and emotions.

Exercise 8—Framework 2 Affirmation

Use the following to affirm Framework 2's infinite potentials, and put them to work for whatever challenges you wish. Feel free to tailor them to suit your own unique situation and needs. For best results, read this first thing in the morning or at the end of the day with a clear mind.

TIP: Your focused intention and desire are critical, and should be reinforced when you read. You don't have to read it every day, just enough to serve as an important reminder. You can even say it out loud to further reinforce your intention. Then, simply forget about it and go about your day or evening.

Personal Well-Being

I deeply and completely trust that my Aspects in Framework 2 will provide me with everything I need in my life. I don't *ever* need to worry about the specifics, as they will be handled instantly no matter how difficult or complicated they seem. In this way, Framework 2 *always* has my best interests in mind.

I am a sacred, unique, and beloved Aspect of All That Is.

I honor and respect all other Aspects.

I completely love and accept myself just the way I am *without* reservation.

It is easy and safe for me to know and express my feelings.

It is safe to be vulnerable because Framework 2 is innately safe and nurturing, and always protects me.

Abundance

My life is a great and exciting adventure. I *fully* understand my intent and purpose for being alive. I live in a world of wealth and abundance, and have great wealth as well. All my needs and desires are provided by Framework 2.

Whatever I can conceive, believe, and receive, I can achieve.

I move with grace and confidence in the world.

I easily articulate even the most complex ideas naturally, in helpfulness to others.

I am at ease in every situation because I know that the things I say and do are helpful in every way.

I see problems as exciting challenges that help me to grow and evolve.

I discover the opportunity for growth in all adversity.

I am receiving ideas right now to help me create what I desire in my life.

I accept these ideas with deep appreciation and take immediate action on them.

The present is my point of power.

Extra credit: Don't undermine yourself by constantly checking to "see if it's working" throughout the day. Instead, state your intent to the multiverse, your entity, higher power—however you imagine those Aspects—and then *trust and allow* nature to spontaneously take its course.[75]

What Are Master Events?

Master events provide the "source energy" that fuel events in all times and periods of history. Recall the matrix of pasts, presents, and futures from the Oversoul Seven story (see Chapter 5). Imagine that each of those boxes has the potential to communicate or transmit inner knowledge to any other box. In this way, not only do all *your* reincarnations communicate, but *all* reincarnations and probable selves have the potential to *communicate with each other*. This functions at the cellular level *within all life forms.* Thus, there is a vast bank of inner potentials, knowledge, and information constantly available to every species.

In this light, master events provide a bank of inner knowledge that is not limited to any particular generation or period of history. So this knowledge is always available, for example, to help during difficult periods when cataclysmic events like natural disasters, meteor collisions, or plagues reduce the living knowledge in physical populations. Therefore, "forgotten knowledge" will *always* bubble up from Framework 2 to help the survivors rebuild and regroup in Framework 1.

Even though we view history as consecutive events in Framework 1, under the surface in Framework 2, all events are nested together. As such, master events form the simultaneous time versions of all the events that our entities jointly create. Historic events are only one version of a much larger multidimensional master event. For example, "before the beginning" was a master event whose "beginnings" never occurred in the world of space-time, but instead *created* space-time.

Afterward, master events continued to fuel history and what appears to us today as evolution. These master events nurtured the "sudden" evolutionary leaps in Frameworks 1's "order of play" that saw the first single-celled creatures and biosphere emerge, and then later, effected how functions like eyes, appendages, and wings emerged. Once conditions were right for human civilizations to form, master events provided the inner impetus for all of our myths, religions, sciences, and arts to emerge, since they *already existed* as fields of probable potentials in Framework 2.

As master events get translated into the events of history, they function like overlapping chapters in a book in what Seth calls *time overlays*. These overlays are not limited to linear, consecutive time. Since all pasts, presents, and futures are intimately connected in the vast communications meshwork of Framework 2, a future self may influence the past self, and vice versa, when fueled by a master event. This is how fresh action can emerge in the past, present, or future.

In terms of Framework 1 history, there are overlapping themes, dramas, and epochs whose echoes slowly die out to be replaced by new ones, like a snake sheds its skin. In this way, even though time appears to flow like a single river, it's really supported by inner processes like master events in which multiple rivers constantly flow in and out of each other in infinite directions. Each river seeks the best outcomes for all involved, through the ever-present embrace of value fulfillment. Such is the beauty, power, and cooperative elegance of Framework 2![76]

KEY IDEAS: Master events are a metaphor to suggest how probabilities, reincarnation, simultaneous time, and value fulfillment function in Framework 2 to fuel events and history in Framework 1.

How Can I Consciously Explore Framework 2?

While master events and time overlays initially seem like abstract metaphysical concepts, Seth provides a map and practices to explore these and other functions of Framework 2. The only tools needed are your conscious mind, curiosity, and desire.

Seth outlined a spectrum of "alternate presents and multiple focuses" called *Alpha states*.[77] Almost any situation can be positively influenced as you learn to tune into them. For example, when faced with important decisions, you can use Alpha states to explore probable outcomes. If you have a health issue, you can use Alpha states to view your body as a "healing mindscape" to discern root causes of challenges caused by this or other lives.

As you go, keep in mind that the Alpha states outlined below don't map *directly* to those of modern dream researchers who define alpha as the relaxed state of reverie that precedes sleep.[78] Seth's Alpha 1-5 states map to what he calls "undifferentiated areas" between Frameworks 1 and 2 that contain vast reservoirs of inner knowledge and serve as a "communication zone" between inner and outer egos.

Psy-time is the inner sense that provides the mental gateway to access Alpha states, because it allows you to focus your attention inward, away from physical reality states (see Chapter 1). Seth is adamant that this is the *only* way to obtain direct experience and conscious knowledge of Framework 2.

While focused intention can be used, Seth also recommends that you access them with *no set purpose*—just keep an open mind and receive whatever inner advice comes your way. Remember, you *always* get what you concentrate on.

There are five main Alpha areas that you can imagine as a series of parallel roads on a map or mindscapes in a psychic ocean. Each has its own unique, discernable feeling-tone:

A1a ~ Good for enhanced creativity, concentration, study, refreshment, rest, and meditation, A1a is simple to enter. For example, it is often the slight alteration you feel when listening to music. Once you recognize it, you can learn to hold it and begin to experiment. You can perceive the present from multiple perspectives. You can see your thoughts clearly, though this may be through symbols, for instance, sensing jumbled thoughts as weeds that you can simply prune away.

You can request that your state of mind (thoughts and feelings) be translated into an "mindscape." Dark and brooding clouds, wildfires, and avalanches alert you to conditions to mentally change into more stable forms. You can become aware of your internal body conditions. You can also perceive other people's mental states and body conditions. Healing may be promoted by manipulating self-generated mindscapes. Some people may not be as visually oriented, and instead may hear sounds or perceive certain feeling-tones, which can also be manipulated.

> **A1b** ~ This is an alternate (probable) present that is not as easy for beginners to enter. It involves group/mass probabilities, racial matters, and civilization-wide issues. This is accessible with practice, and the imagery you encounter here will be significantly different than A1a.

>> **A1c** ~ This has greater mobility, as you move further "away" from Framework 1's physical laws. This is a more expanded version of the previous state, though it borders into realities that have little to do with our root assumptions.

A2 ~ This is a slightly "deeper" area, so its imagery is further removed from physical reality. You can explore the past in terms of Framework 1 probabilities. Reincarnational selves, issues, and beliefs are also available here. If you can't solve a problem in an Alpha 1 mindscape, you may need to go deeper—into Alpha 2—to identify the particular lifetime that's influencing you. This area is characterized by slower breathing, lowered temperature, and slower frequency alpha waves.[79]

A3 ~ Here you access mass issues, geographical histories, racial info, animal species, layers of gas, oil, and coal, and the multiple epochs that have swept the planet and formed it. This is an excellent area for statesmen and politicians to explore to better understand the deeper issues involved in economic, social, and political mass events.

A4 ~ Here you access "beneath" the matter formations of Framework 1. Ideas and concepts appear in symbolic terms here as well. It's also the source of civilization-changing inspiration, and available in sleep states. Personal, life-changing conversions also originate here.

A5 ~ This state is seldom reached in physically conscious terms. It's a meeting ground with clear communication. Out-of-body experiences can occur here, and interactions with other entities imaged as angels, gods, or disciples. Past and future lives of anyone ever born, in any related probable system, can be accessed here. This area is *not* accessed by most mediums or channelers.[80]

Alpha 1 and Alpha 2 are closest to waking state and easiest to access. They are also available from sleep states during periods of dreaming, but you may not remember it. However, you will wake up refreshed and revitalized afterward. Dire probable paths may also be averted here. The results may be translated symbolically into fantasy, fiction or artwork. In this way, Alpha areas serve as sources of artistic inspiration and creativity.

Seth cautions that you may encounter thought-forms in the guise of projections from your subconscious or even the collective subconscious (devils, monsters, etc., as *personified fears*). All you need to do is recognize them as such, and divert your attention away to "deactivate" their power. They are drawn to your desire and intent, and if you encounter them, simply wish them well, and turn your attention away.

There's no need for elaborate protection rituals before you engage Alpha states, as these only tend to reinforce fear-based beliefs in Darwin's battle for survival (meaningless universe), or religion's sinful self (flawed by birth). If you project genuine love, fear-based energies cannot feed off your fears and attention—love conquers all!

There are also deeper areas that you can access. Communication is possible with Aspects that have never been physically manifest, like Seth II, or gestalt energies like Life Clouds. They serve as "custodians" and "guardians" of our system, so they are involved in very deep areas of Frameworks 1-4. In all cases, the idea is to become aware that your reality is never limited to just the five senses and waking state. There is much more to explore!

You will naturally be drawn toward certain Alpha areas over others, so don't expect to instantly access them all or understand their symbols right away. That's not a sign of failure or inability. This is a new mental frontier that takes time and practice to become familiar with. You are learning to interpret the symbolic language of your soul.

Also, you will always interpret your experiences through your belief systems. With Alpha states, you may perceive events that exist side by side with our present history and misconstrue them as something *about* to happen. Your experiences *are* real, they *are* important, and they *are* valid. They are just easy to misinterpret in the early stages. Therefore, it's important not to take your experiences too literally as you begin to explore their symbolic meanings.

In summary, Seth provided a multidimensional "map" in which to explore Framework 2 through Alpha states. As we have seen, the core practices to prepare you are:

1. **Psy-time** (see Exercises 1, 2)
2. **Belief work** (see Exercises 3, 4, 5, 8)
3. **Dream work** (see Exercises 6, 7)

These provide the foundation upon which to learn to discern the symbols your entity uses to communicate with you, and provide inspiration and endless creative energy from Framework 2.

KEY IDEAS: Alpha states outline a map in which to explore Framework 2 through psy-time. Learning to interpret the symbols used by your entity to communicate information takes time and practice.

Exercise 9—Alpha States: Treasure Hunts into Framework 2

Tip: You can record the following, and then play it back over headphones on your iPod or MP3 player. Be sure to speak slowly and clearly, and allow enough time within each Alpha area to become familiar with its unique feeling-tone. As always, tailor the exercise to fit your unique situation and needs.

Now, engage psy-time in a quiet place. Take a few minutes to settle your body/mind down. Once you're relaxed, imagine that it's a sunny day and you're calmly floating on a warm, tropical ocean. There are birds chirping in the distance, and the wind gently caresses you.

Rest here for about thirty seconds. This represents Alpha-1— your home base in physical terms, and closest to normal waking state. Mentally remind yourself that your body will be comfortable and safe, and that your intent is to playfully explore the hidden riches within Alpha states.

Next, use your imagination to project into your first dream body and "dive" under the clear water to a depth of five feet. You're now in Alpha-2. (It's easy to breathe because you're in your dream body.) Take your time and rest here for about thirty seconds. Simply *feel* the subjective difference as you move from the surface to this shallow depth.

Now, dive down a little further to one hundred feet, and rest again for thirty seconds. You're now in Alpha-3. Once again, simply notice the subjective feeling-tone at this depth.

Next, do the same for same for Alpha-4 as you "dive" down to five hundred feet. Don't rush. Just imagine that each time you move to a new depth, you have shifted gears into a deeper Alpha area.

Now, "dive" down to Alpha-5 at two thousand feet for thirty seconds. Then, take a moment to peer "upward" and sense the four other "depths."

Next, begin to *slowly* move back "upward" to Alpha-4, then Alpha-3, then Alpha-2, and finally return to your body in Alpha-1. Again, if you find yourself rushing, slow down and simply notice the differences in feeling-tone as you return through each "depth."

Finally, hold at Alpha-1, take a deep breath or two, open your eyes, and stretch your fingers and toes.

This exercise is similar to practicing scales on a musical instrument. It builds flexibility and "muscle memory," only you're working with the "feeling-tone memory" of subjective areas of your own consciousness.

As you repeat this exercise and grow more familiar with each area, playfully search for hidden treasure in the form of messages, imagery, or feelings within each Alpha state. You will naturally be drawn to some over others.

Do this every day for three weeks to reinforce the new beliefs and behaviors to access a goldmine of inner riches. Use them for problem solving, healing, invention, recreation, inspiration, and anything else you can think of![81]

Chapter 8: The Christ Drama

What is the Christ Material?

Jane Roberts was raised in the Catholic faith, but left it by age nineteen because she outgrew the constraints the Church imposed on her mystical leanings. Still, Catholicism played an influential role in her formative years that would color one of the most controversial areas in the Seth Material—the Christ material—for Seth tells a very different story based on multidimensional personality, reincarnation, simultaneous time, All That Is, and more.

As more information was delivered, Jane grew concerned about the impact that Seth and her own ideas would have as more of their books were published. One night, she mused to Rob that Seth's ideas might provide an alternative to Christianity. Rob acknowledged that organized Christianity left a lot to be desired, but chided Jane that no single person's work had the power to lead our civilization one way or the other, since it's too complex and diverse.

Jane realized that Rob was right: no single person can lead an entire civilization in any particular direction, not even Christ, as we'll see. The nature of mass events, while dependent on individual choices, always follows complex inner rhythms and the guidance of master events to produce a mix of fact, myth, and fiction. Seth said that much of what came to be accepted as the historical facts of Christianity never occurred in Framework 1 terms. They were part of a religious drama within Framework 2 whose symbols, events, and characters became so intermingled that they became facts in Framework 1 terms. As such, they've become impossible to completely unravel.

So what we consider the history of Christianity is really a mixture of actual events colored by mythic intuitions. Therefore, the Christ story wasn't as "singular and neat" as it's made out to be. In fact, there were many probable versions of the story of a god-man that the collective explored before settling into the stories we know today. Certain valid roles and ideas were suggested, tested, and played out over time.

The Christ material is scattered in several Seth books. Though he was ready to dictate an entire book on the subject, the project never came to pass, due mostly to Jane's reservations, as Rob was more than willing to tackle such a controversial topic. That book would have been quite controversial, indeed.

In a nutshell, Seth stated that the historical Christ was only one of "three Christs" who were all manifestations of a "Christ entity," and further, the disciples were also *fragment personalities* of the Christ entity (counterparts, see Chapter 5). As such, there were fifteen "Christs" who were all connected by varying degrees of shared reincarnational memories, dreams, and altered states.

Additionally, the historical Christ was never crucified, but took part in a plot to fulfill Jewish prophecies in which a Messiah would return and be executed. Christ would also "return" by the year 2075, because Christianity had strayed too far from its original ideals, which stressed the immortality of the soul (entity), and love, compassion, and charity for others.

The implications are startling: they suggest that the resurrection was only a symbol of the soul's immortality, not a literal event, and that a "Second Coming" is in the works.

KEY IDEAS: The Christ material is one of the most controversial and intriguing parts of the Seth Material. It is based upon Seth's concepts of multidimensional personality, reincarnation, simultaneous time, All That Is, and more.

What is the Role of the Speakers?

Traditional religious beliefs claim that as the soul develops it "ascends" toward heaven, successively getting "closer to God," since heaven was thought to exist up in the sky. On the other hand, when humans went astray, they "descended" into the fires of hell, which existed in the volcanic bowels of the earth.

However, the entity exists as a multidimensional structure unto itself that simultaneously explores physical and nonphysical domains. There is no overarching single line of development—upwards, downward, or otherwise—that guides its every expression. In this context, there are highly developed Aspects of our entities called *Speakers* whose purpose is to provide helpful inner knowledge for the development of all civilizations. They function as inner translators of master events and teachers throughout every period of history.

In terms of Christian imagery, nonphysical Speakers have been known as "guardian angels." In this sense, Seth is a Speaker. In physical terms, Jane and Rob were also being trained as Speakers. Speakers employ oral traditions as well as written forms, or what Seth calls "Speaker manuscripts," to pass on original knowledge. They include ways to directly experience the inner reality that exists beneath the physical symbols, roles, and stories of all religions.

For instance, there are many still undiscovered manuscripts in monasteries in Spain written by monks who passed on the secrets of reality creation. There were also oral traditions in Africa, Australia, and northern Europe before the time of Christ where the ideas were kept alive and spread by various Speakers.

In this way, the Speakers seeded the ancient world to prepare for the emergence of Christianity. The ancient Druids and Egyptians also obtained knowledge from the Speakers. They existed during the Stone Age, and their abilities helped our dawn ancestors to survive and flourish. Early on, they didn't have the need to write things down. Because they were so well trained, they were able to pass their knowledge verbally with very little distortion.

Over the centuries, however, as their knowledge got translated into parables, tales, and even portions of the Old Testament, distortions gradually diluted their original meanings. And so, the Speakers appear time and again to refresh inner knowledge whenever it's needed.

Since consciousness forms matter, not the other way around, all thought exists *before* and *after* it gets translated into our brains as *ideas*. Thoughts are causal in Seth's definition because they consist of CUs/EEs/QFs, which are not limited to brain processes alone, but include functions of our entities. So our thoughts simultaneously function in Frameworks 1 and 2. This is how the inner knowledge of the Speakers gets translated into practical, physical terms.

The symbols of all the earth gods, including those living in Olympus or manning the River Styx, were originally given by Speakers to help people explain their origins, the forces of nature, death, and the afterlife. Physical Speakers in training would access and memorize crucial information and pass it on. This inner knowledge was reinforced by dreaming "field trips" into other areas of consciousness. Such training still goes on today unbeknown to most.

Some Speakers function mostly in the dream state, and are largely unaware of their abilities or experiences while awake. But due to the simultaneous nature of time the Speakers are active in *all periods of history at once*. They're familiar with the root assumptions of various Frameworks of consciousness, and use them to communicate inner knowledge into culturally meaningful symbols. For example, they may appear as the Christian God, or angels, prophets, or saints to transfer knowledge about our multidimensional heritage to a trainee during dream, alpha, or trance states. Their intent is to help explain the multidimensional nature of reality through meaningful cultural values, stories, and symbols.

In this light, the Seth Material functions the same way. And though there have been millions of Speakers physically manifest to date, according to Seth there have only been less than thirty great ones, including Christ and Buddha. They not only have direct access to inner knowledge, but also are able to perceive much deeper into Frameworks 2, 3, and 4. So much so, they are able to add to the original knowledge that steers the course of an entire civilization.[82]

Even though our entities can never completely materialize into physical constructions, knowledge from our innermost being constantly floods outward to transform everything it touches. In this way, master events within Framework 2 fuel *all* religious dramas. As we will see, the historical Christ was only the tip of a powerful multidimensional entity—a Speaker entity—that played a crucial role in the formation of the Christian era.

KEY IDEAS: The Speakers are Aspects of our entities that exist in nonphysical and physical forms to help nurture humanity by making inner knowledge available throughout all periods of history.

What are Religious Dramas About?

Recall Seth's "time overlays" in Framework 2 that function like chapters of a book that ebb and flow through the great epochs of history. While inner knowledge constantly seeks expression within Framework 1, it's also constantly breaking down, diminishing, and losing its effectiveness over time.

As any great religion begins to lose its potency, the greatest of human yearnings get projected once again from Framework 2 as religious dramas. They are couched in symbols and imagery that will most effectively communicate spiritual knowledge to the general populace. The Speakers and other entities know what kind of personalities and storylines will most affect people. In many cases, prophecies are given to set the expectations for the arrival of new personalities that will symbolize new attributes the collective seeks to explore. This is done with great care and intention. Individuals that take on these roles do so with great responsibility. As certain experiences trigger varying degrees of spiritual remembrance, they begin to function as avatars—human manifestations of All That Is with conscious knowledge of inner reality.

Our beliefs in good and evil, redemption and punishment, gods and demons are mere translations of deeper spiritual values that can never be fully translated into physical symbols. And yet, these translations drive the thematic content of all religious dramas as they unfold.

Some of the "actors" return repeatedly to take on new roles. Therefore, those that arrive on the world stage may have already played earlier roles with reincarnational ties in Framework 2. They may even switch roles, for instance, the traitor in one drama becoming the savior in the next one.

Psychological identification also plays a significant role at the heart of these dramas. We intuitively identify with the gods we create, since their characteristics are *inherent in all of us*. However, we've collectively forgotten that we, too, live forever. So we still project immortality outside of us and onto the characters that populate our religious dramas.

As such, our entities function underneath all the actors of any religious drama, and yet are beyond such role-playing within their native Frameworks of consciousness. These dramas are physical reflections based on the deeper activities of our entities. In every case, they are meant to remind us of our inner heritage.

KEY IDEAS: Religious dramas are always couched in the symbols and imagery that will most effectively communicate spiritual knowledge to the general populace.

What are the Central Themes in the Christ Drama?

Every religious drama attempts to remind people of their relationship to All That Is. While All That Is is *more* than the sum of its many Selves, It is also *within* every Self, in every human, spider, tree, rock, molecule, and QF. Our entities function as the personalized connection to All That Is. Its multidimensional richness and vitality are impossible to fully describe, and yet can be known *through our own direct personal experience*. In this way, we *can* know God. That is the core message repeated in all religious dramas.

In this context, Christ was a living metaphor for All That Is and Its many Aspects. However, there were three individuals whose words and deeds blurred into a "composite" individual that we know today. While the facts of history may be distorted, the deeper spiritual truths expressed were quite valid. John the Baptist, Jesus of Nazareth, and St. Paul (aka Saul of Tarsus) were the primary Aspects of the Christ entity. Together, with the twelve disciples, they worked out a symbolic drama propelled by the unimaginable power of a master event in Framework 2.

For instance, Judas represented the self-betrayer and outer ego greedily focused in physical reality to the exclusion of the entity. He was not a regular man, in our terms, but a fragment personality (counterpart) of the Christ entity. The same is true for all the Disciples. They represented Aspects that were additional qualities of the outer ego of that period, while the three "Christs" represented the entity.

In this light, *there were actually fifteen Christs*, all manifestations of the Christ entity. Of the three main personalities, the first two fulfilled their purposes, but Paul was left unsatisfied because his version of the Church as a "kingdom on earth" eventually constrained and distorted the core teachings. Therefore, it is around the personality of Paul that a new religious drama will play out in the 21st century.

There will be a "Second Coming," though it will not involve the historical Christ. Instead, it will form around the unfulfilled personality of Paul. Two thousand years ago he represented the militant side of humanity, which had to be factored in due to the warring nature and tribal customs of the day. However, that militant quality (masculine) will significantly change and ultimately be overshadowed by more compassionate qualities (feminine). This is another reason why the new religious drama will center on the personality of Paul.

During the 21st century, we will reconnect more deeply with inner source, and a new era will unfold. This will *not* be a utopia, but it *will* initiate a more compassionate, sane, and just era, one in which people become more aware of their relationship to the planet, freedom from time, and connection to their entity. According to Seth, the "new religion" will not be Christian, though the Paul personality will be a catalyst. He will refer to the historical Christ and his relationship with All That Is to promote spiritual remembrance.

This will help humanity move toward a new kind of consciousness, as many of our current problems are the result of spiritual ignorance. Tribal artifacts of racism and misogyny will no longer have merit. As people of all races begin to access reincarnational information, they will come to understand that *all other races and genders are close spiritual relatives*. No one is better than any other, and all are necessary to promote the amazing diversity of our species.

As a result, social, economic, and governmental structures will significantly change. However, there is an innate responsibility and level of development that must first be attained *before* these abilities will blossom collectively. Thus, they will continue to lie latent as probabilities until the proper life conditions occur. As always, value fulfillment (divine love) serves as an inner check and balance to guide these overall developments.

Children will be taught their basic independence from their physical bodies, and also learn that time is a construction we've chosen to collectively explore, but not something we are limited to. New areas of the brain will be employed to process new perceptive abilities using the inner senses (see Chapter 1). It will become possible to evoke past-life memories, though "future memories" will remain veiled for practical purposes. In other words, since each lifetime influences all others within Framework 2, easy access to probable futures must be handled with great care and responsibility within Framework 1. As such, it is possible to abuse this ability and provoke unforeseen and even disastrous consequences.

All of these changes will affect the institutionalized forms of religions we're familiar with. Because the new "religion" will be person-centered—individualized—spirituality will escape organizational bounds as it becomes more mainstream. This is not to say there won't be religious institutions, but that their focus will radically shift to better support a new kind of spirituality. Psychic or inner meshworks will more actively support all exterior structures. Our perceptive abilities will change so radically that we will appear to be a new species.

Again, this will not be a utopia, as there will still be problems to face. For instance, people will still have the free will to create dis-ease and pathological behaviors. However, it will become less probable that warfare will be used to settle disputes. New leaders throughout the world will finally understand that when they kill each other *they literally kill Aspects of themselves*.

All of these changes will be greatly exaggerated in the new "Paul" persona in order to catalyze a collective realization of the same qualities *on a global scale*. Still, the themes of Seth's Christ drama are not set in stone. They exist as strong probabilities on the horizon. The future is always a matter of choice, and nothing is predetermined. So it's important to take this material with a grain of salt, and seek to understand its deeper meanings.

KEY IDEAS: There were three "Christs" or manifestations of the Christ entity that initiated the Christian era. The first two, John the Baptist and Jesus of Nazareth fulfilled their purpose. The third, St. Paul, did not. As such, a "Second Coming" will be based around the personality of Paul to usher in a new religious drama to remind people of their relationship to All That Is.

What About the Return of "Paul"?

There will be no need for a crucifixion in this new religious drama. The returning "Paul" will be aware of all his incarnations in a way the historical Paul wasn't. Even though Seth assigns a masculine gender to this persona, he will not be oriented in terms of a single gender, race, or creed. He will literally redefine human personality as we know it, serving to catalyze the collective toward a new kind of consciousness.

However, Seth cautions that there could be resistance and even trauma for those afraid to encounter Aspects of their "iceberg selves." This is a side effect to be mindful of as we collectively create the birth pangs of this new religious drama. Whether this leads to mass violence, suicide, epidemics, or natural catastrophes remains the choice of all involved. It's also possible that those with traditional religious beliefs will misinterpret these changes as the end of the world ("end times"), when in fact they represent the birth of a new one.

Seth purposefully avoided giving more specific information about the returning "Paul" persona because other personalities may prematurely jump into this role. This is the stuff of prophecy—of probable futures—so Seth only provided a general outline. Since the returning "Paul" will be a composite of the three "Christs" from two thousand years ago, there will be an inner exchange between both "chapters" of this master event within the simultaneous time of Framework 2.

The returning "Paul" will undermine current organizational limits because individuals will reestablish their *direct connection* to All That Is. He will also provide methods to promote direct experience with our "iceberg selves," which will be recognized as the mediators to All That Is. As such, there will be no need for institutionalized mediators.

When Seth dictated this material (July 24, 1971) he said that "Paul" had not yet been born, although his presence was prophesized as the "Second Coming" (Matthew 24). However, these biblical prophecies have become quite distorted from their original contexts. For example, this new Christ persona will not punish evildoers with eternal damnation, nor reward the pious with eternal bliss.

He will also not be generally recognized by the populace. There will be no blaring trumpets or media headlines to globally proclaim his arrival or ministry. His mission will be to straighten out the mess that Christianity is in, and set up a new, more effective spiritual system of thought that improves it. All of this will occur by 2075.

Seth also mentioned that the prophecies of Nostradamus were biased because he couldn't conceive of Western civilization *without* the Catholic Church, and thus he interpreted its dissolution as the literal end of the world *instead of the birth of a new one*. While Seth talks about the end of the Christian era as we know it, he constructively proposes that what follows will greatly enhance humanity's abilities by "straightening out" its deplorable distortions.

Moreover, several will be born to re-arouse humanity's expectations, and pave the way for the full blown drama to unfold. For instance, a man born in India near Calcutta will have an influential local ministry during his lifetime. Another man born in Africa will make his spiritual mark in Indonesia.

However, Seth was intentionally obscure about their dates, as well as the exact date of the returning "Paul's" birth, and said only that they will have occurred by 2075. Given the nature of probabilities and free will, the year 2075 is *only* a ballpark estimate. In other words, to set 01/01/2075 as the "end of the world" or "new beginning" is a distraction at best. This date is meant to suggest only what Seth perceived as most probable futures and to pave the way for yet another religious drama to unfold.

KEY IDEAS: The returning "Paul" will initiate a religious drama in which current institutionalized religions will be undermined, and the entity promoted as the personalized mediator to All That Is. He will provide methods in which to do this. All of this will be accomplished by roughly 2075.

Was Christ Really Crucified?

The crucifixion embodied ideas of crime and punishment unique to Mediterranean cultures of the time. It was a preferred method of execution, because the person was tied or nailed to a wooden cross, which produced a slow and painful death from exposure, dehydration, and asphyxiation. Its political goal was to dissuade local populations from committing serious crimes like rebellion, murder, rape, and so on.

The Jewish prophets laid a foundation of prophecy in the Old Testament that a messiah would come to rescue the Jewish people from their oppressors—which became the Romans during the time of Christ—and be executed. However, the historical Christ had no intention of being crucified, though others felt that a crucifixion had to occur to fulfill the prophecies.

As such, Christ was involved in a conspiracy in which Judas was set up to make him a martyr. The person actually crucified was drugged. This is why he needed help to carry the cross (Luke 23). He actually believed that *he* was the Christ, and thus "the one" to fulfill the ancient prophecies. The group involved tried set up another Jewish sect to take the fall for Christ's death, but never intended the entire Jewish people get the blame.

Christ's tomb was empty because the same sect took the body away. Mary Magdalene did see Jesus after his staged death. He appeared physically and in out-of-body forms to his followers and tried to explain what happened. But those not aware of the conspiracy didn't understand and distorted his actions.

Moreover, when Peter three times denied knowing Christ (Matthew 26), he was being honest. He simply did not recognize the man in custody as the Christ he knew. The cry of "Peter, why has thou forsaken me?" was uttered by the drugged substitute who had been told by the sect that he was in fact the messiah. The substitute was Simon of Cyrene, who in the Bible is said to have carried the cross for Christ (Luke 23), but in Seth's version, never gave it back.

In this context, then, the historical Judas never betrayed Christ, but *actually saved his life*. For the man he turned in to the authorities wasn't the historical Jesus. And yet, the idea of the crucifixion (suffering, death) and resurrection (bliss, immortality) gradually gained enough momentum to express a deeper psychic reality that far surpassed actual historical events.

Christ also had the ability to cause the wounds of the crucifixion, called stigmata, to manifest on his physical body afterwards. This was necessary because many of his followers were convinced that he had been crucified. He intended to stop using this means of identification and explain the true circumstances. But people misunderstood, because they wanted to believe that he had been killed and "resurrected."

In this way, the idea of Christ's death came to dominate, partially because it was symbolic of the deeper truth of the entity's immortality. The message behind Christ's birth—that we are *each* a "son of the Father"—became secondary. In time, when his presence was no longer necessary, according to Seth, he simply willed himself out of his body.

In other words, because the historical Christ was able to project from his body at will, he was able to consciously create his own death (mahasamadhi). This is another important message that was lost, namely, that we each may consciously create our own deaths. Again, once properly understood, death is not something to fear, not an end, but a new beginning of another state of being (see Chapter 5).

KEY IDEAS: While the historical Christ wasn't crucified and resurrected, the psychic vitality and symbolism of crucifixion (punishment, sacrifice) and resurrection (immortality of the entity) reflected core Christian themes of the time.

What Other Themes Propel the New Religious Drama?

All religious dramas are true but partial translations of constantly changing interior spiritual realities. The roles of gods, saints, sinners, and prophets all serve as themes to be explored. These dramas try to translate into meaningful symbols those aspects of inner reality that support collective reality creation.

The symbols are valuable insofar as they accurately reflect the nature of authentic spiritual experience, and serve as a reminder to those who've yet to trust direct experience of their "iceberg self." This has led many to take these symbols in literal rather than metaphoric terms. When this happens, the deeper message often gets lost.

The historical Christ spoke in terms of the "Father and Son" because the social customs in the Mediterranean region were based on patriarchies that emphasized masculine traits and subjugated feminine traits. So this was the form that Christianity took to express the relationship between the entity and physical self, but it was never meant to be taken literally. It could have also been mother and daughter, but those gender roles were not dominant at the time.

This applies to the historical Buddha as well. He also experienced inner realities and attempted to physically translate them into a meaningful cultural context. He understood his identity as much more than the sum of his inner perceptions. Seth said that

Buddhism came closer than Christianity to providing an accurate map of All That Is and reality creation. However, Islam fell short because of its overemphasis on violence and bloodshed.

Centuries earlier, the Hebrews had adopted the notion of a single god (monotheism) that was sometimes angry and cruel, yet always just. As the outer ego became more physically focused and aware of its power to manipulate nature, God became perceived as an ally against nature. He could be petitioned through prayer to help with crops, childbirth, and defeating enemies, for example.

The early Jewish God was also a projection of the outer ego who sometimes behaved like an angry child, soliciting the forces of nature to hurl thunder, lightning, and hellfire at its enemies. As the sense of separation from nature and other individuals grew, nature became the ultimate weapon of retribution.

Long before those eras, however, humanity identified more directly with nature, and didn't feel as separated from it. People identified with a storm or flood directly through inner senses to merge with those elemental forces. In those days, no thought was given to using nature as a weapon because people understood that they were an important part of it. But all that changed by the time of Christ as the outer ego focused more on exterior perception, and less on inner reality. This reflected a new venture in egoic development.

In this way, humanity embarked on a journey toward the type of egoic consciousness we enjoy today. But the price we paid was to forget our direct connections with nature *and* our inner source. By the time of Christ, the outer ego had firmly established itself, and this was reflected in the depiction of the Jewish God.

The Christian God was more merciful and compassionate, and these latent qualities began to bubble up to provide new directionality. In similar fashion, the next religious drama will mirror a new stage of outer egoic development, and open our doors of perception to our greater Selves and the creative thrust of All That Is.

And so we arrive at yet another crossroad in a religious drama (master event) that's been playing out for thousands of years, in yet another chapter in our collective development. In hindsight, we have *always* created God in our own image, not the other way around. For our concept of god has always been based upon the collective projection of outer egoic characteristics to represent what we believe to be the highest ideals, abilities, and qualities of humanity. Since we continue to change and evolve, so too does our definition of and relationship with All That Is.[83]

KEY IDEAS: The Christ drama faithfully reflected the development of the outer ego over thousands of years. This process continues within the new religious drama.

What Does It All Mean?

Prophecy is traditionally used to describe the "revelation" of divinely inspired knowledge through non-ordinary means like channeling, clairaudience, dreams, and other altered states. In other words, a prophet gains access to information he or she cannot know through their normal egoic self. Though best known for predicting future events, prophecy also includes functions like making "God's will" and purposes clearer.[84]

The Christ material is the *only* instance of religious prophecy in over twenty-one years of Seth sessions. Does this make Jane Roberts a prophet? Though she clearly didn't want her work associated with traditional religious beliefs, *within the traditional definition of prophecy,* Seth *does* function as a prophet but in a postmodern way, which we'll explore later (see Chapter 14).

Seth not only outlined a complex story clothed in new symbols about our relationship to All That Is, he even gave a date for its completion with an appropriate disclaimer about the nature of probabilities and free will. Much of the material is very general, and leaves the door open to many interpretations and potential distortions. Such is the nature of prophecy.

In order to adequately discern Seth's intent for providing the Christ material, we *must* factor in the concepts we've explored thus far. As we have seen, there is a rich tapestry of new ideas that explain the multidimensional nature of All That Is within the context of Frameworks of consciousness, reincarnation, entities, master events, simultaneous time, Speakers, and so on.

Therefore, it's crucial to understand that this emerging religious drama will consist of physical symbols and personalities, but also contain deeply symbolic meanings underneath. Seth chose to employ the "messiah mythos" because it appeals to our mythic past and stirs deep intuitions we share about our connections to inner reality. Seth's Christ drama arouses a sense of awe and mystery about the workings of human spiritual experience.

However, Seth's core message is that we each create our own realities. In this light, it is impossible for a "messiah" or anyone else to create your reality *for you*. This is an important conceptual leap. The mythic version of the messiah functions as a superhero like Superman, someone on whom we project all kinds of powers, while too often denying that they *lie within each of us*.

In larger terms, the messiah role functions as a catalyst to stimulate the development of those abilities within us. The Wizard of Oz played the same metaphoric role in pointing out to the Cowardly Lion that he had always had courage, the Tin Man a heart, the Scarecrow a brain, and that Dorothy was always at home.

As such, we must take Seth's Christ material with a healthy dose of skepticism, and not literally. Instead, seek to identify and recognize the deeper themes, roles, and concepts as they *already exist within you*, and do your best to realize them. This promotes a new type of "spirituality without walls" that emphasizes your individual relationship with All That Is, and minimizes an over-reliance on outside mediators (though teachers will always play an important role).

Finally, while cast in the Western symbolism of Christianity, this material takes a "world-centric" perspective—one that doesn't favor any race, gender, sexual preference, or creed over any other, but is intended for *all* people on a global scale. It's remarkably free of the usual negative biases that limit traditional religions in terms of casting others as enemy, infidel, heretic, or unbeliever. In this way, it is inclusive, not divisive, and forms one of the most significant pieces of 20th century revelatory writing.

KEY IDEAS: The Christ material offers a world-centric perspective on religious prophecy. It is not meant to be taken literally, but is symbolic of deeper spiritual themes, roles, and concepts that the collective continues to explore.

Chapter 9: Lost Civilizations, A Dream City, & UFOs, Oh My!

What Are Some of Seth's More "Out There" Ideas?

Jane Roberts had an aversion to the stereotypical occult ideas of her day. For example, she avoided asking Seth about Atlantis, because she was turned off by the superstitious nonsense often associated with it. Jane's natural skepticism, psychic abilities, and strong intellect helped her cope with the challenges presented by Seth's ideas, many of which rocked the boat of accepted religious, philosophical, and scientific explanations. She and Rob learned early on not to rely on anyone's explanations, even Seth's, but to trust their own direct experience. As such, they made every effort to check their facts, and not take anything Seth said in literal terms, annotating the published sessions with their own thoughts and relevant details.

Still, Jane considered some of the material too "out there" to publish during her lifetime. And yet, towards the end of her life she entrusted Rob to publish everything, which he did. This speaks to the high level of integrity and transparency in which they produced the Seth Material.

Seth claims we're not alone in Framework 1, and that sentient life from other planets has interacted with us over eons. He discussed UFO sightings, alien technologies, and Atlantis. As we will see, Seth craftily used such "out there" material to elaborate on *how* probabilities, reincarnation, and simultaneous time have psychically influenced our civilization throughout history.

Recall the probable selves who explore "roads not taken" within any given lifetime (see Chapter 4). This applies to entire civilizations, and their probable successes and failures as well. All of this information is available in Framework 2 and may "bleed through" to influence us in Framework 1.

The civilization-wide themes we typically explore—strong separation from inner source, arts, religion, technology, and manipulation of nature—serve as the main attractors to psychically connect with other probable selves and civilizations. These exchanges are always intended in helpfulness and guided by value fulfillment.

As such, the history of our species is much more entangled in the multidimensional nature of Framework 2 than our religions, sciences, and philosophies presently understand. This material was given to help us learn to develop the psychic abilities (inner senses) required to tap into this rich source of knowledge to help propel our civilization toward as yet unrealized discoveries.

KEY IDEAS: Seth used concepts like alien visitation, UFO sightings, alien technologies, Atlantis, and other lost civilizations to further explain the workings of probabilities, reincarnation, and simultaneous time. Learning to utilize them more directly will provide new sources of knowledge.

What Unknown Civilizations Existed Before Ours?

We still conceive of history as a single, fixed line that unfolds in consecutive stages over time. This kind of one-line development is an artifact of our physical perception, and Seth repeatedly states it is a highly limited view. In the previous chapter, we saw how Speakers reincarnate to participate in different chapters of religious dramas to provide inner knowledge to the collective. Just as individuals reincarnate, so too do entire civilizations.

Probabilities thus play an important collective role as groups of entities manifest to explore infinite arrays of cultural themes and dramas. This overall framework provides many, many different avenues in which to develop our abilities. Seth warned, however, that multiple civilizations have overcome an array of obstacles to reach our current stage of development only to destroy themselves or find ways to grow beyond it.

These civilizations existed on our planet long before our Stone Age,[85] and after working through their themes and dramas, physically left our planet for other galaxies in our universe. They accomplished this only after reaching a stage of spiritual development that utilized psychic abilities and technologies we have yet to discover.

Thus, they have memories of earth as their ancestral home. However, they evolved into forms that could no longer tolerate earth's atmospheric conditions. Some continued within reincarnational cycles elsewhere in Framework 1, while others evolved beyond physical form. These ancestral earth entities are still very involved with helping our civilization within Framework 2's simultaneous time and probability fields, and may be considered "earth gods."

Though Seth didn't provide specific dates, he said that a "long time" before Atlantis[86] there were three highly advanced technological civilizations. They developed ultrasonic forms of sound used in very different ways than we know for healing, war, vehicles, and the manipulation of matter.

The first civilization was concentrated around Asia Minor or modern Turkey. They followed a similar line of technological development as us, and contended with similar problems. They expanded their influence across the earth, and eventually left to live in other galaxies. In this light, those ancestors functioned as extraterrestrials on other planets.

The second civilization was called *Lumania*. It existed in what we now call Africa and Australia, though the land masses and climate were quite different then, and the magnetic poles were reversed. The Lumanians were descended from remnants of the first civilization, but they didn't wish to start from scratch. So their entities imbued their culture with specific innate knowledge that allowed them to rapidly progress through stages of technology to pursue their goal—to experiment with ways to avoid violence.

The Lumanians engineered an elaborate series of underground cities. In this sense *they* were the original "cavemen." They left the surface of the earth to an entirely different race that was primitive by their standards. They peacefully co-existed with this culture, though for the most part, purposefully avoided contact. They did, however, send out emissaries to live and intermarry with surface peoples, hoping to influence and soften their aggressive nature.

Lumanian art was superior to ours because of its elaborate use of technology and their highly developed psychic skills. They used variations of highly compressed color, tone, and shape to create invisible sounds so that, for instance, a drawing of an animal was imbued with "inner sounds" that provided its entire history and background.

The third civilization, which Seth didn't describe in much detail, later discovered this technique. Remnants of their cave paintings that tried to imitate these predecessors still exist today. However, if we were to look at one of these drawings, we wouldn't be able to discern their multimodal elements because we have yet to develop the kinds of psychic abilities required.

Physically, the Lumanians were skinny and weak by our standards, but psychically quite gifted. However, they ran into problems with their desire for peace, as the genetic safeguards against violence began to inhibit their psychic abilities. They ultimately weren't able to properly account for natural aggression in which creative energy naturally seeks full expression (see Chapter 3).

While their technology never threatened to destroy them, as does ours, they gradually realized their chosen course was reaching an endpoint. As such, after death, some personalities returned their attention to remnants of the first pre-Lumanian civilization. Some physically joined those who had migrated elsewhere in the galaxy. Eventually, those who remained abandoned their underground cities to join various groups of the primitive peoples dispersed around the planet. However, due to their inability to deal with violence, they rapidly died off and their civilization ended.

The vitality of Lumanian civilization was hampered because their natural aggressive tendencies were intentionally blocked. Therefore, they never learned how to turn violent impulses into constructive expressions, as we can to varying degrees. So this is something we continue to experiment with and need to further temper to better balance our warlike and violent tendencies.

KEY IDEAS: There were three unknown ancient civilizations that had advanced technologies. The first evolved to where it left our planet to populate other galaxies. Probable variations of these civilizations still exist in Framework 2.

Did Lumanian Traits Influence our Civilization?

The Lumanians' nervous systems were genetically predisposed to avoid violence. When they encountered strong aggression, they instinctively ran away. Since they weren't able to defend themselves, the Lumanian God was conceptualized as a male figure with exaggerated qualities of strength, power, and protection. Memories of the Lumanian God thus served as an archetype for early versions of the Hebrew God, Jehovah, a wrathful deity who protected his "chosen people."

During the Stone Age, our hominid ancestors often lived in the deserted ruins of underground Lumanian cities, tunnels, and caves. Some of the tools they used were distorted replicas of artifacts they found. Jules Verne's sci-fi classic *Journey to the Center of the Earth* (1864) hints at our own mythic memories of these underground structures.

Some of the caves were in parts of Spain and the Pyrenees Mountains (between Spain and France). Some earlier caves in Africa were also of Lumanian origin. Their "cave art" was highly sophisticated and described the local flora and fauna. These drawings were used as models by our early cave ancestors.

While the Lumanians weren't able to channel naturally aggressive emotions into other areas, their strong desire to accomplish this still reverberates throughout Framework 2, and affects us psychically. Seth said that due to reincarnational connections, their multidimensional art and technology has the potential to bleed through to influence our own civilization.

Moreover, there are probabilities in which the Lumanians found solutions to their experiments with nonviolence. In these, a totally different type of probable human being evolved. These traits are available to us today as we explore our unique type of consciousness and its abilities to cope with natural aggression. We don't yet realize that such a broad array of psychic potentials exists for us to employ because we don't yet recognize the nature of probabilities.

As we become more aware of other probable selves and civilizations in Framework 2, like the Lumanians, we will begin to recognize the psychic influence of what Seth calls "benign intrusive impulses." They will seem to have nothing to do with our current activities or interests. Yet they will come quickly and vividly into our awareness and *feel as if they're not our own.*

For instance, you might have a sudden impulse to buy a flute, having never played a flute before. This is an indication that a probable portion of your entity is gifted with that instrument. If indeed the impulse originates from this probable self, you would be able to learn the flute much quicker. As such, there is an array of probable variations of the Lumanian civilization that exist in Framework 2. Their advanced technologies, high psychic development, and nonviolent traits still exert psychic influences on us.[87]

KEY IDEAS: Various traits from the Lumanian civilization influenced our past, and still exert a psychic influence on us within Framework 2.

Did Atlantis Really Exist?

Seth said he had a lifetime as a Lumanian, and was later born in Atlantis. Again, these kinds of statements always made Jane and Rob cringe because of their connotations with the cultish belief systems of their day. Yet in hindsight, we can see that Seth introduced this "out there" material to further develop his map of our multiverse based on the core concepts of:

- **Probable Selves** (Chapter 4).
- **Reincarnation** (Chapter 5).
- **Simultaneous Time** (Chapter 5).
- **All That Is** (Chapter 5).
- **Frameworks of Consciousness** (Chapter 7).

As we have seen, only by exercising our intuitive and psychic abilities (inner senses, dreaming, and altered states) will we better understand these functions of the "unknown reality" and begin to put them to practical use. So the Seth Material is designed to arouse various subjective states to help us to widen our awareness, because our civilization is at an important crossroads.

There are scattered references to Atlantis in the Seth Material, some of which appear contradictory in Framework 1 terms. For instance, Seth referred to Atlantis ten times in *The Seth Material* (1970) and *Seth Speaks* (1972) as being *in the past*. However, in *The "Unknown" Reality* (1979) he described Atlantis as existing in a *probable future*.

Is it possible to be *both* at the same time? Only when we factor in the multidimensional nature of All That Is—probable and reincarnational civilizations in Framework 2—do Seth's explanations become plausible. They are intended to purposefully stretch our preconceived notions of single-line development (evolution). That is, they are designed to help us conceptualize nonlinear functions of our "iceberg selves" like probabilities, reincarnation, and simultaneous time. Just as Lydia could die in the 20th century and reincarnate as Tweety in the 17th century (see Chapter 5), so too can Atlantis exist as a probable future that serves as the basis for a new probable past to emerge *in our present*.

However, we still conceptualize the earth in terms of geographical traits like land masses, bodies of water, and climates because that's what we still perceive in Framework 1 terms. In Framework 2, our planet also exists in terms of "time and probability areas." In this way, many civilizations can exist together and bleed through to cross-pollinate each other in different periods of history in Framework 1.

Therefore, Atlantis exists as a probable past, present, *and* future in Framework 2. It can thus function as a future attractor—an impetus for development—in Framework 1 to create a mythical, yet precognitive yearning *for the kind of civilization we hope ours to be.* It also mixes in a blend of elements from various civilizations in our past, like the three versions of Lumanian culture.

This hints at the mechanics that underlie collective reality creation in which Framework 2 influences Framework 1. In this light, Atlantis exists as a probable future reality whose greater validity lies in its potential to influence our civilization today, even though we place it in our mythic past.

In Framework 2, simultaneous civilizations spiral outward within each "moment" of divine creativity to create pasts, futures, and other species of time we don't yet recognize. Again, there is no single-line evolution in any absolute sense, just the surface level appearance based on our limited physical perception in Framework 1.

As such, Atlantis also serves as a psychic blueprint in Framework 2 for the new type of consciousness Seth predicted to emerge in the Christ drama in terms of psychic abilities, advanced technologies, and coping with natural aggression. Probabilities now exist for us to begin to utilize these traits to solve our most important problems, and propel our civilization into as yet undreamed of achievements and fulfillment.[88]

KEY IDEAS: Atlantis is a blend of fact and myth in which our civilization projects its ideal characteristics upon the future. Based upon the traits from as yet unknown civilizations in our past, as well as the "pull" of probable futures, Atlantis serves as an impetus for future development.

What is the Dream City?

Seth's Dream City bears an interesting similarity to his Atlantis material, in that both concepts were introduced to help us break out of the linear modes of perception that currently limit our civilization, and to further explore the rich potentials inherent in Framework 2.

In October 1974, Seth encouraged ESP members to build an inner city—a "Dream City"—as a destination for group dreamers to jointly explore. It was a clever and exhilarating way to entice class members to continue their dream work. As always, Seth made it a playful endeavor, one that promoted creativity, curiosity, and spontaneity. He challenged them to explore the nature of inner dream symbols in the process.

In the weeks and months that followed, class members reported a variety of dreams that dealt with city imagery—a university, and even shared dreamscapes. Seth also hinted that this dream city would serve as an inner destination for group activities, similar to those in Framework 1.

Seth teased class members that he would appear as a loving "bum" in their city who snooped through garbage cans, yet kept an eye on things. He challenged people to not only remember their dreams every night, but to create the desire to consciously participate more in group dreaming environments. (Recall that we use our second dream body to access group dreaming environments, see Chapter 4.)

As the months rolled by, Jane and Rob moved from their Water Street apartment to the Hill House in Elmira, New York. ESP class was beginning to wind down, and there were only occasional classes thereafter. Seth's final remarks on the city came nine months after introducing the concept. In the end, Seth revealed that he knew class members weren't ready to complete the task he assigned them. And yet in hindsight, he cleverly outlined an excellent way to begin to probe Framework 2 from the dream state, and put theory into practice.[89]

KEY IDEAS: The Dream City is a way for group dreamers to jointly explore Framework 2.

What Are Dream-Art Sciences?

Seth introduced another group dreaming concept during this period to suggest other ways to explore Framework 2. While many scientists work alone at times, they always share their findings and go through a peer review process to reach a consensus. The method they use has three main steps:

1. Devise an experiment, paradigm, or activity to test a hypothesis or theory.
2. Do the experiment to gather evidence.
3. Draw conclusions that are verified or falsified by a group of peers.

In this, science is a highly specialized group activity that scientists train for over many years. What if the same discipline was applied to sciences that included dreaming and other altered states? In other words, what if sciences included not only physical (five senses) and mental senses (intellect), but also the inner senses (deep intuitions)?

This is the essential premise that underlies what Seth calls *dream-art sciences*.

Modern sciences are still very limited because they completely ignore subjectivity, dreaming, and inner sensing. For instance, scientists in current dream laboratories only study *other* people's dreams, not their own. They focus on physical changes in subjects, but exclude all subjective reports.

The arts open the doors of perception to subjective experience, because they directly identify with a subject. On the other hand, modern science still tries to divorce itself from its subject to maintain objectivity. And so it misses crucial dimensions of the subject's interior states and processes. It deals with only the objective half of reality, and ignores the rest.

By excluding the interior universe, modern science reduces all reality to exteriors—to the thin outer crust of Framework 1's QFs. By exploring Framework 2, scientists will discover the *blueprints for reality* or root assumptions "beneath" the surface of QFs. They function as the set of intentional constraints upon which our civilization has agreed to explore, as we saw with the Lumanians.

Learning to develop group dreaming capabilities would lead to entirely new solutions to some of the challenges we face. For example, recall the rich areas of inner information available in Alpha 1-5. Racial knowledge lies just underneath the personal subconscious that could help social psychologists. And beneath that lies knowledge of the entire species. Further inward is knowledge of the entity and functions of Framework 2, 3, and 4—that is, the mechanics of reality creation and how our entities manipulate CUs/EEs/QFs. This is the kind of "mind treasure" waiting to be mined as we widen our consciousness to master Alpha states, inner senses, and group dreaming—the basic tools of dream-art science.

As such, a dream-art scientist must first learn how to lucid dream and *sustain the state*. There are many techniques now available to learn how to do this.[90] In the process, they will naturally develop what Seth calls the *high intellect*—a new form of cognition that integrates a magnificent balance of physical, mental, and inner senses.

The dream-art scientist then learns the subjective alterations that occur when dreams start, continue, and finish. They familiarize themselves with their own dream symbols and discern how they do or don't match physical symbols in waking state. These symbols serve as agreed upon signposts for group dreaming and communication. They form the basis of an inner commerce similar to any physical city or market. In one sense, these inner "places" will also serve as a learning center (like the Dream City).

Next, the dream-art scientist begins to discern many different layers and types of dream activity. They begin to seek the blueprints (root assumptions) that govern Framework 1. For example, as they learn to identify those dream dimensions that coincide closely with physical reality, they'll discover that in some, future events become realized, while in others, they don't.

Seth provided three exemplars of dream-art scientists:

1. **Dream-art Scientist** (A generic scientist, already described.)

2. **True Mental Physicist** (A physicist who explores the basic functions of CUs/EEs/QFs involved in the mechanics of reality creation.)
3. **Complete Physician** (A healer that understands how body/mind/entity dynamics maintain health and are used to promote physical, emotional, psychological, and spiritual healing.)[91]

In the three decades since this material was first dictated, we've barely begun to scratch the surface of the "unknown" reality in any collective sense. And yet as Seth points out, there are new art-sciences that now lie on our horizon. If humanity undergoes the kind of psychic transformation hinted by Seth, dream-art sciences are likely to play a major role in those probable futures. Only then will we begin to jointly explore the "final frontier"— not space in Framework 1 terms—but Framework 2, the "hidden domain" that is its source.

KEY IDEAS: Group dreaming is an ancient art that can be used in a variety of new sciences to help unlock the secrets of reality creation in Frameworks 1 and 2.

Do UFOs and Extraterrestrials Exist?

As we have seen, early civilizations on earth are the ancestral home of extraterrestrials that migrated to other galaxies. But how did they travel there? Moreover, what kinds of dream-art technologies did they develop? How can we learn their core principles? The core principles in the Seth Material we've explored thus far lay a foundation in which to begin to explore them.

In terms of space travel, our current technologies travel *around* space-time. But the distances between habitable solar systems, even at or near the speed of light, are incredibly vast in Framework 1 terms. Therefore, Seth suggests we learn to travel *through* space-time by psychic manipulation of its camouflage constructions (CUs/EEs/QFs).

This is another reason why Seth outlined dream-art sciences: to further our development and help our civilization reach the stars. In the mean time, we *have* been visited by others, though it's not as simple as our one-line thinking suggests, because there are different modes of space-time travel. Some involve present time, some involve past or future times, and some involve other Frameworks of consciousness. In this way, Seth doesn't limit visitors to inhabitants of other planets as in classics like H. G. Wells' *War of the Worlds* (1898).

Moreover, some visitors are intentional and some are accidental, the side-effects of early experiments with dream-art sciences. These involve sudden transformative experiences triggered by the entity that reveal *how* all boundaries within All That Is may be pierced. As dream-art sciences progress, then, these kinds of accidental tourists become more controlled, and less frequent. But inhabitants of any Framework 1 are bound by the native attributes of their camouflage (primary constructions). As such, they must take those attributes with them, and learn to adapt to the new ones they encounter.

Because CUs/EEs/QFs have the ability to move and change forms between different Frameworks of consciousness, what we perceive as a UFO does not originate in our Framework 1, but one parallel to ours with more highly developed technologies. As such, its primary constructions become quite visible, much to our amazement. The QFs that make up the craft are imbued with the native characteristics of its Framework 1. As it bends space-time to enter our present, its native QFs encounter distortion effects from our QFs. The craft experiences a paradox of form that's literally stuck between the forces of the earth and its original QFs.

What we perceive, then, is something that's a hybrid of both Framework 1s and yet resembles neither. As such, the craft retains some of its original structure, and changes whatever's necessary to adapt to ours. This explains many of the different shapes, sizes, and colors of crafts reported over the years. Crafts that move quickly at odd angles do so because they retain some of the native functions (root assumptions) of their original Framework 1.[92]

KEY IDEAS: We have been visited by others throughout our history. They come from a variety of Frameworks, but all travel through—not around—space-time as we know it.

Did Our Ancestors Originate on Earth?

As we saw in Seth's creation myth, our universe, galaxy, planet, and species were all created in a dreamtime by Aspects of our entities known as the Sleepwalkers (see Chapter 6). There was an "order of play" in Framework 1 terms as our planet developed a biosphere to support early hominid life forms. But did the human race originally manifest solely on earth?

Seth said that not all human stock races originated on earth. Evolution actually involved several "beginning points." Though he never specified exact points, Seth repeatedly mentions that there were indeed visitors from other planets in Framework 1. While some visitors were more evolved than others, all appeared superhuman—even as gods—to the locals that encountered them. There were deliberate, humane experiments performed on local populations, as the visitors always tried to promote human knowledge.

Since the dream-art sciences that develop interdimensional travel always involve highly developed psychic abilities (group dreaming, inner senses), a preferred method of first contact is during the dream state when aggression is lessened, and there is less danger to the visitors, some of whom have been attacked and killed by "locals." As such, out-of-body interactions are a common method of contact, since space suits are clumsy attempts at imitating primary constructions suitable for interdimensional travel.

Visitors even presented our ancestors with an early code of ethics that was customized for the locals and cast in useful terms of their cultural development. Seth said these visitors came from "another star," and were involved in the origins of Atlantean culture. While put into written form initially, these ethics were later spread in oral form by various Speakers.

Visitors also taught some of our ancestors to manipulate matter through sound. For instance, the ancient Egyptians used this to build some of their pyramids, to irrigate their crops by "pulling" water over distances, and to accelerate crop growth. The "overenthusiastic" use of this technology resulted in the biblical flood, as these sounds required highly targeted precision, and when they overreached, they caused a disaster of literally biblical proportions.

Remnants of spaceships were also incorporated into ancient temples. The death and recovery of some visitors were the basis for the Egyptians' belief in the afterlife. Due to the nature of time's relativity, a visitor might come to earth as a young man, and return forty earth years later, but only age several months (as Einstein understood). This fueled early legends about the immortality and eternal youth of the gods.[93]

Clearly this material begs more questions than it answers, but it lays an important conceptual foundation on which to build. Given the multidimensional nature of All That Is, there *were* various interactions between physical races, some of which originated on earth, some that didn't. But they were all physical manifestations of our entities. So in that sense, we're *all* related through probabilities, reincarnation, and simultaneous time frameworks.

Our current beliefs in evolution limit stories of our origins to single-line thinking. Religious beliefs in creationism, and Adam and Eve, are even more simplistic. As we have seen, Seth repeatedly cautions that there is no single moment point in which our universe, our planet, or species began because our Source Consciousness—All That Is—has *always* been. While we continue to wrestle with the self-imposed boundaries of Framework 1 perception, we hold the means to expand it through new ways of knowing (high intellect).

In closing, we've explored some of the most "out there" parts of the Seth Material in this chapter. As such, it's important to be discerning, and continue to probe its deeper meanings and practical applications through our own personal experience. It hints at the many avenues of creativity that lie latent on our collective horizons, and more importantly, the idea that we exist in a multiverse that is far more complex and sophisticated than our current sciences, religions, and philosophies understand.

KEY IDEAS: Our ancestors come from a mixture of races from the earth as well as other planets, all of which are related through probabilities and reincarnation to our entities in Framework 2

Chapter 10: Our Animal Heritage

What Role Do Animals Play?

Life on earth consists of a spectrum of *nested* consciousness that extends from QFs to molecule, mineral, plant, animal, and human forms. Each type serves as a steppingstone for increasingly complex constructions that emerge over time, as we saw in the "order of play" in Seth's creation myth (see Chapter 6). Each plays a vital cooperative part in the whole, and helps form the world as we know it.

Within this spectrum, animals are closely related to humans.[94] The cells in our bodies consist of QFs, molecules, and minerals. We eat insects, plants, and other animals. We share similar abilities such as inner senses, dreams, "emotions," imaginations, free will, "morality," social orders, reproduction, reincarnation, and reason.

These traits are moderated by the types of bodies and brains unique to each species. What distinguishes human from animal consciousness, in general, is our self-reflexive awareness, belief systems, and intellect. Therefore, we are the only creatures on earth with the ability to conceptualize "I think, therefore I am," write symphonies, and build space shuttles.

While we tend to believe that these achievements make us the most highly evolved life form on the planet, Seth paints a different picture. He acknowledges our sophisticated abilities, but suggests that animals experience incredible variety, richness, and fulfillment in their own ways. For example, they surpass our current stage of development in other probable systems (parallel Framework 1s) that would be quite alien to us.[95]

In addition to animals' ability to perceive their own alternate advanced cultures, they also play a major role in our own, sometimes in very different ways. We raise them for food, domesticate them as pets, study them for medical cures, and even worship them as gods. They are also used as symbols in our myths. For instance, the serpent in the Garden of Eden story was the character who enticed Eve to eat from the Tree of Knowledge.

According to Seth, the serpent represents the knowledge and wisdom of our entities in Framework 2—the *source* of male and female principles. Its natural inclination toward transcendence represents the evolutionary impulse within all primary constructions to evolve, symbolized by Adam-as-outer-ego who first recognized itself in the world as being different from our dawn ancestors.

And yet, it's the feminine aspect of Eve that initiated our dawn ancestors' "departure" from the dreamtime into Framework 1. This feminine aspect listened to the inner wisdom of our creature selves and sparked the transition toward self-aware humans. Ironically, in a misinterpretation of this myth, women and the feminine, intuitive principle were blamed for "disobeying the Father" *instead* of being honored for *birthing* this crucial step into physical reality.

The serpent would later represent Satan in religious stories—the personified source of temptation and evil—whose early depictions included half-animal, half-man forms. In this way, the traditional creation myth reflected what we considered negative human traits based upon our animal heritage.[96]

KEY IDEAS: Animals are part of a spectrum of consciousness that makes human life possible. They play crucial roles in all human cultures, and serve as important symbols in our myths.

Why Are Cats and Geese Prominent in the Seth Material?

The Seth Material is full of stories about Jane and Rob's cats (Rooney, Willy, Billy, and Mitzi). Seth humorously referred to Willy as the "beloved monster" because he could see Willy's cat nature through the eyes of the mice and insects he hunted and occasionally used as toys. *A Lyric to Rooney* is a poem from *Dialogues of the Soul and Mortal Self in Time* (1975) that deals with his death. While the mortal self (Jane) decries the loss of her beloved pet, the soul (Ruburt) reassures that Rooney doesn't even realize that he's dead, but instead has simply changed form.[97]

As we've said, there are many different kinds of psychological characteristics within animals. Though we think of human consciousness as rich and diverse, we tend not to grant animals the same qualities. Yet many of their qualities may be considered more potent than our own at times. For instance, they perceive cycles of dis-ease and health as natural body rhythms, and their instincts guide them in ways to cope. When animals get sick, they automatically begin their own therapy. They intuitively understand that illness serves as a means to correct systemic imbalances, individually and within herds, which promotes better health in the long run.

Humans experience disease differently than animals because we feel separate from nature, and have a unique type of memory that makes intense emotional associations with past events. This has led humans to recall those diseases that caused death in the past and become more fearful of them, as in the case of plagues. This was, and continues to be, a side-effect of moving away from animal instincts into the self-reflexive perception of past, present, and future.

Another theme that permeates the Seth books is Rob's love of geese and his notes about the noisy spectacle of their seasonal migrations. These served as reminders of his deep connections to the outdoors and nature. They reinforced Rob's sense of creaturehood, and their seasonal movements reflected inner movements toward as yet unknown dimensions of experience and existence.[98]

In this way, Seth often used the creatures in Rob and Jane's lives to show how human consciousness evolved in relation to nature and our deeply felt connection with it. While the theory of evolution overemphasizes the competitive aspects of animal-human relationships (survival of the fittest/most adaptable), Seth always emphasizes the cooperative nature of the deep connections between *all* species. Without such cooperation, there would be no way to sustain *any* life on earth.

KEY IDEAS: Seth used some of the creatures in Rob and Jane's lives to show how human consciousness developed and exists in cooperation with all species.

What Key Relationships Do We Share With Animals?

The Bible tells us that we have dominion over all the animals on earth, and science tells us that animals have no larger purpose than to serve as pets, entertainment, food, beasts of burden, zoo inhabitants, or subjects for medical experiments. In other words, we still believe that animals exist merely to serve us because we assume they are lower, inferior life forms.

But there have *always* been mutual human and animal benefits based on value fulfillment. Recall the nature of the sub-cellular meshworks of communications in Framework 2 (see Chapters 2, 6). In this light, animals are not only in constant communication with each other but with *all* species on the planet. As such, they are much more in tune with the deeper purposes of all species, even if humans don't acknowledge that they are conscious, have emotions, and suffer pain.

Still, many animals enjoy their relationship with humans and share deep emotional bonds. Dolphins and whales react with their own types of emotional expressions to human interactions. Farm animals frequently have deeply felt connections with the families that care for them.

If we were to learn to communicate more directly with animals, profound changes would result in how we treat them. For instance, our ancestors often used animals to learn from because they had a deeper empathic connection with them. They learned which plants were poisonous, and which were safe to eat or use as medicines.

Our pets and other domesticated animals have unique reasons for cooperating with us. If they were in the wild, they'd have much different existences. Cats would eat rodents and insects instead of canned food, and would not need inoculations. Populations would be limited by available food, water, and other predators. In this way, they purposefully explore a different kind of relationship with humans, and their consciousness changes as a result.

In larger terms, however, animals and humans are simply one of the many forms that All That Is manifests to know Itself. There is nothing predestined in terms of what kinds of animals or humans manifest in Framework 1, as consciousness always seeks myriad expressions. As such, there is really no specific dog or hamster consciousness per se. Instead, they are unique forms of consciousness who choose to experience life on earth. The same holds true for humans, as there are endless potentials for consciousness to take on physical forms.

Also, while animals will reincarnate *as* animals, they may select different species in which to reincarnate. So a cat may also manifest as a pig or bear, but they will *not* reincarnate as humans. In this sense, there is no transmigration of animal souls into human form or vice versa, though a human entity *may* project a fragment into an animal (see Chapter 5).

On the other hand, there is a constant intermixing of the molecules that make up a human body that may be used to form the body of an animal, and vice versa. This is also true for minerals and plants. So there are many different relationships and deep connections between all living species in Framework 1.

Seth didn't go into further detail about other species' reincarnational relationships, or the Framework 2 structures that support them. However, the main point is that reincarnation links animals and humans together because it allows the exchange of information and experience between all species in Framework 2.[99]

KEY IDEAS: Animals and humans share a variety of bonds and reincarnational relationships in which all species are enriched.

Do Animals Have a Soul?

As is often the case when Seth uses paradox, the answer is, "Yes *and* no," because it depends on how "soul" is defined. Yes, in the sense that animals *do* have nonphysical consciousness, a *kind* of "iceberg self" that allows them to reincarnate. No, in the sense that their *type* of "iceberg self" is different than humans (though Seth didn't provide much detail).

Therefore, if we use Seth's definition of the human soul (entity) as a baseline, then no, animals don't have a soul, because it's *different*. But if we use Seth's definition of CUs as primal cause, then yes, animals and humans are *equally* made of this "soul stuff."[100]

CUs *are* the primal vitality—the "I AM"—of All That Is. They permeate and support all Frameworks of consciousness and probable systems to fuel *all* reality creation. CUs are not "miniature people," nor are they clumps of passive energy. CUs form *all* the psychological boundaries within our multiverse, as well as the inner communications meshworks between them. They contain the infinite potentials to explore all probabilities, and yet maintain their unique sense of individuality, which can never be destroyed.

In this light, CUs represent the irreducible "unit" of interiority within All That Is, which Seth considers "soul stuff." By that definition, *everything* in Framework 1 contains some type of "soul," and yet these naturally differ in terms of complexity and function. For example, we know that QFs form the most basic kinds of matter and as such are in *all* matter. An elephant consists of cells made from QFs, molecules, and minerals that, in turn, form its organs and nervous system. In that sense, an elephant is more complex than a rock, raindrop, or oxygen atom. It is "one-made-of-many"—a gestalt consciousness—a unified whole that is *more* than the sum of its parts.

Seth admits that his definition of "soul stuff" based on CUs alone has limits because there are more highly developed "personality gestalts" like Seth who have finished their reincarnational cycles, and some that never experience physical reality like Life Clouds or Seth II (see Chapter 5). From that perspective, humans are perceived as less evolved entities, as "junior souls."

Most religions have a partial understanding that human and animal "souls" are different. In Christianity, only humans may enter heaven—no pets allowed—which reinforces beliefs that mankind is superior to animals. The belief that an animal, or anything, is "less than" human has led to needless philosophical questions like "When does the soul enter the flesh?" and "When does a fetus become a human being?"

Seth's definition of CUs as "soul stuff" applies to *everything* in Framework 1. All insects, plants, single-celled creatures, rocks, water, air, fire, all molecules, atoms, subatomic particles, down to the most basic QFs *are thus conscious*. This core truth has also been expressed in the mystical traditions, that God—or whatever name you prefer—exists *within all* physical reality. For example, the Gnostic Gospel of Thomas says:

It is I who am the light which is above them all. It is I who am the all. From me did they all come forth, and unto me did the all extend. Split a piece of wood, and I am there. Lift up the stone, and you will find me there.[101]

While the mystics share Seth's view, modern science presents a more limited perspective. The cognitive sciences in the West based primarily on brain research, claim that human consciousness is the result of brain chemistry and five sense inputs. Thus, they define it as a side-effect of the QFs in the brain, and there is no need for a soul or anything nonphysical that transcends the material world, such as Framework 2, to explain how you create your own reality. In other words, they still believe that form evolves consciousness, not the other way around, as Seth and the mystics maintain.

As such, because animals are considered "soulless" and therefore inferior to humans, abuses such as inhumane conditions at slaughterhouses, food-raising farms, use in medical experiments, and other horrific treatment is perpetuated. Seth wryly noted that Hitler's Germany was made possible by similar beliefs that equated certain races of humans to nothing more than inferior animals, while perpetuating the insane delusion of a Master Race based on social Darwinism's survival of the fittest (see Chapter 13).

Moreover, modern biologists still operate under the assumption that they can learn "how things work" by studying the effects of induced disease and traumatic injuries. However, when you kill a lab animal and extract its inflicted heart, eye, or brain you still deal *only* with the exteriors of QFs, and *never account for its consciousness*. Humpty Dumpty can never be put back together again because *the whole is always greater than the sum of its parts*.

Therefore, when we infect and injure lab animals as a means to cure human disease and injury, the results are second-hand knowledge at best. As such, we are still far away from first-hand knowledge of the deeper connections between human and animal consciousness. Only when scientists wake up to the fact that not only animals, but all things in Framework 1, are made of "soul stuff" will they take steps to treat animals more humanely.[102]

KEY IDEAS: Seth uses paradox to answer the question, "Do animals have a soul?" Yes, in the sense that animals are made of the "soul stuff" of CUs. No, in the sense that their type of "iceberg self" is different than humans.

Did Humans Evolve From Animals?

As we have seen, Seth continually stretches our beliefs in linear thinking with concepts like simultaneous time, probable systems, and Framework 2. Therefore, linear concepts that involve the "beginning" of time, the universe, or any species, are extremely limited. As such, we are faced with yet another Sethian paradox in which the answer is, "Yes *and* no," that depends on the definition of "time."

Because there is an "order of play" in linear time in Framework 1, then it is true that humans *did* evolve from animals. But they also *did not*, in the sense that all species co-exist in simultaneous time in Framework 2 "before the beginning." As such, all species lie latent within infinite probable forms (blueprints) until life conditions are right for them to physically manifest. Therefore, there is no single line of development since probable pasts, present, and futures are *ever-changing* and simultaneously influence each other. Again, these functions are made possible by CUs, so the notion that reptiles turned into birds, then mammals, then apes then humans is highly limited.

According to Seth, there were also multiple species of half-animals and half-humans that co-existed for many centuries.[103] These multiple species lived side by side 50-30 million years ago, much earlier than is currently believed. Some species reached dead ends as their lineages became extinct, and they simply *moved into other probable realities parallel to ours.* In larger terms, this means that no species ever goes extinct. They simply no longer fit the life conditions in one probable system, and move to a parallel Framework 1 where conditions are better suited.

As human consciousness gradually emerged in Framework 1, our animal instincts had to be diminished, even though they had been extremely acute and useful. For many centuries, there was no clear cut separation between certain human and animal species, as emergent hybrid species explored various postures (bipedal, quadrapedal), types of memory, senses, instincts, brain sizes and structures.

One way to imagine how this may have occurred is based on genetic research like the Human Genome Project. For example, we know that we share roughly 96% of the *same* DNA, genes, and chromosomes as chimpanzees, and yet they are clearly *not* human. In this way, species that are highly related in genetic terms can still manifest *quite different types of consciousness.*

CUs are aware of every grouping or system they ever create. Their freewheeling nature allows some of the lessons learned by one probable species to serve as the "instinctual" basis for others. Therefore, species don't develop in one-line sequences, like ape to man. Instead, they *precognitively select future probabilities to alter their present form.* In other words, the genetic mutations that produce new species are not driven by chance at all, they are *purposefully chosen* at the cellular level from the most fertile probable futures that *already exist in Framework 2.*[104]

Again, consciousness is not an after effect of more complex groupings of matter over time. Consciousness existed first and dreamt up the forms in which it manifests (see Chapter 6). In this light, our modern scientific beliefs in single-line evolution are as distorted as the biblical creation.

Though this sounds like the stuff of science fiction, the mechanics of collective reality creation incorporate the functions of simultaneous time, probable systems, and Frameworks of consciousness. All of this is managed by our entities, Sleepwalkers, and others like Seth II, who play supporting roles. In this way, Seth reinforces the crucial role played by consciousness, one that remains missing in action in mainstream sciences.

KEY IDEAS: Seth uses paradox to explain that humans did evolve from animals in the sense that there was an "order of play" in linear time in Framework 1, but did not in the sense that all species co-exist in simultaneous time in Framework 2.

Is Bigfoot Real?

There are new species discovered every year in our oceans, rain forests, mountains, and deserts. So we still don't know everything about life on earth, much less its history and origins in the linear sense. While there are mythical stories of unicorns and fire-breathing dragons, there have also been numerous reports of an upright, bipedal ape in the Himalayas of Nepal and Tibet, and the Pacific Northwest for centuries.

Due to the lack of fossil, carcass, or skeletal evidence, most scientists remain skeptical of its existence. Typical explanations cite misidentification, hoaxes, folklore, and overactive imaginations. And yet, Seth claimed that there are indeed two species of what is called Sasquatch or Bigfoot. He presented this material after Jane watched a TV showed hosted by Leonard Nimoy called *In Search Of* in 1984.

He said that two kinds of mammals exist that walk upright like humans, but are physically larger and have more highly developed senses. For instance, their sense of smell can track a human several miles away. They thrive on a vegetarian diet and use ingeniously designed, tree sap-laden traps to catch large numbers of insects, which they consider a delicacy. The traps are camouflaged within trees to protect them, and are not obvious to the untrained eye. The creatures also have a kind of rapid-fire memory system that processes sense data almost instantaneously.

Though Seth didn't cite specific ages, they mature later than we'd expect for normal breeding purposes, and mate in similar ways to humans and apes. If we account for normal territorial variations, they exist in *many areas* throughout our planet, which would account for reports of the Yeti or Abominable Snowman in the Himalayas. Their total population remains relatively small, so small that we'd likely consider them an endangered species. Seth claimed there were only "several thousand" alive in 1984.

They don't gather in herds or large groups, yet maintain family groups with a maximum of twelve adults in any particular area. As the group expands through new births and maturing adolescents, they break up into smaller groups. They use tools, forage for food, and live in harmony with nature and other animal species. That is, they don't compete for food, shelter, or reproductive resources with other animals.

They're naturally docile, though if cornered or protecting young they are capable of being ferocious, like most species. In the winter months, their body metabolism slows down due to the colder climate. As their body temperatures drop, like many animals they will hibernate for weeks, even months at a time. They don't have a spoken language, and instead rely on their keen senses.[105]

The existence of these bipedal primates is consonant with Seth's claims that there have been multiple species of man-animal hybrids that have shared the earth with humans for millions of years. It's possible that fossils of their ancestors have been mistaken for early species of humans as well.

KEY IDEAS: There are many species of life on our planet we have yet to discover, two of which are bipedal primates. This is consonant with Seth's claim that there have been many species of animal-man hybrids that lived alongside of humans for millions of years.

Why is Seth's View of Our World So "Out There"?

Shakespeare's Hamlet famously said, "There are more things in heaven and earth, Horatio, than are dreamt of in your philosophy." As we have seen, the stories told by mainstream religions, sciences, and philosophies are filtered through the limits of cultural belief systems. And yet, the mechanics of reality creation—*the blueprints for reality* that lie buried in Framework 2—await those bold enough to seek them, though this requires a major shift in consciousness. Areas of our brains remain latent, waiting for the proper life conditions to activate them.

Seth is ever optimistic that we will activate those latent probable futures to develop as yet undreamed of abilities that are inherent in our spiritual and animal heritage. They exist *right now* in Framework 2, and exert an inexorable pull to inspire the emergence of a new type of human consciousness that can better mine the riches within Framework 2. Seth also encourages us to *fully embrace* the fleshy aspects of our creaturehood, for *to deny them is to deny spirit*. They form the basis of what we are, and what we have yet to become.

We are on a collective journey to learn *how* we create our own realities, jointly and with All That Is. In that sense, we are in the process of becoming conscious co-creators. We have chosen a unique type of consciousness, replete with its own challenges and rewards. We knew that we would "forget" parts of our animal nature, a necessary tradeoff for our continued development.

In Part 2, we explored some of the most difficult and challenging concepts in the Seth Material. They are intended to outline a new story—a new worldview—to help us better understand the journey we began countless eons ago in the dreamtime, and the probable futures that await us:

- **Creation Myth** (Sleepwalkers)
- **Frameworks of Consciousness** (1, 2, 3, 4)
- **Christ Drama** (Speakers)
- **Lumania, Atlantis, UFOs, Bigfoot**
- **Probable Gods, Systems, and Species of Man-Animal Hybrids/Humans**

In closing, Seth did an excellent job to hint at the origins of All That Is, and outline the "hidden" functions in Framework 2 that have fueled mass events throughout history. He encouraged us to joyfully and heroically explore this "unknown" reality for ourselves. As always, just because Seth "said so" doesn't mean it's true. He left that part up to each of us to verify or falsify. And so our continued journey will always be a matter of individual and collective choices.

But one thing is certain—the maps of our world presented by traditional religion, modern science and philosophy remain incomplete and are in serious need of updating. Whatever we can imagine and dream of, we *can* create. Therefore, the potentials of learning to tap more directly—more consciously—into Framework 2 loom large as a means for new solutions to the many challenges we now face on a global scale.

KEY IDEAS: Seth used a mixture of paradox, intellect, and direct experience to explain the origins, hidden source, and history of our world to update our current maps and suggest new ways for problem solving and innovation.

—PART 3—

DISCOVER

HOW WE CAN

LIVE IN HARMONY

Chapter 11: Sethics

What is Truth?

Answering this question is the goal of every religion, science, and philosophy, for they all seek the answers to life's most important questions, "Do I survive death, or is that the end of existence?" "Does my soul really exist, or is my life the result of some cosmic accident?" "Is there a Creator "within" physical reality?" "If so, what's the ultimate meaning and purpose to my life?"

The answers to these and other questions are really quite simple, for they are within you all along, closer than your breath and heartbeat. For it is only through your own direct experience and knowing that you discover "the truth." This perennial wisdom has been expressed in all the world's mystical traditions for thousands of years.

And yet, what if my truths are different than yours? It seems that so many people spout their truths and seem so sure that they're right, but lead people down a primrose path of fundamentalism, fanaticism, or violence. Moreover, as we have seen mystics, scientists, and philosophers provide partial, even *contradictory* truths because they use different ways of knowing truth (physical, mental, *or* inner senses, but rarely all three). So what's going on?

Seth points out that "the truth," while very important and written in every cell, is relative to the perceiver. In this way, we each hold beliefs that all our truths are based upon. These types of truths are known as *relative truths*. Note the plural: *truths*. There are as many different sets of relative truths as there are perceivers.

So what about Truth with a capital "T"? Is there some kind of Absolute Universal Truth that is *never* false, and never changes?

Yes.

All That Is—the eternal I AMNESS within all things, the Whole that is more than the sum of its parts—is One Truth.

While the traditional definition of *God* is too narrow to fully express One Truth, Seth understood that we often cast God in masculine clothing, and thus used the term "He" on occasion because he felt that "It" was too impersonal.

Whatever way you describe It, *all* other truths are relative to this One Truth. This in no way diminishes the nature of relative truths, however, for they are *very* important. They form the foundations from which we create our own reality through our belief systems in Framework 1. As such, our truths—our beliefs—are the crucial parts of our perception we use to shape our lives.

Therefore, it's important to *always* question those truths you hold to be self-evident. When we hide behind the shield of absolute certainty, we automatically filter out any questions and information that threaten the validity of our truths. Questioning requires a skeptical attitude, which drives human development, the process of old truths giving way to new truths *based on direct experience*, not an expert or authority's "say-so." This applies equally to religious truths taken "on faith," and scientific truths based on "facts," because *both* can be twisted to suit hidden agendas that may not serve our best interests.

As such, Seth encourages you to explore altered states in which you may "encounter living truth" through your direct experience (physical, mental, *and* inner senses). These will initiate "expansions of consciousness" that widen your awareness. However, he cautions that any knowledge gained this way will *always* need to be interpreted through your belief systems—your truths. So you need to be as aware of your own limits—your *prejudiced perception*—and make every effort for honest self-examination and reflection.

While "the truth" may be relative to your beliefs in Framework 1, the more you know them, the wider your awareness becomes, and the *deeper* you will understand *how* they create your own reality.

KEY IDEAS: There is only One Truth that never changes: All That Is, which can be known only through direct experience. However, you will always translate that experience into your own belief systems, which in Framework 1 are relative and subject to change.

What is Natural Law?

Seth's definition of *natural law* follows that of truth. There are many, many relative laws and yet only One Law: All That Is. Therefore, what we consider laws, like the speed of light (a scientific law), is also *relative* to Framework 1. It appears absolute within Framework 1, *and is*, but "outside" of Framework 1, *it simply doesn't exist.*[106]

The same holds true for religious and secular laws. What we refer to as "God's Law," or a secular law like the voting age, are belief systems within Framework 1. Just as the speed of light doesn't exist in other Frameworks, neither does an absolute "God's Law" or the voting age.

Again, this doesn't mean these laws aren't important or real; they *are*. It's just that they're not as absolute as we've been taught to believe. For instance, while secular laws are understood to be changeable, both scientific and religious laws are believed to be absolutes, and yet they are *only relative to Framework 1*.

Seth took this one step further when he presented the laws that govern *all* Frameworks of consciousness. He called them *laws of the inner universe* (and later, *natural laws*). Again, note the plural. These are not *the* One Law in the Absolute Universal Truth sense. They, too, are relative, applicable only to the Frameworks of consciousness in Seth's awareness.

He initially outlined ten natural laws, and later said there were others, but never specified them.[107] Value fulfillment was the first law introduced. As we saw, this also forms the basis of the divine love that nurtures *all* reality creation (see Chapter 3).

Seth's intent was to help us understand that there are deeper principles that promote all reality creation in Framework 1 and underlie the rest of our multiverse. As such, these laws don't favor any race, creed, nor are they limited to humans, animals, plants, or rocks. They apply to *all* constructions—including entities and Life Clouds—within All That Is. So they may initially seem abstract, general, or even alien, because they *embody the primal creative forces of All That Is within all Frameworks of Consciousness.*

- **Value Fulfillment** (fuels all action, all development in relation to everyone and everything's best interests).
- **Energy Transformation** (the forces in which "no-thing" creates space-time frameworks: CUs => EEs => QFs).
- **Spontaneity** (the infinite unpredictability that prevents predetermined outcomes and closed systems of reality).
- **Durability** (the results of transformation of inner energy: idea constructions).
- **Creation** (all probabilities seek expression through expansion: infinite becoming).
- **Consciousness** (the Essential Interiority/I AM *within* All That Is).
- **Capacity for Infinite Mobility** (the ability to transcend or take form: all boundaries are psychological in nature, there are *no* closed systems).
- **Changeability and Transmutation** (a capacity to take on any pattern or to form an infinite number of energy fields: allows entities to create physical constructions).
- **Cooperation** (a force that nurtures all value fulfillment).

- **Quality Depth** (a force of powerful psychic motion in which all consciousness constantly expands and creates).[108]

In this light, we can see that CUs—the "building blocks" of reality creation—are actually imbued with *all* of these natural laws, which also contain an ethical component based upon value fulfillment.[109] Thus, what we've defined as "divine love" can now be expanded to include the nine other laws, in addition to value fulfillment. Together, they guide the functions of all CUs, and contribute to the ethical underpinnings of our multiverse.

In other words, *there are innate ethics imbued in all CUs that result from natural laws.* As we will see, they form the basis of the *innate moral intuition* that guides all Framework 1 reality creation, including human beings.

Though natural laws are relative, they are still *more* fundamental than the so-called laws of physics (science), "God's Law" (religious), or voting ages (secular) because they apply to *all* Frameworks, and are not limited to human belief systems in Framework 1.[110]

In this way, natural laws innately guide all social cohesion, growth, and fulfillment in Framework 1, but are subject to the vagaries of belief systems that change over time. The main point, however, is that while natural laws innately fuel human morality, they don't operate in the absolute way that most religions and sciences have taught us to believe.

KEY IDEAS: The laws of the inner universe (natural laws) express the primal characteristics of All That Is that guide all reality creation. They also express an innate ethical foundation that forms the basis of all moral belief systems.

What is Sethics?

The term *Sethics* is used to outline a form of ethics based on the Seth Material.[111] It's a play on words to describe how Seth's natural laws impact our moral and ethical belief systems. The terms "morals" and "ethics" are tricky words that, like "myth" and "God," come with preconceived notions and baggage. As such, for purposes of overview, we'll use them interchangeably to mean the same thing—an innate value judgment (belief system) of good and bad, and right and wrong that reflects the overall stage of development of any individual's or group's worldview.

As mentioned earlier, even animals have a type of morality or "code of honor" that guides their instincts and choices. These, too, are fostered by natural laws. While their code doesn't need to include a legal age for voting, for example, human moral codes *do*. So there is a kind of sliding scale that influences the emergence of morals and ethics within *all* Framework 1 consciousness. That is, morals don't just "poof in" full-blown, but develop and change over time as consciousness evolves.

As such, morals and ethics need to be understood in relation to the three main cultural worldviews—traditional, modern, and postmodern (see Introduction, Chapter 6)—because they contain very different belief systems (relative truths).

Traditional morals are codes of conduct and punishment based on divine revelation—"The Word of God"—through acknowledged prophets. For example, the ten commandments of the Abrahamic religions "delivered" to Moses influenced Judaic Talmudic law, Christian Canon law, and Islamic Sharia law. This worldview believes in forms of *moral absolutism* because its moral codes are considered "perfect and unchangeable." As such, traditional moral beliefs distinguish between "God's Law" (religious) and "man's law" (secular).

Modern moral theories are based upon reason, not divine revelation. For example, German philosopher Immanuel Kant (1724-1804) believed that all moral principles (good and evil), laws, and punishments could be determined by "pure practical reason," which he called *categorical imperatives*. This is another form of moral absolutism, though based upon the cognitive powers of the intellect.

Postmodern moral theories are based upon reason *and* subjective experience. For example, integral psychologist Ken Wilber (b. 1949) outlined what he called a *basic moral intuition*.[112] He defined morals as the belief systems *throughout the entire spectrum* of traditional, modern, and postmodern worldviews that deal with moral principles (good and evil). Absolute standards are less important than the context of a particular situation, and therefore standards may vary from one situation to another, and even contradict each other. They employ pluralism (many truths) and contextualism (situational) that result in *moral relativism.*

Therefore, in the context of these three main cultural worldviews, the word "morals" is *not* limited to only the traditional worldview's definitions of moral principles (good and evil), laws, and punishments. It *applies to all three worldview's* definitions of those belief systems. As such, we don't want to limit the definition of morals to *only* traditional (religious) or modern (scientific) absolutes, because all three worldviews are very active today. They form a vast probability field in Framework 2 that fuels mass events.

Sethics thus deals with the emerging postmodern worldview's morals *and its differences* from traditional and modern worldviews. Sethics includes *all* three worldviews, and together they outline the "belief framework" in which Seth so often criticized traditional (religious) and modern (scientific) beliefs. As we will see throughout Part 3, he exposed their contradictions and limitations based upon his map of multidimensional identity (Your Self) and the multiverse (Your World) that we explored in Parts 1 and 2.

In this light, Sethics shows how your ethical belief systems create your own reality *in relation to self and others*, and suggests some new ways to approach how we can all get along to make the world a better place.

KEY IDEAS: Sethics deals with the emerging postmodern worldview's ethics, its differences from traditional and modern worldviews, and suggests new ways to help us all get along.

How Did our Innate Moral Intuition Emerge from our Animal Heritage?

In *The Nature of Personal Reality* (1974) Seth introduced additional concepts that show how moral and ethical beliefs emerged in our dawn ancestors from what had previously been animal instincts. When we think of animal instincts, we may incorrectly assume that some, like aggression, are "lower" or undesired, but that is not accurate.

As we saw, *natural aggression* is the principle that provides the great creative thrust for all life to *take action* (see Chapter 3). Thus, aggression is not innately bad or to be avoided, because it is foundational to all biological life from which human consciousness emerged. Physical birth is a good example of the raw power of natural aggression. Likewise, the manifestation of any idea into physical form reflects its innately creative thrust. As such, any attempt to deny or repress naturally aggressive acts inevitably backfires to produce a kind of pseudo-aggression. This creates an array of psychological imbalances that result in war, violence, and other pathological behaviors.

So there is an important distinction between natural aggression, designed to promote creative action, and pseudo-aggression, the side-effect of blocked impulses, repressed emotions, and anger that explodes into violence to gain release.

With the emergence of the conscious mind (outer ego), early humans began to experience a new type of free will. What had previously been instinctive animal moral codes became suggestions instead of hard-coded guidelines. As a result, the healthy emotions of *natural compassion* and *natural guilt* emerged.

While animals have an instinctual sense in which they know that death is not annihilation when they hunt prey, humans made a conscious leap outside of that framework. Early human hunters were thus forced to empathize with their prey. The new emotions of natural compassion and natural guilt produced an innate sense of *violation* in our dawn ancestors. It provided a check and balance in which it was understood that there was no need to kill more than was necessary to sustain life. Therefore, a biological, emotional, psychological, and spiritual knowing arose: *don't violate*. As animal instincts receded, human consciousness developed the flexibility in which to interpret this innate sense of violation.

Therefore, stealing, sex, or farming the land may or may not be a violation, because it depends on the context of each situation. Seth humorously said that not attending church on Sunday is *not* a violation, though there could be a situation where it is.

While normal aggressive thoughts are not a violation, committing a violent act to your or someone's body or spirit *is*. As such, killing anyone, even in self-defense, *is* a violation whether it seems justified or not.

Additionally, the new ability for early humans to perceive past, present, and future sparked the further development of natural guilt and violation, which were designed *as a means of prevention*. In other words, as the human brain evolved a complex memory system, new situations could be compared with past ones. A moment of reflection allowed the conscious mind to evaluate the consequences of any imminent action, and if a violation previously occurred, then that action was *not* to be repeated.

This "moment of reflection" was something that animal consciousness didn't need. Natural guilt thus emerged from animal instincts as the ability to pause and reflect, to remember the past and visualize probable futures. Without it, humans would be unable to recall past acts, compare them to the present situation, and imagine the future emotion of regret triggered by a natural sense of violation.

As such, an innate moral intuition based upon free will and memory emerged: don't kill more than you need to eat, don't kill each other for blood sport. And yet, when that happens, *there is no innate need for punishment*. Natural guilt alone prevents the recurrence, so no punishment is necessary. In this way, natural guilt was *intended to prevent violence, not encourage it*.[113]

Since early humans lived in foraging groups made up of small families, natural compassion and natural guilt insured that most would kill only what they needed to live, and if things occasionally got out of hand, provided checks and balances like natural aggression to prevent further violations.

KEY IDEAS: The emotions of natural compassion and natural guilt, developed in early humans as cognitive abilities based on memory and free will, emerged from animal instincts. These produced a sense of violation that formed the basis of an innate moral intuition.

What Other Gifts Did We Inherit from our Animal Heritage?

Animals and humans exist in a state of *natural grace*, made possible once again by divine love (natural laws). This state infuses the effortless, transparent, and joyful foundations of physical existence. Since it's innate, it's impossible to ever leave it, and *no one can ever take it away*. You were born and will die in a state of grace no matter what words are incanted or rituals performed. However, you have the free will to deny its existence during your lifetime, and lose touch with its divine presence.

In this light, the traditional belief in "original sin" is a distortion that has led to much unnecessary suffering. The state of natural grace actually serves as an "original blessing," literally a *gift* of divine love. Beliefs like original sin—that alienate us from natural grace and natural guilt—were a side-effect of the conscious mind's emerging beliefs, thoughts, and emotions.

As the Paleolithic Age ended around ten thousand years ago, metal replaced stone technologies, and farming replaced foraging economies. Human societies became more sophisticated and supported larger populations that evolved consensual belief systems about moral behavior. At some point, what we consider *conscience* emerged from *artificial guilt*— a sense of false contrition and guilt *dissociated* from natural compassion, natural guilt, and natural grace. This was a side-effect of the ability to pause and reflect that led to mass beliefs in punishment and penance.

Thus, ideas of crime and punishment developed over time, but are relatively recent human belief systems. However, Seth pointed out that punishment makes no sense in the context of simultaneous time because, as we saw, all incarnations occur simultaneously within Framework 2 and the belief system of karma (reincarnational punishment and reward) is highly distorted (see Chapter 5). In larger terms, each personality must eventually reconcile the impact of all their actions on themselves and others in Framework 2.

Still, in practical terms, we must deal with the apparent nature of cause and effect in Framework 1, but there is no innate need for punishment *when we are fully in touch* with our natural compassion, natural guilt, and natural grace. People will naturally self-correct when their innate sense of violation acts as a deterrent. In effect, they use their innate moral compass to prevent further violations, which fosters social cohesion and harmony with self and others.

However, as we can see from the past six thousand years of human history, these natural instincts can become blocked by the same conscious mind that distinguish us from animals. As such, belief systems in crime and punishment, and individuals who are out of touch with their natural moral instincts are realities we must cope with today.[114]

KEY IDEAS: Natural grace is an innate state of being that can never be taken away because it is made possible by divine love (natural laws). Conscience based on artificial guilt has led to beliefs in crime and punishment (karma) that developed over time. Natural compassion, natural guilt, and natural grace provide self-correction mechanisms in every individual, but are often blocked.

Exercise 10—Notice and Identify Natural Grace

Engage psy-time. As you settle down, pay attention to your breath as it comes and goes. Notice that while you are not your breath, it makes your physical consciousness possible. Do this for a minute or two, and continue to relax.

Next, imagine what happens to your breath after it leaves your body. Sense how it disperses like clouds in the sky in the air around you, or as bubbles underwater. Imagine what other forms it may change into. Do this for a minute or two.

Next, imagine that each breath is one of your own lives, and that *you* are the entity from which they are all birthed into the world of space-time. As your breath moves away, so do you move through vast psychic and psychological domains. Do this for a minute or two.

Next, as you expand your awareness into your entity, simply notice your state of grace. It is within the simple feeling-tone of your be-ing. There will be no artificial guilt present, for example, thoughts in which you berate yourself for perceived faults or inadequacies. (If there is, slowly take several deep breaths, *relax*, and then start over.)

Finally, feel as deeply as possible into your entity and state of grace. Do this for several minutes, and then simply rest in that grace as long as you wish.[115]

What About Good and Evil?

As we've seen, the character of Satan as catalyst for temptation and evil represents the humanized projection of our deep seated archetypal fear of separation from All That Is and the Sleepwalkers (see Chapter 6). Seth repeatedly states that there is *no innate evil within All That Is*. There is only divine love, which is based upon natural laws that can be equated with innate goodness.

Hatred, fear, and evil are the results of beliefs in separation from our entity and All That Is. Recall the end of the dreamtime (Garden of Eden) in which our dawn ancestors first found themselves in physical bodies that required food and shelter, and experienced pain, hunger, and alienation. That primordial "separation from God" is what led to our initial beliefs in good and evil as reflected in the myth of Adam and Eve (see Chapter 6).

Still, if there's no innate evil, then why doesn't our innate sense of violation prevent all of the murder and mayhem in our world? Because the conscious mind is imbued with free will, and can make choices that override or suppress it. This is the double-edged nature of our free will, something that's necessary to allow us to make the "wrong" choices and learn from them over time. This is how we grow as individuals and as a civilization.

While our free will may at times seem limited in relation to our entity's amazing abilities, the fact that we can override natural compassion, natural guilt, and natural grace and create the many problems we face speaks to the *power of choice* we have with free will. It is a gift of All That Is, and as such, we each bear the responsibility to make our choices in ways that provide our greatest fulfillment. Just because there's no eternal punishment doesn't mean there's no accountability for our actions.

Seth says that evil, as we conceptualize it, is the *absence* of knowledge, fulfillment, and growth. In larger terms, a murderer can never annihilate anyone, but in any case, they will inevitably deal with the consequences of their actions. Though crime is not punished in the afterdeath environment, knowledge must be gained about how every action, thought, and behavior has an impact on *others*, for in larger terms, *the other is you.*[116]

Most importantly, while there is never a "final judgment," because consciousness is never static, there is always movement towards growth, wisdom, and spiritual remembrance. A major problem with understanding this idea is that, once freed from the absolutes of religious dogmas, people often *get lost in its relativity.*

For example, they may believe that since there are *no* Absolute Moral Truths, and therefore violations don't result in eternal or other cosmic punishment, then anything goes. *But they still don't understand the workings of innate moral intuition.* Put simply, you have a natural moral compass that identifies not only if violations exist, but what to change and avoid the next time. In this way, you can live in healthy, abundant, and fulfilling ways. When you ignore or suppress that compass with an "anything goes" approach, you inevitably create artificial guilt, which always results in needless pain and suffering.

Therefore, this doesn't mean that hatred, fear, and evil don't exist or don't take a physical, emotional, and psychological toll. They're very real and *must* be addressed because they exist in some form within *your* belief systems, as we will see in the next chapter. Even though Seth talks about Framework 2 and other nonphysical domains, that doesn't make Framework 1 experience any less real or important to your entity's overall growth. So you must always apply these ideas *in practical terms to your everyday experience*. Otherwise, they're useless.

This is also why Seth puts the onus *back on you* in terms of constant movement towards wisdom and remembrance. For there are important lessons to be learned from every action you take and ethical decision you make. All your beliefs, thoughts, and emotions not only affect yourself, but also ripple out into the world to affect others.

KEY IDEAS: While there's no absolute good or evil within All That Is, and there's no eternal punishment for any violations we commit in Framework 1, all of our actions have consequences that contribute collective value fulfillment. There are important lessons to be learned because every action you take has an ethical dimension to it.

So What?

In summary, divine love (natural laws) forms the basis of your innate sense of natural compassion, natural guilt, and natural grace. Together, these form the moral and ethical basis of *how* you create your own reality. However, because of your conscious mind (memory and free will), you also create artificial guilt (conscience) that colors all your belief systems about good and evil, right and wrong, and crime and punishment.

While Seth didn't detail an explicit moral theory, an implicit foundation was outlined in the Seth Material. As such, Seth offered a "moral imperative" and even used biblical language to express it: *"Thou Shalt Not Violate."*[117] While this principle guides your innate moral intuition, collectively it also forms the basis *for how we all get along,* which we'll explore in the rest of Part 3.

While Seth didn't go into detail about specific moral issues like cloning animals, stem cell research, or euthanasia, he did discuss several mass events and violations against humans and nature, which we'll investigate in the coming chapters. He also didn't specify if some violations are worse than others, and thus leaves the door open to use your own moral intuition to discern the differences. As such, Seth leaves moral interpretations *up to you.*

In this way, he *challenges you* to develop your abilities to intuit and discern violation and take appropriate actions to the fullest extent possible in this and every lifetime. As we saw, it's one of the requirements agreed to when engaging a cycle of lifetimes (see Chapter 5). Though it takes time, effort, and commitment, to do anything less is not facing up to your own abilities, or your responsibilities to your self, your world, and how we all get along.

KEY IDEAS: Divine love (natural laws) forms the basis for your innate sense of natural compassion, natural guilt, and natural grace. Together, these form the moral and ethical basis of how you create your own reality in relation to self and others (how we all get along).

Chapter 12: Why Do Bad Things "Happen to" Good People?

What Do You Mean I Create My Own Good and Bad (Evil)?

You create your own reality through your beliefs, thoughts, emotions, and moral intuition: that's the central message of the Seth Material. While most of Seth's books focused on *individual* reality creation, you also create your own reality in relation to *6.5 billion others*. As such, there is no reality creation without simultaneous co-creation, and therefore, you find examples of good and bad things that "happen to" people every day.

But wait a minute! Did you catch the invisible belief expressed in the previous sentence?

The fact that you create your own reality means that *nothing ever "happens to"* you. You create *everything* in your life: health, abundance, fulfillment, *or their lack*. So why do people, regardless of whether you consider them good or bad, create good *and* bad things in their lives? Seth said that we each choose a religious, social, and political belief framework in which to explore our own personal challenges in relation to the collective. So there is a tremendous ebb and flow between personal and mass belief systems.

As we saw, there are three main cultural worldviews whose mass belief systems currently dominate global reality creation (traditional, modern, and postmodern). They each have their own types of creation myths (see Chapter 6) and moral codes (see Chapter 11). In similar fashion, each worldview creates mass belief frameworks of good and bad to test out various kinds of experience.

Traditional worldviews believe in the literal existence of God and angels (good spirits) and demons (evil spirits) that are a source of human joy and suffering. These supernatural beings cause things to happen like healthy babies, abundant crops, new jobs, or injuries, accidents, and natural disasters. They possess superpowers that *cause things to happen to you*, and as such, most events are beyond your control. In that light, *they create your reality for you*. You can petition them with prayer, sacrifices, and other offerings, but if you don't have adequate faith or behave according to their laws, you will be punished by poverty, disease, or death in this life *and* the eternal afterlife. Traditional mass beliefs of good and evil have existed for thousands of years, and remain *quite real* today.

Modern worldviews don't believe in God or the soul because they can't prove their existence through the use of five senses and reason. Therefore, good and evil get expressed in belief systems of health (normal function) and pathology (dysfunction). Pathology is seen as the result of physical causes like viruses, parasites, defective genes and DNA, or psychological causes like neurosis, psychosis, and other mental illnesses. Health is simply their absence, and the result of superior survival skills and adaptive intelligence based upon Darwin's evolution (natural selection and genetic mutation). Therefore, illness is still inflicted by outside forces, though they are no longer personified as demons.

Moreover, altered states and dreaming are considered useless by-products of evolution, Freud's unsavory subconscious, or pathology. Traditional beliefs in good and evil are seen as superstitious nonsense based on primitive thinking. Since there's no afterlife, you may as well seek all the wealth, pleasure, and benefits of youth while they last. Since there's no God looking over your shoulder to judge you, you might even lie, steal, or break the law, as long as you don't get caught.

Postmodern worldviews are still emerging. They perceive traditional and modern belief systems in good and bad (evil) as relative and thus subject to change as consciousness develops. However, "bad things" are still very real, and need to be dealt with. Therefore, *working with beliefs becomes paramount to help transform consciousness into a wider perspective.* The beliefs that All That Is bestows an "original blessing" upon all existence, you create your own reality, and have an innate intent and purpose, are great places to start.

Further, the challenge is *not* to repress your beliefs in bad (evil) things, and pretend they don't exist. It's also important to allow and express resulting emotions. Repression and denial are two of the most powerful psychological actions that lead to artificial guilt, pain, and suffering because they inhibit naturally aggressive impulses that allow you to blow off steam before it builds up into more serious symptoms like violence and dis-ease (see Chapter 3).

As you learn to notice and identify the beliefs you hold in good *and* bad, and recognize how they help to form your reality, you will begin to understand that, in larger terms, bad things really don't ever "happen to" people. If people concentrate on good, they will find plenty of evidence for its existence (the half-filled cup). But when they focus solely on bad (evil), they will find plenty of evidence for its existence (the half-empty cup).

Therefore, Seth suggests that you concentrate upon the innate goodness that exists within *every* Aspect of All That Is, though never at the expense of denying that bad or evil things happen. As we will see, there are larger reasons for why they occur as expressions of individual *and* collective value fulfillment.

KEY IDEAS: "You create your own reality" means that nothing ever "happens to" you. You create <u>everything</u> through your beliefs. Beliefs in good and bad (evil) abound in a multitude of belief frameworks to test out various kinds of experience.

Exercise 11—Identify Beliefs in Good and Bad (Evil)

The belief system of duality deals with morals and ethics. All your beliefs in better/worse, good/bad, right/wrong, and so on, orbit around this "belief planet" within your "solar system" of core beliefs. There are two basic techniques that can help you begin to identify those beliefs and how they affect your life.

1. Have a series of talks with yourself (use your intellect).

2. Work backward from your emotions to your beliefs (use your feelings).

In either case, one method will lead to the other, as beliefs and emotions go hand in hand. Both require an honest self-appraisal and direct encounter with emotional, mental, and psychic aspects of your reality.

To begin, make a list of your beliefs in good and bad, or right and wrong. Spend about fifteen minutes and *simply list them in your journal*. As you go, you may discover that you hold different beliefs in different circumstances. Some will even be contradictory (conflicting beliefs). Simply notice that as you go.

Next, examine any conflicting beliefs. Invisible beliefs will appear that connect those seemingly opposite expressions. Again, they are beliefs you hold in your conscious mind but intentionally ignore and repress, because they reflect challenge areas that you have not yet been ready to face.

For example, you may be the world's greatest manager in the eyes of others, and yet feel that you are really a bad one. Or you may tell yourself that age is meaningless and think young thoughts, and yet you really are afraid to admit that you're getting older and your body and mind are changing.

Next, simply *notice* the next time they arise in your daily experience. Notice how they are ingrained in your language. For instance, have you ever said, "Money is the root of all evil?" Write that down in your journal as well. Don't overlook anything. Don't assume anything you say or believe is too small to notice. You will be amazed at the belief trails you will identify as you repeat this practice.

One caution: it may seem initially that you have so many different beliefs at different times that it's impossible to correlate them all. Give it time. If you make this a regular practice, in time you will begin to see clear patterns in which your beliefs in good and bad orbit around an even deeper core belief "planet"—the belief system of duality. It's innate, and we all have our own versions of it.

Therefore, the goal is not to repress or marginalize your dualities, but to *own them as fully as you can*. Again, you can't eliminate beliefs—that's not the point! You simply neutralize their power by addressing them—making them objective in your conscious mind—and learning to recognize them the next time they arise in your awareness. Once recognized, then you can change them, and your life in the process.

Extra Credit: Explore your beliefs in good and bad (evil) in relation to:

Sex (Pleasure/Pain)

Money (Wealth /Poverty)

Politics, Religion, Gender, Ethnicity (Us/Them)

Relationships (Love/Hate)[118]

What about Incurable Diseases, Birth Defects, and Other Handicaps?

If we create our own realities, why would anyone choose to be born with, or develop, a severe handicap? The reasons are as varied as each individual. Again, each life is planned "ahead of time" and thus chosen to develop overall abilities throughout a cycle of manifestation. From your entity's perspective, all your lifetimes exist simultaneously within Framework 2, and as such, there is no predestined cause and effect like karma that inflicts handicaps or disease as punishment for past deeds (see Chapter 5). Therefore, a lifetime that involves disability is chosen because it provides a challenging framework for reality creation that benefits you, your entity, and other individuals.

Seth chided those who hold onto the infantile notion that there is a state of bliss in which all questions are answered and challenges solved, as if someone outside of you will do this *for you*. This also reflects beliefs in God as an omnipotent Mommy or Daddy. As you learn to take responsibility for everything in your life, and understand the difference between what you can and can't control, you will connect with the true power of your being and your divine heritage. As such, you realize that any challenge you face is an opportunity for growth and fulfillment.

Challenges are *never* inflicted by God or randomly "happen to" anyone. However, what provides a challenge for one person may seem unnecessary or even ridiculous and never be chosen by another. In this way, *we would need to examine each situation on a case by case basis to understand why they are chosen.* But in every case, as you learn to tap into the power of the moment point, you learn that all your limitations are self-imposed.

Again, Seth points out that in practical Framework 1 terms, the *present is always the point of power* in which to act based upon your beliefs (see Chapter 2). As such, you are never at the mercy of other lifetimes, even though they simultaneously work out their own challenges in Framework 2. Nor are you at the mercy of past or future events.

A person with several lifetimes that emphasize intellectual development may purposefully choose a lifetime in which their cognitive abilities are downplayed in order to allow the emotions freer rein. In the context of simultaneous time, this simply means that you have set up certain limits in this lifetime that balance out challenges in other lifetimes not currently available to your conscious mind. In each case, there is purpose, meaning, and value fulfillment. Nothing is thrust upon you, nor predetermined, because your free will *always exists within these constraints.* As such, there are infinite probable paths of exploration within any life choice.

Some people prefer lifetimes in which accomplishment follows a steady, even course. Some prefer great contrasts. One life may include severe poverty, another luxurious splendor, or a series of lives with great athletic achievement may include a life as a quadriplegic.

In cases of severe mental handicaps, it's the family who often seeks to understand the choice. Again, not only do parents select their children "ahead of time," but their children select them. As such, there are no accidents of birth. In every case, there is group fulfillment being worked out for one and all. Some of the most rewarding lifetimes involve these kinds of challenges.

A disability thus provides a framework in which to limit certain abilities while simultaneously emphasizing others. The physicist Stephen Hawking (b. 1942) is an example of how a disease in adulthood can provide a context for great discovery and accomplishment. He was seemingly "struck down" in college by ALS (Lou Gehrig's disease) that reduced his muscle control and bound him to a wheel-chair. It was only *afterward* that he made incredible scientific breakthroughs, which may not have been possible without the constraint of his disability.

Seth compassionately pointed out that all situations are intentional, a choice made by your entity, which *is you*, to experience a framework that enhances certain abilities, and limits others. The idea, then, is not to focus upon the half-empty cup, but to develop whatever abilities come naturally, for your entity will always direct its vast energies to fulfill those probabilities.

Finally, this doesn't mean that you need to choose a disability to be great at something! It is just a way to understand why some may create their realities this way. As we have seen, each case is based on individual desire and intent, which means in the larger picture, our challenges and how we deal with them add greatly to the fulfillment of the collective. There are no accidents in this regard.[119]

KEY IDEAS: Disabilities are chosen because they provide great creative challenges for reality creation. Each choice is individual, balanced over an array of simultaneous lifetimes, and supported by the vast energy of your entity.

What about Natural Disasters?

Why would anyone choose to experience the horrors of a flood, fire, earthquake, tornado, or tsunami? According to Seth, every person has some reason to participate in a natural disaster. Again, the reasons are varied and highly individualized. For example, sometimes there are precognitive dreams or an inner knowing to help someone to avoid a disaster. Unconscious knowledge may be either accessed or blocked depending on your beliefs. Still, no death is accidental, and at some level everyone who dies makes the choice to do so.

The earth has its own "body" made of atoms and molecules. It experiences day, night, lunar, and solar cycles throughout varying climates. The wind and ocean currents that create its weather patterns function as a kind of circulatory system. Human consciousness evolved to uniquely fit within this biosphere and is perfectly suited to exist in those conditions. In this way, the rhythms of your body and mind mirror those of the earth, and there is a great give and take between them.

Your beliefs generate, focus, and direct your thoughts and emotions. They are expressed in your body in terms of neurochemical reactions that impact your perception of physical reality. Your thoughts and emotions have electromagnetic properties that must rid themselves of excess chemicals in similar fashion to the way land clears itself of excess water after a rain storm.

Seth said that there are nonphysical "chemicals"—functions of EEs not yet understood—that morph into electromagnetic structures that release energy from your body into the atmosphere. Just as your cells influence your body consciousness, so too does your body affect the body of the earth. Just as your body exists in a dynamic flux of chemical interactions, so too does the earth's atmosphere exist in a flux of psychic, electromagnetic, and chemical currents.

These forces work together to generate natural disasters. However, there are always hidden reasons involved, for people will respond in a variety of ways that they otherwise would not. A natural disaster provides a highly concentrated challenge in which to grow and use certain abilities that may be lying latent or unused.

Thus, in the long run there are *always* benefits that result from natural disasters. This is another example of our ever-present half-filled cup. Seth used the example of the Chemung River flood that devastated Jane and Rob's home town of Elmira, NY, in June 1972. The region had been economically depressed, and local businesses and industry were moving elsewhere. Unemployment was on the rise, and many people felt depressed and mired in hopelessness. People were moving from the city to the suburbs. The ruling elite and well-heeled that populated the city council didn't have the best interests of impoverished citizens in mind. The whole region was out of balance in a variety of ways.

The region was ripe for riots to break out, as they also release tremendous amounts of pent up hopelessness, powerlessness, and despair. But due to their unique feeling-tones, the tensions of the people of Elmira were expressed and transformed into the atmosphere to co-create a catastrophic flood. Their unconscious needs and pent up desires fueled the storm system through hormonal and chemical reactions naturally released into the atmosphere.

The crisis forced all involved to examine previously hidden personal values and priorities. For instance, those used to luxury had to do without, and came to realize the importance of family, friends, and community. Those used to poverty were surprised to learn that they had leadership abilities never realized before. The business district qualified for government funding that had long passed it by. Daily routines were radically changed, and forced people to see things in new ways.[120]

In this light, similar factors are in play in *every* natural disaster, whether humans are directly involved or not. All species have similar relations to the earth, and strive to create their best fulfillment. While floods, fires, tornadoes, earthquakes, and tsunamis often leave great destruction and death in their wakes, no death is ever an accident or in any way meaningless. Whether chosen consciously or subconsciously, each person and creature innately knows its death occurs within a larger framework in which nothing is ever really destroyed.

Moreover, the close of any chapter *always* leads to the beginning of a new one within Consciousness, for the loving presence of All That Is constantly supports its creations. As such, the explosive release of energy in any catastrophic event is *always* nurtured by divine love (natural laws). Though it's difficult to lose a loved one in any circumstance, there is always a larger constructive purpose involved. Seth is always sympathetic to our present belief systems in good and bad events. But death and destruction are two of the greatest teachers we have in life. They force us to ask many questions that we might not otherwise have the courage to ask, and make changes in our lives that we otherwise might not have the courage to make.

KEY IDEAS: You co-create the weather and other natural events through your beliefs, thoughts, and emotions' effect on the

Earth's environment. Every natural disaster has a silver lining (half-filled cup) that promotes deeper growth, balance, and understanding within All That Is.

What about Suicide?

Your body is innately designed to remain healthy throughout your lifetime. In all cases, your beliefs play a central role. Western culture places a premium on the vitality of youth, material wealth, and good looks, and chronically reinforces the fear of their loss through old age.

Thus, when old age is equated with deterioration, disease, and death, it becomes a self-fulfilling prophecy. These are the *belief systems* that create conflict in young adults taught to fear their first facial wrinkle or grey hair. However, there are no diseases that are the direct result of old age. In fact, there are always opportunities to create disease at any stage of life, but old age by itself is *completely neutral in this regard.*

Given this belief framework, many suicides are based on the belief that life has hit a dead end, and there's no future as adults, or in an afterlife. There may be an underlying belief that life is ultimately meaningless. Some individuals may be highly gifted and yet feel they are lost in a pointless world in which their talents will never develop. Some become depressed and begin to concentrate *exclusively* on the half-empty cup (see Chapter 2). They see the planet as overpopulated, and chronically project probable futures with dire man-made or natural catastrophes. Who would want to raise children in that kind of world?

Such beliefs inevitably lead people to a state of depression. The half-empty cup blinds them to the innate heroic qualities in themselves and people all around them, to their love for their fellow creatures, their wonder, compassion, and the redeeming qualities throughout the natural world. Yet, the creative, life-affirming aspects of life *are ever-present*, and focusing on them—the half-filled cup—can revitalize, refresh, and release the grip of depression.

We are each imbued with a natural spontaneity and vitality that, when fully engaged, leads to a deep trust in the energy, power, and strength of our being. Learning to trust and allow—to "let go" and abandon yourself in the energy of your being—will *always* lead to a deep acceptance and affirmation of life.

Personal and global problems always represent great challenges. Individuals are *always* needed to work towards solving them, which requires action, and the tiniest bit of appreciation for life to invoke the desire to do so. As such, the more fully you embrace the vagaries of life and death, and all things beyond your egoic control, the more easily the secrets of reality creation will become known to you. The simplest action like a leaf blowing in the breeze, smell of a rose, or the sun on your face can trigger a sublime understanding and deep appreciation of life *on its own terms*, which in turn reinvigorates the life force *within you.*

There are as many reasons for the choice of suicide as there are individuals. But no matter how depressed someone gets, there is always an innate part that seeks life and vitality. The important thing to realize, in all cases, is that *you always have a choice.*

What will an individuals' life be like if they do commit suicide? As we have seen, your immediate after-death experience will be based upon the expectations set up by your beliefs (see Chapter 5). If deep down inside you believe that you will be punished for your sins, or believe that suicide is a mortal sin as taught in many religions, your immediate experience *will* occur in your own privately created version of hell. But again, this is not permanent, as there are always guides to help you understand your predicament so that you may transition into a less stressful and more joyous state.

In this light, there is no set punishment to be doled out in cases of suicide. They are always treated with care and respect. However, any challenges not dealt with in the life just ended will be dealt with in another. This is not limited to suicides. Seth also pointed out the irony of those who severely limit their experience during life as a form of "living suicide."[121]

As always, you create your own reality through your beliefs, thoughts, emotions, and moral intuition. There are *no* exceptions! You have the free will to make choices within the root assumptions that govern Framework 1, the life choices you made before you were born, and most importantly, throughout your physical life. If you are dealing with any kind of illness or depressing circumstances, keep in mind that you always have the power to change things in an instant through affirming the vitality, joy, and creativity that are your natural heritage. The Exercises in this book are designed to help you do this.

KEY IDEAS: We are all imbued with a natural vitality and joy that reinforces a deep acceptance and affirmation of life. Though suicide can become a choice when we lose touch with that, it is never punished in any absolute sense, but serves instead as the basis for continued growth and understanding in the after-death environment and beyond.

Exercise 12—Create Your Own Healing Mindscape

Seth cautions that his exercises are never intended to replace the advice and care of conventional doctors, especially since those beliefs may still exert a *strong* subconscious influence. Again, these simple exercises are introductory and allow you to test the waters through your own experience.

As we have seen, you can focus on the half-empty *or* the half-full cup. There are times in life when things get the best of us, and we create depression or physical illness as symptoms designed to get our attention and help us make important, life-affirming changes.

This exercise is designed to facilitate that process. It helps to release tension and anxiety, and promotes the acceleration of the healing process. (Again, you can record the following and listen to it on headphones.)

First, relax yourself as deeply as possible. Take 2-3 slow, deep breaths, and just let your concerns go for now, as you can always return to them later. The idea is to access the surface of Alpha 1, but remain awake and aware of your body.

Now say, "I completely trust, accept, and love myself." And just feel into that statement for a few seconds.

Then say, "Whenever I explore my abilities, I express the deepest, loving energy of my being." (You can adjust the language to whatever works for you, as it's the intent behind the statements that are important to set the stage for what follows.)

Next, if you are dealing with a specific dis-ease, use your imagination to shrink down and project your awareness into the affected area of your body. If it's depression, project into the feeling or emotion within your heart or mind, whichever one feels appropriate.

Then, allow any images to arise for 2-3 minutes within this mindscape *without judging or interacting*; simply observe. Notice what kind of environment arises. It could be a field, lake, room, road, etc. This imagery will represent your condition.

During this time, also notice as many details as possible. Be on the lookout for kinds of inner imagery that represent old growth that needs clearing, obstacles removed, or doors to be opened. You may also perceive invading armies, swarms of buzzing bees, or storm clouds that represent energetic blocks that need to be addressed.

Next, begin to mentally clear, open, or remove whatever "inner debris" arises. Simply use your imagination to restore your mindscape to its normal, healthy condition. Take your time. Be mindful and creative. In this way, you begin to engage the deep power of your entity, and reopen doors of communication to ignite channels of healing energy and loving vitality

Finally, open your eyes, stretch your arms and legs, and take a couple of deep breaths to return to full waking awareness.[122]

Do You Create Your Own Death?

If you create your own reality, then you create your own death. It's simply your choice how deeply involved you wish to be. *But that's a double-edged statement*!

Each person creates their own death in unique fashion according to their desire, intent, and beliefs. It's a natural and valuable experience. For example, when Seth reviewed each of his deaths, they each seemed a perfectly natural outcome, an inevitable result of each life's choices. He experienced a deep sense of awe and humility as he became aware of his entity—his inner self. He also noted that while he could relive portions of any life, all his personalities continued in an independent fashion.[123]

Jane Roberts also channeled *The Afterdeath Journal of an American Philosopher: The World View of William James*

(1978). James (1842-1910), founder of American psychology, detailed his life, death, and afterdeath experiences. It's a highly recommended book for anyone interested in a first-hand account of a skeptical scientist who realized only after the fact that death is not an end, but a new beginning. In James' case, his death became the crowning achievement of his life when he shockingly discovered the afterlife was real.[124]

One of our biggest challenges is the *fear of death*, which is the outer ego's fear of annihilation. Often people hold the contradictory beliefs that death is real but "it won't 'happen to' me." And yet, death is a practical part of life, for if no one died, the world would quickly over-populate to the point where all natural resources would disappear. It is a biological necessity that ensures the continued vitality and life of all species. In this sense, death is a natural expression of divine love, because natural laws *include* death so that others may take their turn living, while we move on to experience other lives and potentials.

As such, we all have an innate desire for death, not necessarily a "death wish," but a natural, inbuilt knowledge that while the entity is immortal, the flesh is not, and thus there is a time to move onto the next chapter of existence. According to Seth, at some point it is quite natural and healthy to desire an exit from physical life, especially if you have direct knowledge that life continues. This involves a reduction of bodily functions, and gradual or even sudden disidentification with the body and its senses. While your body dies in Framework 1, your dreamtime body lives on in Framework 2—nothing is ever lost (see Chapter 5).

Understanding this can help you cope with your own death, and others', in healthy ways. The sad fact is that too many individuals believe there is no afterlife, or equate death with punishment, even when directly faced with it. They deny, repress, and block out any thoughts of their eventual deaths, and don't even discuss it with family members, leaving one and all unprepared for the inevitable, which "happens to" them as a needless shock. They may live out their days desperately clinging to the hope that scientists will find a "cure" for death.

Like everything, however, this a choice of experience based upon beliefs. Eventually the truth of continued existence is always discovered, for no one remains ignorant of their immortality forever. Those who are have yet to recognize their true multidimensional identity.

Jane Roberts also wrote a beautifully illustrated children's book that explains the biological necessity of death and the natural role it plays in maintaining equilibrium in the earth's biosphere. It's called *Emir's Education in the Proper Use of Magical Powers* (1979). It instills healthy beliefs about life *and* death in a playful and highly educational way that children easily understand. It also includes an introduction to the dream body that is used after death.

Can you imagine how your life and beliefs would be different if your parents had raised you with this kind of book, one that instilled realistic and healthy beliefs about life and death? Life is meant to be lived with all the vitality and gusto at your command, no matter what age you are, and in full acceptance of life *on its own terms*, including the fact that we all die. In this light, not only is death a natural part of life, but it's also a *healthy* part of life.

Again, there is no inherent dis-ease or dysfunction hard-wired into the aging process. It is possible to live much longer, and at a much higher standard of fulfillment. The more closely you're in touch with your beliefs, the more willfully you can *direct your energies* to heal any life-threatening illness. In this way, you can create a more fulfilling life, one that will naturally and perfectly end with a fulfilling and less traumatic death.

As we saw, the historical Christ was a great psychic who held the ability to simply will himself out of his body when the time was right (see Chapter 8). However, this was the willful act of a highly evolved being, and most of us don't believe we have that ability. But what if you believed you could do that, or something close to it?

The belief that you create your own reality goes a long way to *reorient* your beliefs about life and death. Doing the exercises that Seth outlined can provide the kinds of direct knowing through regular *and* altered states that will neutralize any beliefs about "death as annihilation." They simply become as moot as the belief that the earth is flat.

The exercises are *designed* to prepare you for the after-death environment (see Chapter 5). There may be nothing more profound and exhilarating than to willfully exit your body during a projection of consciousness, explore inner realms, meet deceased relatives, and subsequently reenter your physical body! That experience dispels *any* doubt that your consciousness exists "beyond" your body and survives physical death.

People who engage near-death experiences also create a profound knowing that they exist beyond their physical body. However, there is often severe physical or emotional trauma involved in experiences like a car accident, surgery, or heart attack. But there's no need to engage trauma to project out of body. You can learn to trigger this during sleep or meditative states.

Again, you don't need to take Seth's or anyone else's word on faith alone. With direct experience this knowledge becomes self-evident. As always, you are your own best authority.

KEY IDEAS: "You create your own reality" means that you will create your own death. The fear of "death as annihilation" can be neutralized by learning to engage psy-time, inner senses, and dream work.

Chapter 13: The Practicing Idealist

What about Conflict, War, and Dis-ease?

In Part 1, we explored the metaphysics, physics, biology, and psychology of reality creation (Discover Your True Self). In Part 2, we explored the cosmology, anthropology, and sociology of reality creation (Discover Your Place in the World). In Part 3, we've been exploring the morals and ethics of reality creation (Discover How We Can Live in Harmony). These are the key "domains" of self that work together in *cooperative* fashion to help you create your own reality—*all* of it—in relation to 6.5 billion other humans. In this context, there is no reality creation without simultaneous co-creation.

So what happens when *any* of the elements within these domains don't get along? The result is always some type of conflict. Yet conflict—in itself—is an inherently *neutral* aspect of cooperation, value fulfillment, and the natural laws that guide all reality creation. That is, conflict is not inherently good or bad; it is your belief systems that interpret your experiences as such. Therefore, you can utilize conflict as a constructive *or* destructive tool, one that heals and promotes growth *or* destroys and limits growth.

For example, at the biological level, a cold or intestinal virus may correct imbalances in your respiratory or digestive system and leave them healthier as a result. While most would agree that the resulting pain and discomfort are bad, most would also agree that the return to improved health is a good outcome. Additionally, viruses can be used as a means to create your own death. On average, over 36,000 people die in the United States from the flu each year.[125] But as we just saw, death is not a bad thing when it is self-evident that you are more than just your physical body. Death is a wonderful transition to a new life—a good thing.

Further, at the psychological level, conflicting beliefs, thoughts, and emotions may precipitate the emergence of a new stage of development *or* create mental dis-ease and dysfunctional behaviors. For instance, adolescence is one of the most challenging and transformative stages of human development. New hormones get released, the body grows adult features, and a new array of adult experience begins. However, that process can be confusing, difficult, and leave emotional scars that lead to psychotic breaks or addictive behaviors—bad things. Or, an individual can address their issues and heal themselves to thus create the means to help others based on lessons learned—a good thing.

This scales up into collective co-creation as well. At the sociological level, conflict may be used to create a new social order *or* degenerate into a hellish war. A public dispute may lead people to blow off steam, air their grievances, and eventually reach a mutually beneficial solution, like when South Africa outlawed the racist injustices of Apartheid without civil war in 1994. Or it can lead to the horrors of Auschwitz, Stalingrad, and Hiroshima in the 1940s.

In this light, we have nested "social orders" within our own cells, belief systems, *and societies* that work together to promote mass reality creation. Therefore, when we limit or deny the cooperative aspects of value fulfillment, we can be "at war" within *any one of those domains*. The result can be destructive forms of physical, mental, or social dis-ease.

A major contributor to these kinds of "war" is the belief system of social Darwinism—beliefs that we live in an unsafe universe and that humans are innately murderous, selfish, and must compete for survival and limited resources. Life overall is characterized as "poor, nasty, brutish, and short."[126] When there is little reason to live, no species or civilization will flourish. When the quality and meaning of life become overshadowed by the chronic "struggle for survival," considerations for what makes life worth living become secondary, which in turn limits choices for growth and fulfillment. For the collective always reflects the private belief systems of each individual.

Unfortunately, Darwin's original research was biased by his over-emphasis on the *competition* between and within species. This blinded him to the innate cooperation between all species of life in the biosphere. Darwin also projected the darkest of human traits upon the many species he studied. Thus, he over-emphasized violence and murder, and completely missed the inner laws which allow every species to exist in the first place.

Some variation of Darwinian concepts has fueled scientific belief systems since the late 19th century. As we have seen, modern scientific beliefs are based upon a limited view, one that conflates Framework 1 as "all that is"—an expanding universe based upon cause and effect, with no larger purpose than to ultimately destroy itself through the loss of all energy (entropy).

Darwinian beliefs also permeated the World Wars in the 20th century and were used to justify the violent deaths of millions. They became so deeply ingrained in the modern worldview that we now have a "war on . . ." drugs, poverty, terror, cancer, and so on. Ironically, the United States, which was founded on the noble, egalitarian ideals of life, liberty, and the pursuit of happiness, has been at war with other nations for the majority of its short existence.

Seth considers war a social dis-ease—a form of mass suicide carried out with the full resources of each nation. Wars can only be perpetrated by people who believe the universe is not safe, and therefore, live in a state of constant threat. Others—always vilified—are out to usurp your treasured "way of life," and must be stopped at all costs. This, in turn, justifies the insanity of murder, rape, and collateral damage—the endgame of modern warfare.

Darwinian beliefs fuel the continual surveillance and expectation of each new "inevitable" threat, which perpetuates the misinterpretation of sense data and daily events. The result forces *everything* to conform to preconceived notions of competition and survival. Anything that doesn't fit is simply ignored and literally ceases to exist.

But in all cases, you create what you concentrate on through your belief systems. The limitations you place upon yourself are the result of the limiting beliefs you refuse to let go. When you obsess about potential threats, the continual mental reinforcement actually *creates* them in your reality through natural hypnosis (see Chapter 2). As such, the hatred of war will never create a lasting peace, only the "love of peace" can do so.[127]

Therefore, when you concentrate upon a "war on terror" or "war on cancer," you actually *reinforce* their continued psychological power and manifestation. However, you can just as easily use natural hypnosis to concentrate on a *love of peace* or *health* and you will manifest those conditions as well.

War and dis-ease have been with us for thousands of years, and are very important issues to address. Seth provides a unique perspective to help us understand why we individually and collectively create them. Only when we learn to take full responsibility for *everything* we create will we find new ways to reduce their impact.

KEY IDEAS: There are nested "social orders" within our own bodies (biology), minds (psychology), and culture (sociology). When we limit or deny the cooperative aspects of value fulfillment, we can be "at war" within any one of these domains.

Do You Live in a Safe Universe?

The traditional worldview promotes religious beliefs like "original sin" or "karma as punishment" that demean your physical nature and reinforce limiting beliefs that you are *flawed from birth*. The modern worldview promotes scientific beliefs in the "survival of the fittest" and "life as a cosmic accident" that demean your innate intent and claim that your life has no meaning or purpose.

While both worldviews reinforce beliefs that the universe is an unsupportive and unsafe place, the emerging postmodern worldview seeks to shed these limiting beliefs because they no longer serve our collective needs. This is why Seth reinforces the belief that we live in a safe universe, innately designed to nurture individual and collective fulfillment.

When you believe in an unsafe universe, you fall prey to belief systems that overemphasize competition between biological, psychological, and sociological aspects of your life. Nature seems "out to get you" through natural disasters, wars, and dis-ease. The constant threat of viral pandemics, cancers, and competing social systems hangs over you like a dark cloud. Therefore, it's only logical to rely on inoculations, chemotherapies, and strong homeland security. The amount of time, effort, and financial resources dedicated to these types of "protection" is enormous.

On the other hand, what if we were to concentrate on the many examples of innate cooperation that exists between *all* the cells, minds, and social groups that make life possible in the first place? Without it, life as we know it couldn't exist. For example, viruses play an important biological role. They are highly intelligent and have a social, cooperative function that helps us maintain healthy bodies. As such, they are *not* inherently destructive.

According to Seth, viruses must be activated into their lethal forms, and this occurs only when individuals or social groups reach a crisis point in their quality of life. Degrading social conditions are always involved, for example, when the bubonic plague wiped out an estimated one third of the population of 14th century Europe. Overall life conditions were very difficult for the average person, and the gap between rich and poor was high. This changed the course of Western history, because the Catholic Church lost credibility as sole purveyors of "God's will" when the dis-ease struck pious and impious, rich and poor alike.

New causes, reasons, and answers were sought out to explain why so many could die, for what kind of God would allow so much suffering? As a result, the modern scientific worldview emerged to provide new answers and technologies to deal with such viral contagions. Life conditions gradually improved for the average person. In this way, the virus functioned as a means for important social change to occur, and thus the "silver lining" (half-filled cup) within this tragic mass event.

Once you understand this, you can reorient your entire approach to individual and collective health and well being. Since this works on our bodies, minds, and social groups, it's important to understand the impact that beliefs, thoughts, and emotions have at all levels. That is, when you *fully believe* that you live in a safe universe made possible by cooperation at all levels of existence, you will more clearly see how beliefs in an unsafe universe *serve as self-fulfilling prophecy.* When you focus on the half-empty cup, you shut out those probable potentials for greater happiness in the half-filled cup. As Seth said, "you get what you concentrate on!"

The process of reorientation is valuable, but takes time and practice. Seth repeatedly stated that you have to make a conceptual leap and be unequivocal, for it's impossible to live in a safe and unsafe universe *at the same time.* Beliefs that make sense in an unsafe universe have no place in this new orientation, for they become meaningless.[128]

In this light, health is the ideal situation in which *all* aspects of self cooperate on biological, psychological, and social levels. Dis-ease occurs when various portions of self get out of balance. In all cases, your beliefs, thoughts, and emotions play a crucial role. It is possible to *return to health* at any time once limiting, invisible, and conflicting beliefs are identified and addressed. Therefore, the belief that the "universe is safe" will not make any sense when there appears to be so much evidence to the contrary. Instead, affirm to yourself that you "live in a safe universe" and what formerly appeared as threats will simply melt away.

This is a complex and nuanced topic, and Seth always recommends that if you are suffering from any kind of illness to continue to work within your regular health care system. While it is entirely possible to cure almost any dis-ease (except those purposefully chosen before birth to explore as incurable, see Chapter 12), Seth cautions that the power of ingrained cultural attitudes and beliefs in the unsafe universe, survival of the fittest, and flawed selves *run very deep.* As such, it's easy to kid yourself into believing that you've identified and addressed *all* core beliefs that relate to any particular situation, when in fact certain invisible belief complexes remain that continue to influence your situation.

As we will see in Chapter 14, much of the later Seth Material was intended for Jane Roberts and Rob Butts's personal use to help them deal with Jane's worsening health and restricted mobility from the complications of rheumatoid arthritis. Thus, even Jane and Rob weren't able to put all of Seth's ideas into practice all the time. However, this in no way diminishes the life-affirming and healing potentials of Seth's ideas. It simply reinforces how deeply ingrained and affecting beliefs systems are, and how important it is to learn how to work with them.

KEY IDEAS: Deeply ingrained beliefs that the universe is unsafe are found in various guises in traditional and modern worldviews. To counter that, Seth promotes the idea that we live in a safe universe, one that is innately designed to nurture individual and collective fulfillment.

Exercise 13—Natural Hypnosis: Accepting Desired New Beliefs

As we saw, natural hypnosis is simply the unconscious acceptance of conscious beliefs. You give yourself hypnotic suggestions all the time as you concentrate on aspects of your core belief systems. When you hold your own *undivided* attention, you function as hypnotist *and* subject. You can use this natural function of your conscious mind to reinforce newly desired beliefs, such as "I live in a safe universe."

Again, Seth chides that some people have lazy mental habits, because they have not yet learned to consciously examine their own beliefs, thoughts and emotions, which requires a process of introspection. Ironically, many who "deny" negative suggestions, and assert positive affirmations instead, are actually convinced that those negative beliefs have *more* power than beneficial ones. As such, they continue to manifest them.

Similarly, your habitual thought patterns, backed up by conditioned behaviors, continually reinforce *negative* beliefs because you concentrate on them to the exclusion of anything that contradicts them. Therefore, this practice is designed to help you concentrate exclusively on changing limiting beliefs.

Now, engage psy-time. For five to ten minutes only, concentrate all your attention on the following statement: "I live in a safe universe." You can speak it out loud, or say it mentally.

Repeat it over and over, like a mantra meditation, and focus on it *exclusively*. If your mind wanders, simply take a deep breath or two, settle down, and return your concentration to the affirmation. You can substitute another phrase or try a different wording until you settle on something that *feels* right to you.

When you finish, don't check to see if it's working yet, simply forget about it and go about your day.

Again, there's no need to spend any more than five to ten minutes as longer periods will simply reinforce your limiting beliefs. Seth suggests that within three days you will begin to see results, but you can continue to practice it for greater results. You will find that your subconscious begins to generate new impulses in line with your new beliefs.

The challenge is to *notice* those new impulses and to *take action*. Don't ignore them!

(Finally, Seth cautions to *not* do this practice along with Exercise 4—The Point of Power, see Chapter 2. They may be done on separate occasions during any twenty-four hour cycle. However, realize that you always use the "present as your point of power" to neutralize old beliefs and activate new beliefs.)[129]

What is a Practicing Idealist?

As we begin to reorient our beliefs, thoughts, and emotions to live in a safe universe, we must learn to cope with various types of conflict in new ways. It's naïve to think that we can change our beliefs and wars, violence, and dis-ease will *collectively* disappear overnight. As we have seen, reality co-creation doesn't work that way. While you may be able to do that on an individual basis, the collective has chosen a particular set of challenges and unique type of consciousness in which to explore various types of conflict.

So the question becomes, "What's the best way to deal with conflict, even though I live in a safe universe?" As always, Seth concentrates on the individual to provide an effective way to address this challenge: become a *practicing idealist*. That is, if you want to reduce conflict and make the world a better place, then *strive to realize your own ideals in the world.*

Ideals are very important, for while we know they may never be fully achieved, they stimulate our deepest potentials and growth. Ideals fuel a kind of *hero's journey* to "boldly go where no one has gone before," and discover new things about our selves, our world, and how we all get along. But we need to anchor our ideals for a better future on *what is* in relation to *what could be.* Our ideals thus need to be practical, no matter how lofty or far-fetched they may seem initially, for in time they can literally change the world.

For instance, in 1776, the founders of the United States sought to create a radically new form of democratic rule based on ideals of social equality that outlawed monarchy and eventually slavery. By 2007 there were one hundred and twenty-three democracies across the globe, with only traces of monarchy and slavery remaining.[130]

In 1899 at Kitty Hawk, North Carolina, the Wright brothers began testing the ridiculous idea that humans could fly. By 1947, Chuck Yeager broke the sound barrier, and by 1969 the first men landed on and returned safely from the moon.

Framework 2 supports the infinite, endless probable paths that any individual and civilization may follow in the pursuit of their ideals. The process always includes successes *and* failures which serve as lessons that we all can learn from. As always, the process is driven by value fulfillment (natural laws).

The pursuit of ideals is one of our noblest characteristics, truly a gift from All That Is. The key to manifesting them is self-knowledge, for it is only when we learn to *trust our private self* that we learn to trust others. When people become convinced that their private self is untrustworthy, then they deny their own abilities. As a result, probable choices and new opportunities for growth become limited.

Groups or organizations that reinforce these kinds of limiting beliefs are largely based on fear and mistrust that further limit choices, which in turn limits the innovation, creativity, and problem solving necessary to move from *what is* to *what could be.*

Thus, social groups who subscribe to beliefs in an unsafe universe begin to over-control their religious, political, and economic structures to the point where they constantly reinforce unseen threats and generate fear. Fearful people become more willing to give up their personal liberties for rules that promise order and security. In the process, they give up their own authority to leaders who promise these things.

Frightened people thus become vulnerable to fall under the sway of charismatic leaders whose ideals always sound good at first because they hold the enticing promise of better things to come. However, in practice, their actions often lead to conflict, even violence and war, as their ideals become perverted into excuses *to use any means* to achieve them. As such, what initially may have been a noble set of ideals becomes a justification to remove any perceived threats to attaining them. This results in fanaticism between leaders *and* followers.

Therefore, an idealist nurtures constructive choices that lead to growth and fulfillment that allows individuals to move closer from *what is* to *what could be*. Fanatics, on the other hand, pervert their ideals by making destructive decisions based on their ends justifying their means.

In simple terms, this means that there is never any spiritual justification for the murder of abortion doctors, for example, or the use of animals in medical experiments in order to "save" human lives. Seth says these are forms of fanaticism to avoid. Even if you entertain the notion of killing someone in the pursuit of your ideals, you *are* a fanatic.

In this context, Seth once again offers a commandment in biblical language: "Thou shalt not kill even in the pursuit of your ideals."[131]

However, it's important to take what "Seth says" here in its proper context, or else it becomes easy to distort. When he says, "Thou shall not kill . . ." he understands that death is a natural part of life, and there are circumstances we deal with daily in which we inadvertently may kill. For instance, when you brush your teeth you kill bacteria in your mouth, or when you eat *any* food you have to kill it. So he's not saying to stop brushing your teeth or stop eating in the pursuit of your ideals, but to become as aware as possible of the potential for violence and murder in the pursuit of your ideals.

Moreover, in larger terms nothing is ever destroyed because consciousness only changes form, but that requires a deeper understanding of All That Is, and doesn't mean that violations don't exist. In any case, you must deal with the consequences of every action you take.[132]

In this, Seth offers another important, broader moral imperative: *"the end does not justify the means.*[133] If the means toward an ideal is based upon moral violations like violence and murder ("thou shalt not violate"), then you're dealing with fanaticism, not idealism.

KEY IDEAS: A practicing idealist seeks to make the world a better place by realizing their own ideals in the world. They understand that the difference between idealism and fanaticism is that the end never justifies the means. It means "thou shalt not kill in the pursuit of your ideals."

What Were the Lessons of Jonestown, Guyana?

In *The Individual and the Nature of Mass Events* (1981) Seth discussed several examples of what can happen when idealists turn into fanatics. The first was the mass suicide at Jonestown, an experimental religious community based upon ideals of racial, economic, and social equality led by Reverend Jim Jones. Originally based in California, they moved to Guyana to escape public scrutiny and, ostensibly, political and religious discrimination. By 1978 there were just under 1,000 members living in Jonestown.

Once isolated, Jones subjected his followers to indoctrination methods that included behavior modification and brainwashing. The group got caught up in the "cold war" mentality of competing capitalist and socialist ideologies. Some members wanted to return to the United States, but were not permitted to "defect."

Eventually, US Congressman Leo Ryan flew to Jonestown to investigate mounting complaints. His trip triggered a hostile reaction by Jones and others that led to the shooting deaths of five members of Ryan's group, including Ryan on November 18,

1978. This, in turn, led Jones to order a mass suicide in which 909 men, women, and children took their own lives by drinking cyanide. The news made headlines around the world.

What are the belief systems that lead so many people to make this kind of desperate choice? Were there no alternatives?

Seth said that people will join together to "die for a cause" when they feel powerless and lose their reason for living. This attracts like-minded individuals who think in terms of black and white absolutes (right/wrong, good/evil). They also seek out the comfort of a rigid social framework, and thus attract a leader who fulfills their needs, and vice versa. A cult-like mentality is then formed that severely limits choices and the potentials for growth.

Such was the case with Jonestown. But what began as a noble social experiment and ended with 914 deaths still has important lessons for us today. Jonestown remains a powerful example of what can go wrong when individuals give up their personal power to misguided leaders and jointly believe they live in an unsafe universe. Their beliefs gradually closed off all possibilities for further fulfillment. As such, they fell prey to a "belief epidemic" in which their mass suicide became the only means to achieve their grossly distorted ideals.

However, in a safe universe, *no death occurs in a vacuum.* Seth repeatedly stresses that each death, no matter how tragic, *always* carries a deeper purpose and meaning.

Jonestown's mass suicide was a powerful testament to the kinds of beliefs that deny personal authority and limit growth and fulfillment. Therefore, their deaths made a collective statement that literally shook the world, and made people question the validity of their social, religious, and political beliefs. In this context, their deaths continue to make us question our own ideals in relation to those they sought in the jungles of Guyana.[134]

KEY IDEAS: Jonestown serves as a reminder of what can happen when a group of people succumbs to an epidemic of beliefs that creates a closed mental and physical environment. It also shows that when individuals give up their personal power to a fanatical leader whose ideals become destructive, choices for growth and fulfillment become severely limited.

What Were the Lessons of Three Mile Island?

Six months after Jonestown, there was a nuclear accident at Three Mile Island in Harrisburg, Pennsylvania. There was a partial core reactor meltdown that released radioactive gases into the local community. While there were no fatalities, the threat of a nuclear disaster far overshadowed local events and made international headlines. Ironically, a movie called *The China Syndrome* had its public release just twelve days before the accident. It eerily portrayed a similar type of nuclear disaster, and helped to stoke the social, political, and economic issues surrounding the use of nuclear energy.

Seth pointed out that while we're more familiar with religious cults (traditional worldview) there are also scientific cults (modern worldview) who operate under similar assumptions. As we have seen, both approach their truths as absolutes, instead of strongly held beliefs about reality. In the case of science, it constantly reinforces beliefs in an unsafe, uncaring, and unfeeling universe with no spiritual purpose.

Scientists are trained to be objective, to deal with only verifiable or falsifiable facts. This is an ideal by which modern science defines its truths and progresses ever forward. However, this approach also *separates* the scientist from the natural world, because it treats everything as an external object "out there" without understanding that they *always* create their own perception of anything they study. So it's a disastrous mistake to believe that stars, flowers, people, or fish have no intrinsic value or meaning beyond their objective characteristics.

In this context, modern scientists artificially divorce themselves from any subjective identification with the objects and processes they study. Since they don't value the deeper meaning of life, a nuclear accident that might kill thousands of people becomes a justifiable means of doing business.

Rob Butts astutely pointed out that the relationship between Jonestown and Three Mile Island represented destructive *extremes* in terms of religious (traditional) and scientific (modern) belief systems. Seth commented that the scientists at Three Mile Island held contempt for those who weren't privy to their elite knowledge and expertise. They looked down upon the people who controlled their funding sources, and who didn't fully appreciate their technical knowhow. Their own arrogance and false sense of power blinded them, and thus they made mistakes that nearly cost thousands of local residents their lives. Though they didn't consciously wish to hurt anyone, some felt an accident of that magnitude would serve people right for not giving them more power and money.

In spite of the potential threat, the situation at Three Mile Island quickly stabilized, though it took fourteen years to clean up and retire the contaminated reactor at a cost of almost one billion dollars. As a result, there was a halt on all new nuclear power plants in the United States and stricter federal regulations on existing plants. Again, there was a silver lining, as there *always* is, in a safe universe.

Additionally, recall the Christ drama in which a master event and mass dreaming in Framework 2 mixed with historic events to change the course of Western civilization (see Chapter 8). Seth said that the Three Mile Island accident unfolded in similar fashion, though on a much smaller scale. In all cases, individuals collectively co-created their own reasons for participating.

Nuclear energy didn't exist before the 1930s. It represented a vast source of power that was originally something we could only dream of. Since moderns feel so separated from nature, they feel separated from its elemental power, which also represents the "power of God." Nuclear power thus came to symbolize a new way for moderns to control this power. Various probabilities were then activated to explore the potential rewards and dangers through the active imaginations of scientists *and* lay people alike. In this way, nuclear power originated as a dream symbol that slowly manifest into Framework 1 to affect billions of people.

Therefore, individuals *always* play a crucial role in any mass event. Those involved contribute through private and mass dreaming, as well as their physical actions. Again, all events originate as master events in Framework 2 in conjunction with our entities. Dreaming serves as a connective tissue between Frameworks 1 and 2 in which probable variations are explored and selected for manifestation. In this way, the safe universe is innately designed by us to help us pursue our ideals and collective fulfillment.[135]

KEY IDEAS: Three Mile Island serves as an example of what can happen when rigid attitudes, emotionally-charged states, and compulsive behavior become the means to achieve scientific ideals. It also showed what can happen when any elite group develops a false sense of comparative omnipotence.

What about Hitler's Germany?

No discussion of fanaticism would be complete without a brief look at Adolf Hitler (1889-1945) and Nazi Germany (1933-1945). Hitler started out as an idealist who sought to return Germany to world power status after its humiliating defeat in World War I. The Treaty of Versailles had imposed harsh political and economic penalties on Germany, and along with the global economic depression that began in 1929, the German people suffered greatly. They looked for a strong personality to lead them back toward prosperity and a respected place on the world stage.

The Nazi party was based on socialist ideals that criticized democracy and free market capitalism. The party promoted a vision of ethnic purity and began to systematically persecute anyone it perceived as enemies or threats to their ideals. This was the environment in which Hitler became the leader of Nazi Germany in the 1930s. While the German people believed they needed an iron-willed but fair leader to guide them back to greatness, by the time World War II began in late 1939, his ideals were seen by many in the world as quite evil.

Seth said that Hitler's vision of Aryan ethnic superiority combined the darkest pitfalls of scientific *and* religious beliefs. In his rise to power, Hitler's daydreams became increasingly grandiose. His racist views labeled anyone not of Aryan descent as the enemy. The Jews bore the brunt of this racism because of their financial power, ethnic cohesion, and beliefs that they were "God's chosen people." Further, because of the Jews' culturally ingrained beliefs in victimhood, Nazi Germany became, in effect, a 20th century Egypt that they became willing martyrs to escape from once again. Both groups, for all their ideals, subscribed to pessimistic views of humanity.

Hitler also promoted the belief that war was an acceptable means for a nation's inalienable right to conquer the world. Hitler's Germany thus became an incubator for a fanatical form of nationalism. It was a "perfect storm" that unleashed humanity's worst shadow elements in an ethnic fury of unparalleled scope and devastation, facilitated by the lethal weaponry of modern science. To this day, it remains a hard-earned lesson of what can go wrong when a rogue nation pursues its fanatical ideals.

Hitler's Germany serves as another important reminder of what can go wrong when individuals give up their power to a fanatical leader. What began as noble ideals gradually degenerated into oppressive and unsustainable goals. In the end, fanatics *always* sabotage their efforts because they suffer from so many conflicting beliefs, the result of their fears and delusions. According to Seth, this was also the reason that Germany did not succeed in developing the atom bomb before the United States did.

In the end, as the saying goes, we must either learn from history or we are doomed to repeat it.[136]

KEY IDEAS: Hitler's Germany was founded on a fanatical form of nationalism. It fueled a "perfect storm" that unleashed humanity's worst shadow elements in a lethal ethnic fury of unparalleled scope and devastation facilitated by the weapons of modern science.

How Can You Become a Practicing Idealist?

Given the complexity of mass events, international politics, and global economics, it's easy for an individual to feel overwhelmed and powerless to effect any positive change in the world. Why bother when it seems so hard or sometimes even pointless? Because in the long run, it's only through individual action that we ever create change from *what is* to *what could be*. Again, this is why Seth spent so much time to explain the mechanics of *individual* reality creation.

What can you do to achieve ideals that will make the world a better place? You follow your own heroic impulses to become a *practicing idealist*, for there is nothing more fulfilling than the impulse to make the world a better place. Seth challenges each of us to make this our unique "mission in life."

But what's the best way to proceed?

You start from whatever situation you are in right now, and build from there. You begin by taking small steps. It's not enough to simply meditate upon or dream about your ideals, you *must also take action toward realizing them in the world.* You will always get feedback from your actions that serve as a barometer of your progress.

Seth discussed two additional functions of your conscious mind to help you realize your ideals: *imagination* and *impulses.* Both allow you to explore new choices and probabilities. Let's begin with imagination. Its great power lies in its ability to manifest anything within the scope of probabilities in Framework 2. Thus, all reality creation utilizes imagination to help you trigger inner events into physical manifestation. When combined with the intellect's cognitive power, it opens the doors of perception to untold inner resources, knowledge, and wisdom.[137]

Therefore, imagination, like dreaming, can be used as a tool to navigate through the probable fields and infinite potentials in Framework 2. It seamlessly unites the reality creation power of your conscious mind with All That Is. As always, your belief systems play a crucial role in *filtering* or *interpreting* the products of your imagination within Framework 1.

In this way, anything you can imagine, you *can* create! It takes time, practice, and a practical approach. Too many people give up the moment they run into obstacles, but this is always the result of limiting and negative beliefs, which can be addressed. As such, it's important to be persistent in the pursuit of your ideals. Obstacles are only self-imposed challenges to overcome along your journey. The hero always gets tested along their journey, but in the process of overcoming obstacles, transforms into a wiser, more powerful self.

In complementary fashion, impulses are an avenue of direct communication from your entity, also meant to help you actualize your ideals. They may arise as actual words or a sudden knowing, but far more often appear as spontaneous *urges to do something,* such as the urge to call a family member or make an important decision. They also occur within the larger social framework of the species and planet to promote not only your fulfillment, but that of world. Therefore, it's important to learn to recognize them, and discern their purpose.

In this light, *original* impulses are directly tailored to your situation and needs, but will also benefit others because they are inherently altruistic and unselfish. But again, to be a practicing idealist means that *you must act on your impulses*, and learn to trust their spontaneous and altruistic nature. This is *how* you gain the confidence and wisdom required to choose the best outcomes within an array of probable futures.

But what happens when you notice impulses that seem conflicting, dangerous, or even "evil"? In a safe universe, your entity *naturally* provides the inner urges for your deepest fulfillment. But you—the outer ego—have the free will to ignore or repress them. Therefore, "dangerous" impulses result from the chronic denial of earlier impulses deemed too difficult to act upon, because they went against the grain of cultural beliefs. For instance, if you believe that you are flawed by birth (sinful self) you may inadvertently demean your physical body, its sexual nature and natural needs, and deny your ability to act upon healthy sexual impulses.

This is another reason why it's so important to do belief and dream work to more deeply examine these kinds of urges, because with time and practice, you *will* trace their origins to blocked realizations of some ideal. Since All That Is *is within you* always, as is your entity, they support your innermost desires through constant impulse communications intended to help you realize your ideals.[138]

Therefore, the original impulses don't go away! They get pushed into your subconscious mind where they fester to create physical, emotional, or spiritual symptoms, such as impulses to intentionally hurt others. These types of impulses are symptoms of pathology that result when you artificially splinter off aspects of your own conscious mind into your subconscious. In this way, *beliefs play a crucial role in the way you interpret your natural impulses toward action.*

As you begin to experiment with impulses, Seth encourages you to question, assess, and choose among them. You can always try to ignore them, but original impulses, direct from your entity, will knock repeatedly on your head *until you learn to listen and take action.* They are intended to nurture your best interests no matter how strange or weird they may seem at first. While they may appear contradictory at times, they will inevitably point the way toward constructive action that promotes your growth and fulfillment.[139]

Therefore, your beliefs, thoughts, and emotions work in complementary fashion with your imagination and impulses. Guided by your innate moral intuition, these aspects of your conscious mind *are the most important tools you can use to pursue your ideals.* But you must also rise to the challenge, take bold steps when necessary, and have the courage to do what you know in your heart is right. All change begins with *you* in the moment point.

Seth also encourages you to be *reckless* in the pursuit of your ideals, but always respect the sacredness of all life, and be mindful that killing in the name of peace, or whatever ideology, will *always* prohibit the realization of your ideals.[140] By reckless, Seth doesn't mean to act rashly or without thinking about consequences. He means for you to be committed enough to get back on the proverbial horse when it throws you off, and to use experience as your best teacher to guide you along the way. By reckless, Seth challenges you to identify the divine spark of All That Is within you in the pursuit of your ideals to cultivate a raging wildfire of love, grace, compassion, spontaneity, creativity, humor, and deep appreciation for the endless wonders of All That Is.

Practicing idealism is what fuels the hero's journey. It will help you to take appropriate action in the midst of *all* circumstances, even in the darkest night of your soul when all hope seems lost, and you feel like giving up. Your ideals, when approached this way, will *always* guide you to discover the very best in yourself and others. In the process you *can* make the world a more just, sane, and compassionate place in which to live.

KEY IDEAS: Realize that your life is a personal kind of hero's journey. As you pursue your ideals, you will change your self and your world in beneficial ways.

Chapter 14: The Birth of Aspect Psychology and a New Worldview

Why is Aspect Psychology Important?

Though we have focused on the Seth Material thus far, we also need to consider the heroic effort of Jane Roberts to assimilate and apply Seth's ideas. It's easy to imagine the excitement that Jane must have felt as Seth provided new material week after week for over twenty years. And yet, Seth's ideas challenged the foundations of everything she believed, and pushed her even further to seek her own answers.

This creative tension sparked Jane's psychic development and inspired her to create her own theoretical framework to explain her experiences. Recall that each entity agrees to develop its abilities to the fullest through each lifetime (see Chapter 5). In this light, Jane certainly rose to the challenge! In fact, she became one of the greatest psychics of the late 20th century. By 1972, eight years after Seth's first appearance on the Ouija board, Jane's skills had blossomed to include what she identified as twelve states and Aspect selves that she could, more or less, access at will:

1. **Seth** (a robust personality with full emotions, masculine qualities, and low booming voice)
2. **Seth II** (an asexual personality, soft spoken, unemotional, further "inward" than Seth)
3. **Sumari (*Cyprus*)** (included singing, chanting, and pantomime in ESP class)
4. **Sumari Poetry & Math** (poetry and evocative material on mathematical principles)
5. **Sumari** (inner silence transformed into inner sound)
6. **"Seven"** (a distinct personality tone, featured in automatic writing)
7. **Helper** (a sensed energy form, volitionally projected to others)
8. **Special State** (stronger, deeper version of Sumari, never accessed from waking state)
9. **Reincarnational Dramas** (therapeutic role-playing of different personality Aspects)
10. **Reincarnational Selves** (past lives, Aspects of her entity)
11. **Worldviews** (psychic "energy deposits" of past lives, Aspects with their own entities)
12. **Probable Selves** (distinct selves that spin off during each lifetime and develop on their own)

Jane used her experiences and Seth's ideas to create her own "map of the entity" and called it Aspect Psychology. It was first published in *Adventures in Consciousness* (1975). In this framework, each lifetime exists as a unique *Aspect* of the entity. Thus, her Jane Aspect functioned as a *focus personality*, and her entity (Ruburt) functioned as the *source self* who managed her reincarnational cycle. The focus personality serves as the primary Aspect with the potential to communicate with various Aspect selves, through altered states and dreams, depending on its overall stage of development.

A healthy psychological balance is achieved when the primary Aspect is able to access various Aspects at will and maintain its sense of identity. Pathology results when the primary Aspect fragments, or loses its "center" within an ocean of Aspects, and confuses various Aspects *as the primary Aspect*. For example, this confusion can lead to claims of being Christ, Buddha, a space brother, Napoleon, or any probable personality. It means that other Aspects are no longer being properly integrated within the primary Aspect, but dominating and splintering it. Therefore, Aspects therapy involves reintegrating the primary Aspect by teaching it to properly discern among various Aspects and maintain its sense of personality (outer ego).

Additionally, Jane made a unique contribution to the field of what was called para- or transpersonal psychology during her lifetime. She discovered what she called the *nuclear self*—an expanded version of Seth's subconscious mind—that reached *far deeper* than anything earlier psychologists like James, Freud, or Jung had discovered. For example, it goes deeper to transcend yet include what Jung called the collective unconscious and archetypes.

The nuclear self not only manages all cellular activity in the physical body, but also manages all probable bodies and events from birth to death for *each* lifetime. As such, your nuclear self remains underneath, invisible, or subconscious to your outer ego, because it manages the vast field of probabilities within Framework 2. And yet, it also allows the outer ego to emerge and function within Framework 1.[141]

This structure also explains how your entity functions within simultaneous time and is able to perceive probable selves and events within the spacious present (see Chapter 5), as well as worldviews (which we will explore in this chapter). Therefore, your nuclear self functions as the "psychological connective tissue" between your entity and outer ego, and plays a crucial role in your physical, emotional, and psychological health.

Aspect Psychology also provides a new way to model mental health in relation to altered states and various psychological diseases that may occur over the course of human development. Imagine what it might be like to suddenly experience simultaneous time, multiple memories of past and future, or other incarnations through your inner senses in waking state. It can be a shock to the system, especially if your cultural worldview provides inadequate explanations for these kinds of phenomena.

As such, Aspect Psychology provides an expanded framework to understand them and ourselves more deeply. It was also a significant discovery and contribution to Western psychology. Though Jane did her research outside of academia, and therefore it was not highly visible, this gave her the freedom to pioneer her own phenomenological path. Her Aspects books document the results for anyone interested to verify and refine.

Although Jane was *not* interested in founding a new religion, Aspects provide a new way to model and integrate scientific (rational) and spiritual (inner senses) ways of knowing. It legitimizes altered states and dreaming as normal psychological states with the potential for great individual and collective benefit. Aspect Psychology also foreshadows the psychological foundations of Seth's dream-art science (see Chapter 9), and may hint further at the kinds of human abilities that become the collective norm during the next stage of human evolution.

KEY IDEAS: Aspect Psychology is the theoretical framework invented by Jane Roberts to explain the psychological structures outlined in the Seth Material. It is based upon her own psychic development, research, and experience.

Why are Worldviews Important?

Earlier, we defined a worldview as "the sum total of all intention, behavior, cultural values, and social systems from which any individual or civilization creates their reality" (see Introduction). At the individual level, your worldview also includes your belief systems (see Chapter 2). In Parts 2 and 3, we emphasized the importance of the three main cultural worldviews whose belief systems influence global reality co-creation. We can now expand the definition of worldview to include "living or dead, and in waking or dreaming states."

Your personal worldview functions like your favorite local television station. It serves as your home base in Framework 1, but you may also access other worldviews in other Frameworks of consciousness by switching channels. Like television stations, you can think of various Frameworks in terms of different frequencies and states of psychological focus.

As you move away from your home station, you may begin to experience "unusual" events, for you always interpret your experience through your core beliefs, no matter what state you're in. If you have the courage to leave expectations of the familiar behind, you can learn to access other helpful states of reality. In all cases, Seth says that personal worldviews can only be accessed when a personality holds similar intent and is sympathetic to its content.

For example, Jane wrote the "after-death journal" of William James by tuning into his worldview and a version of a book he had mentally drafted during the action of transition (see Chapter 5). As such, this was not a direct communication with James in his "present" or evolving state. But it required that Jane be open-minded enough to merge with his worldview without panicking and losing her own center of identity.

Seth also humorously cautioned to be careful what you ask for because you *will* get it, in terms of contacting the dead or accessing alternate and probable realities. So if you have the burning desire to explore your psychic abilities, always do your best to remain grounded and be discerning as you begin to experience new realities ("you get what you concentrate on!").

Lastly, the potential to access past, present, or future worldviews through altered states also provides an excellent explanation for the multidimensional nature of creativity and inspiration ("there are no closed systems"). This has been described in the past as communication with Greek Muses or Tibetan Dakinis, in modernity as objectified scientific discovery, and in new age circles as access to the Akashic Records. In each case, Seth's notion of personal worldviews and Jane's Aspect Psychology provide new ways to conceptualize these as communications between various Aspect selves.[142]

KEY IDEAS: Worldviews function as a kind of "psychic energy deposit" that contains the core belief systems through which we interpret our experience. These Aspects are a multidimensional source of inspiration and creativity.

Exercise 14—Visualize Your Own Worldview/Shift Perspectives

Engage psy-time. Take your time, and settle into your relaxed yet aware state (Alpha 1). Close your eyes and imagine a recent picture of yourself.

(If necessary, take a good look at the picture before you engage this practice. Or you can take an imaginary snapshot of yourself. In either case, pay close attention to all the elements in your picture and mental environment.)

Now, take a minute or two to playfully imagine the picture sitting on a shelf, desk, or coffee table—a place where you normally have pictures—so that it's easier to visualize. Just view it there.

Next, take a minute to observe all the other items in the picture. Notice how they are a natural part of that environment.

Next, look at your mental picture or environment and notice its natural boundaries. Its span is limited by the four corners of the picture frame. There may be water, land, or sky in the frame.

Next, project your consciousness into the image in the picture. That is, mentally shift your perspective to a first-person perspective *within* the picture looking out.

Now, mentally walk out of the picture onto the shelf, table, or whatever it stands on. The environment of the room will feel gigantic. Simply become aware of what it feels like. The sizes and proportions will be quite different from what you're used to in the confines of the picture.

Next, visualize your miniature self playfully investigating the new room, then find a door or window, open it, and go outside. Take a few minutes to experience the expanded worldview in this new environment.

Finally, open your eyes, take several deep breaths, and return to waking state.

Tip: use your dream journal to record any significant experiences. This exercise can also be done before going to sleep, when the mind is more settled from the day's events. Do the exercise, and finish with the suggestion to have a dream in which you explore new environments and worldviews. As always, finish with the suggestion that your dreams are very important and you wish to remember them when you wake up. Be sure to record them in your dream journal.[143]

What was the Negative Impact of Freud's Psychology?

When Jane tapped into the worldview of William James, she received some important critiques of the mass belief systems that influenced global politics, economics, and psychology during the 20th century (see Chapter 13). Along with the disastrous effects of social Darwinism, James also had a lot to say about the negative social impacts of Freudian Psychology and Protestantism on American democracy.

For instance, Freudianism replaced the theological hell of Protestantism with a psychological hell. Instead of demons, there were now unsavory animal impulses inherited by birth to contend with. In this way, the dark side of Protestantism was given a scientific "facelift." Protestantism's negative beliefs about humanity's sinful appetites formed the foundation for newly minted Freudian theories clothed in the respectability of modern science.

Simultaneously, Protestantism's push for salvation became entrenched in American churches and optimistically expressed in democracy's potential to abolish poverty, unfair class distinctions, and master nature through industrial technology. However, the United States' hidden fears that its ideals were impossible to achieve were reinforced by Freud's hypnotic emphasis that the subconscious, left alone, would always lead humanity astray.

Moreover, Freud reinforced the Puritan belief that human nature is essentially untrustworthy, because of hidden subconscious drives that masked Darwinian motives. Psychoanalysts became the new priesthood who served as new middlemen for salvation from the unsavory subconscious. The Catholic confessional became replaced by the psychoanalyst's couch.

By the 20th century, Freud's psychoanalysts successfully carved out a new economic niche to provide "salvation" from new dis-eases like neurosis, psychosis, and hysteria, which reinforced beliefs that the subconscious, dreams, and altered states were best left alone. These natural gifts from your entity became demonized—culturally stigmatized—as chaotic amoral animal urges that, once unleashed, would undermine a civilized, moral society.

When combined with Darwinism's emphasis on competition and survival, the results were a horribly pessimistic view of human nature that has *inhibited* human evolution for more than a century. Freudianism emphasized that human nature is fundamentally amoral, animalistic, and selfish. It purported that while these traits promote survival, they must be constantly reigned in, forced into a type of morality that keeps a lid on our dark subconscious urges in order to promote social cohesion. Spontaneous, impulsive behaviors became taboo, symptoms of a deeply flawed humanity.[144]

This dark side of the modern worldview fostered a cultural belief climate that led to the unchecked greed of the robber barons, the development of weapons of mass destruction, the widening gap between rich and poor, and more, during the 20th century. The ideals of a young and hopeful nation were sadly hijacked by the very dark side from which religion and science ostensibly promised salvation.

On the other hand, though the general public was sold a bill of goods that neither religion nor science could ever deliver, there *were* benefits provided. Religion has provided a sense of purpose and meaning fueled by its mythic soul and God (Consciousness with a capital "C" remains in this form today). Science has provided wonderful inventions that improved the quality of life for millions (better foods, sanitation, medical care, mass transit, etc.).

In a similar vein, Freud and Darwin didn't get it all wrong either. Both men were geniuses who made great contributions in their respective fields. For instance, Freud discovered "the shadow": how feelings, hurts, and trauma get repressed in the subconscious mind and fester to cause emotional problems if not properly reconciled. He also pioneered the use of dreams as therapeutic tools. These were further developed by Jung and remain important today. Darwin discovered legitimate biological functions of evolutionary change between species, and in 1996 Pope John Paul II declared that the theory of evolution was not in direct conflict with Church doctrine.[145]

Therefore, while James and Seth criticized the *negative effects* of the mass belief systems nurtured by the dark side of Freud and Darwin's work, it's a mistake to vilify them to the extent that we ignore their positive contributions.

KEY IDEAS: Freud took religion's sinful self and reliance on spiritual middlemen (priests) and dressed them up in the respectable clothes of modern science (psychoanalysis). This further marginalized beliefs that the subconscious, dreams, and altered states are valuable tools for personal growth, healing, and innovation.

Why Are the Codicils Important?

As we have seen, the Seth Material clearly outlines a personal, social, and moral framework to help us move beyond the limiting beliefs of traditional (religious) and modern (scientific) worldviews. Given their dark sides, is it any wonder that people continue to seek new ways to get along? But *how* can we translate Seth's suggested ideals into practical action to make our world a better place to live?

As Jane Roberts sought answers to these questions, she expanded Aspect Psychology to include the "psychic politics" of reality creation. In late 1974, while pondering her next book project, *Psychic Politics* (1976) was born with the vision of a "psychic library" full of new ideas and solutions. Jane engaged an altered state in which she saw a library transposed over the southeast corner of her living room. She "saw" her own psychic counterpart in the library and realized she could deliver new material similar to the way she accessed worldviews. In her initial encounter with her library, Jane was presented with a "model" for *Psychic Politics*. She felt as though she had "finally come home," and it was her mission to translate these inner books that had their origins in other times and civilizations.[146]

Jane was hesitant to assign an occult label like "Akashic Records" to this new development, because her library was couched in personal symbols. She knew that others who access this state might perceive different environments, or rely on auditory information instead of visual, and so on. In other words, she understood that her psychic library didn't exist "out there" in a pre-existing form *or* state, but was co-created through her own inner senses and belief systems, and thus could be perceived differently by others.

At one point, Jane received the word "codicil" several times, but nothing more. So she looked it up, and it turned out to be a legal term defined as "an addendum or refinement to a last will and testament." Curious but determined, she continued book work and put it out of her mind. One day she "saw" her counterpart reading a library book, and the word "codicil" grew mentally louder. Suddenly she knew the material she was about to access outlined a different direction for humanity, one that would provide new concepts upon which to create a better world, one that we had yet to explore in Framework 1.

Thus, she wrote *the Codicils*—eleven new hypotheses for the individual and collective—to serve as refinements to the "human will" that pave the way toward enhanced governments, economics, educational systems, and so on.

In summary, the Codicils declare the interdependence of matter and Spirit—that *everything* is connected within a magnificent web of life that is conscious and therefore sacred. While our political, economic, and social structures are by-products of our current cognitive functions based on physical senses and separation from nature, there are new neurological pathways in the human brain not yet developed that will activate increased use of our inner senses. Our "iceberg selves," while dependent upon space-time, are ultimately free of it. Our entities use reincarnation, simultaneous time, and probability fields to develop their abilities.

In this light, there are probable models of our self, world, and innate moral intuition from which we can choose to create an entirely new worldview and civilization.[147]

However, the Codicils are *not* to be directly compared to the Ten Commandments, for while both have moral implications, the Codicils are amendments—refinements to a path *already chosen*. They are *not* intended to usurp the moral foundations of Western society, but are offered instead as a mid-course correction.

The emerging postmodern worldview will by definition *transcend yet include* the best practices of the traditional and modern worldviews because, in Framework 1 terms, they are deeply rooted in our world. Therefore, the Codicils were Jane's suggestions for the kinds of new ideals that could change *what is* into *what could be*. They outline noble ideals that, if followed, will promote the development of new abilities and means for problem solving.

The Codicils are offered as suggestions from an avant garde visionary who sensed deeply those probable futures that could realize humanity's greatest potentials. The rest is up to each of us to create, since our future is *always* a matter of choice, not chance. In this way, the Codicils foreshadow the kind of evolutionary shift in consciousness required to create a *mature* postmodern worldview, which is still in its infancy.

KEY IDEAS: The Codicils are refinements to the traditional and modern worldviews that serve as alternate hypotheses for private and public experience based upon the Seth Material and Jane Roberts's Aspect Psychology. They foreshadow key ideals that may form a mature postmodern worldview.

Why is the God of Jane Important?

Jane Roberts's final Aspects book is appropriately dedicated to "those individuals who insist upon interpreting the nature of reality for themselves."[148] *The God of Jane* (1981) reflects the final stages of the hero's journey in which Jane shared her struggles and triumphs to put Seth's ideas to work. It wasn't always easy, and her physical symptoms continued to worsen. Her joints were sore, and she began to have visual and auditory problems, but soldiered on with Rob and Seth's loving support.

Jane was intrigued by Seth's material on impulses and Framework 2 in *Mass Events*. She worried that her readers might misinterpret his words to mean that impulses to harm others could be considered acceptable. Of course, he didn't mean that at all, as we have seen. Seth reminded Jane that Framework 2 always provides the best outcomes for everyone in relation to the whole. But we need to become mindful that the authority of the individual continues to be undermined by religious and scientific beliefs that deny the important, positive influences of our natural impulses. The underlying fear is that if impulses remain unchecked, they inevitably provoke antisocial behaviors that undermine the social order, when just the opposite is true, as we just saw.

Again, working with impulses and learning to utilize the benefits of Framework 2's constant, loving support is a process that takes time and persistence. However, Jane's doubts remained as she wrestled with the social, political, and moral implications of Seth's ideas. Was she leading people down a primrose path like so many others had? How could she best avoid that?

Jane knew that she and Seth *had* identified some of the major flaws within religious and scientific worldviews, but struggled with what to offer as alternatives. She was hesitant to rock the boat, because what if she got it wrong and made things worse?

One morning, as she pondered her own connection with All That Is in her writing studio, sipped morning coffee, and listened to the first bird songs echo from the hill, Jane felt a *deep mystical connection to everything*. She realized that her individuality was a unique and precious perspective *within* All That Is, as an Aspect of All That Is.

In a moment of inspiration she named that portion of the multiverse from which she emerged the *God of Jane* to symbolize her private, personal connection with All That Is. There was also a God of Rob, a God of Billy and Mitzie (her cats), and so on. The idea was to personify each individual's direct access to All That Is to emphasize the important distinction between the private "God"—the entity Aspect—and the universal All That Is within *every* Aspect.

The "God of You" puts the emphasis on *your* entity which, again, serves a *mediating function* between the physical you and All That Is. But the crucial thing here—an evolutionary leap forward—is that when you engage any kind of "conversation with god" (like the biblical or new age "prophets"), it is now understood that *you do so through the filters of your own beliefs systems and worldview*.

Therefore, no single individual can *ever* claim to speak in Absolute terms for God to the *exclusion* of all others. Thus, we each speak "God's truth" through our Billhood, Janehood, Christhood, Buddhahood, and so on, but no single definition can be considered Final. The God of You levels the playing field and opens the door to a more democratic vision of Spirit-in-flesh, one that promotes new interpretations of the divine.

As such, your divine "piece of the rock"[149] *can never be taken away from you.* No one can excommunicate you from The God of You *unless you give up your authority.* Again, no one else can ever create your reality for you. You *always* have the free will to choose to follow a different set of ideals that promote your best fulfillment.

While Martin Luther's reformation was centered in Christian Germany (he also believed in burning witches), Jane's vision was global (world-centric) and not limited to any single religion, creed, or ethnic group. Thus, the belief in "god's chosen people" becomes obsolete—too limited and self-serving—since *God is within everyone equally.* This also puts the onus back on each individual to develop their abilities to realize that Divine-Spark-within and stop blaming God or their entities for their problems.

The God of Jane dared to suggest we consider a new ideal, one that prohibits the centralized control of our souls by middle-men—priests, mullahs, and gurus—no matter how noble their ideals may sound, or how well-meaning they may be, because we have been witness to their chronic perversion throughout history *in the name of* God, Christ, Allah, Jehovah, and so on. Most of the wars in the past six thousand years have been fought in the name of a god that played ethnic and regional favorites. That kind of god is tribal, ethnocentric, and undemocratic. The God of Jane paved the way for a more egalitarian, world-centric, and democratic vision of All That Is.[150]

KEY IDEAS: The God of Jane is a way to conceptualize your entity as your own "piece of the rock," one that provides direct access to All That Is and requires no middlemen. It promotes a decentralized relationship with All That Is, one that transcends the limits of any organization that claims to hold the only True Path to spiritual salvation.

Why is the American Vision Important?

The process of globalization continues to exacerbate regional and global conflicts generated by the worldview dynamics of traditional, modern, and postmodern belief systems. Though it's been close to thirty years since *The God of Jane* was written, the underlying core beliefs of the major worldviews *remain very much the same*. Jane keenly intuited that the collective was indeed struggling to birth a new worldview like a root-bound plant needs a larger pot.

Though Europe was mired in a history of authoritative traditions and doctrines, the United States was founded as a country of do-it-yourselfers who sought religious freedom and economic prosperity. The democratic ideals that so brilliantly instituted the legal separation of church and state also made Jane, Rob, and Seth's work possible. It was no accident that these same ideals, along with the Seth Material, inspired Jane to offer her own vision—an American Vision—that was based on a democracy of Spirit-in-flesh. In this context, the notion of an Absolute God as King, Dictator, or Grand Poobah becomes obsolete.

Even though the founding fathers of the American Constitution were wise enough to separate church and state, there was still an implicit undercurrent in which the Christian God supported our presidents and people. As such, when they spent American blood and treasure on warfare, it was with the implied consent of God's blessing.

But that reflects a limited, parochial God who is for and against "His" own creations. What kind of God plays favorites like that? One who works in mysterious ways, who common folk can never know? Or one cast in man's own image based upon his worst shadow elements? Such narrow definitions continue to limit our choices and potentials. Jane sought a wider view, a new vision bold enough to transcend yet include the boundless optimism of the American spirit.

Jane couched her American Vision in the world-centric ideals of the founding fathers: egalitarian ideals of life, liberty, and the pursuit of happiness for all citizens. The God of You provides a check and balance to prevent any single person, group, dogma, or book to speak for All That Is in Absolute terms, because God is *equally inside us all*. As such, no single interpretation, including Jane or Seth's, can carry the final stamp of Divine approval.

For example, we saw that Seth's Christ drama was a legitimate instance of prophecy as defined by traditional religions (see Chapter 8). But in light of the American Vision, it is not intended to be the final say, or be taken in literal, absolute terms. Therefore, it is up to each of us to interpret within the context of the God of You to seek its *deeper* metaphoric meanings and *avoid* the kind of religious fundamentalism that results when prophecy is taken as literal fact.

Moreover, just as there is no longer room for kings or dictators in a democratic nation, there is no longer any room for a Dictator God. The God of You also limits the abuses of any group who claims to own "*the* word of god" or any individual "son or daughter of God," because that unduly privileges a "dictator" group over all others. Therefore, the God of You allows us to more accurately conceptualize ourselves as a healthy family— "sons and daughters of the Mother *and* Father"—and extend that privilege to *all sentient forms of life*.

Jane's Vision suggests the ideals that founded the United States may pave the way for new approaches for living, but does *not* suggest that Americans hold the moral high ground over the rest of the world. It suggests, however, that the democratic ideals we can trace back to our Greek and Roman roots have flowered in the United States and may serve as the basis upon which to build a new global worldview.[151]

Finally, keep in mind that Aspect Psychology was birthed by a woman with no formal political, religious, scientific training or affiliations. She heroically confronted her own psychic experiences, battled her own demons, and did her best to make sense out of the Seth phenomenon. Taken as a whole, Jane's three Aspects books present a personal legacy that offers many valuable insights into the important issues that underlie the birth of the emerging postmodern worldview.

KEY IDEAS: The American Vision offers an inspired approach to living that is world-centric and based upon democratic and relativistic—not authoritarian or absolute—ideals.

Why is Jane Roberts's Death Important?

As work on *The God of Jane* finished, Jane's physical symptoms worsened. She had trouble taking more than ten steps at a time. It hurt to use the typewriter, wash dishes, and even use the bathroom. Though there were periods of respite and improvement, her health gradually deteriorated to the point where she was hospitalized for the last eighteen months of her life.

Jane Roberts died on September 5, 1984 at the age of fifty-five. The official cause was due to "complications from [protein depletion, osteomyelitis, and] soft-tissue infection, arising out of the rheumatoid arthritis she'd suffered from for so long."[152]

The unofficial cause was due to a psychological condition that Jane, Rob, and Seth came to identify as "the sinful self"—a psychological "sub-personality" that restricted Jane's natural impulses to exercise, and blocked out anything her spontaneous self suggested that competed with her writing regimen.

Jane's death raised the uncomfortable question: "Why didn't she use the Seth Material to get well"? The subtext is, of course, "Does it really work?" It's important to first understand that Jane and Rob were *the* front line who produced the material day after day for over twenty years. For much of that time, Jane was in a dissociated state, and it took her time and effort to assimilate Seth's ideas into her own work.

As we just saw, Jane's Aspect Psychology revealed her incredible ability to synthesize Seth's main concepts and brilliantly speculate on their many implications (as did Rob). But there is a difference between being able to intellectually explore the material and to change core beliefs, which Jane did extremely well! But the nagging question that perplexes Seth readers to this day is, "Why did Jane choose to die so young, and in such a painful way?"

Her friend and student, Susan Watkins, said that Jane understood the nature of her problems, and had analyzed them thoroughly with Seth over the years. So it wasn't a question that she couldn't properly apply the Seth Material. In short, "she never quite made it out of the thicket of her own beliefs, which served not only Jane, but Jane and Rob as a couple. Difficult to say, but true—and they knew it."[153]

Additionally, we each have a natural fear of the unknown, and death is perhaps the most mysterious unknown we must face. Therefore, when we contemplate someone else's death, we tend to subconsciously project our own future death onto their situation. Our own defense mechanisms then kick in to convince us that we'd naturally have done something different to avoid such a fate. But fate has nothing to do with it.

Once you understand that you create *all* your own reality, you realize that each death is the perfect expression of the life one chooses to live. Jane's life and death were no different. To judge her death as some kind of failure reflects your own beliefs in death as annihilation, the result of a meaningless universe, and a loss in the battle for survival of the fittest. Again, there is no loss, with every ending comes a new beginning, and from every death comes new life.

Seven books were posthumously published called *The Personal Sessions* (2003-2006) that contain all the "deleted material" from the regular Seth books. They detail the ways that Jane, Rob, and Seth addressed Jane's dis-ease for almost two decades. Rob also published extensive notes on Jane's symptoms and her "sinful self" in *Dreams, "Evolution," and Value Fulfillment, The Way Toward Health*, and *The Magical Approach*. Susan Watkins penned an excellent memoir that revealed parts of Jane's private and public life in *Speaking of Jane Roberts* (2000).

In this light, the chief legacy of Jane's death actually helps us to better understand *how* the mechanics of reality creation really work. Rather than overanalyze Jane's choices, understand that she created her own reality perfectly, as we all do, until our last breath. Jane's choices will forever be her own, as will yours.

Another fringe benefit, perhaps, is that by dying at such a young age, Jane ensured that her life wouldn't be unduly canonized because of the seeming contradictions involved. By showing that she had her own flaws, death made her seem more human, and tempered the mystique surrounding her virtuosic psychic abilities.

To the bitter end, Seth was present and did his best to be helpful. He even dictated a book Jane had considered for years during the last months from her hospital bed (*The Way Toward Health*).

It contains helpful information for anyone who has chosen to deal with serious health problems.

Taken as a whole, the personal material on Jane Roberts's death contains many valuable lessons. It captures the human elements involved—the pain, fear, uncertainty, confusion, anger, and resignation—that we can all learn from with grace. It was made public by Jane's own request during her final days, with Rob's permission, so that we could each learn from their successes and failures, joys and sorrows, and search for answers to life's biggest questions.

KEY IDEAS: Jane Roberts's death contains many valuable lessons about some of the most mysterious unknowns that we all face. The personal material revealed a very human side to the woman behind the Seth Material.

Chapter 15: The Secret Revealed

What is the Magical Approach?

Seth spoke about the art of creative living in one of his last books *The Magical Approach* (1995). This is not a Seth-dictated book like his earlier books, but a series of "connective sessions," as Jane called them, from 1980. In them, Seth fleshed out some of his earlier ideas to help Jane cope with her worsening health issues. As such, its main focus was to provide a simple method in which to put his core ideas to work.

For example, since the material on Framework 2 and the entity (the "God of You") was so new at the time, neither Jane nor Rob had been able to put them into everyday use. They had been cautiously testing the waters like most beginners. The magical approach was a way to take the necessary leap of faith to radically reorient their approach to daily life, and consciously tap into the healing potentials available in Framework 2.

Seth pointed out that Jane and Rob held deeply entrenched beliefs in the importance of *cultural time* (clocks and assembly lines) instead of *natural time* (sunrise, sunset, tides, seasons, and planets). The "Protestant work ethic" cautions that "the devil finds time for idle hands" and reinforces the primacy of assembly-line time and the forty-hour work week. This belief system influenced how Jane's sinful self approached her writing to such an extreme that, in effect, it made her a prisoner of her writing studio. It eliminated all other acceptable outlets for her spontaneous self's artistic impulses that, in a vicious cycle, fed her symptoms.

While assembly-line time works well in an industrial orientation—it makes the trains run on time and mass produces factory goods—it frequently blocks natural impulses from the entity toward creativity and spontaneity. When they become blocked to the extreme, they inhibit the body's natural healing abilities. Therefore, if Jane had followed a magical approach, one that enabled her spontaneous self to flourish, her symptoms would have lessened.

Seth said that the magical approach required a new way to cope with life's challenges, one that integrated a *natural approach* to life based upon our natural instincts, which contradicts the conventional approaches we've been taught. The magical approach is a natural approach because it activates our own natural abilities. On the other hand, the rational (scientific) approach can become a conflicting belief system when it claims to be the *only* way to solve all our problems. But it omits our feelings, emotions, and deep intuitions (inner senses), and often forces the conscious mind to overly concentrate upon a problem or set of symptoms to the extent that it *actually perpetuates their manifestation.*

Seth emphasized the magical approach to buffer Jane's (and our) reliance on reason alone, over-thinking and endlessly analyzing a problem to seek its solution. More importantly, it is based on the assumption that we live in a safe universe. It provides a natural trust that there is *always* a solution to *any* physical, emotional, mental, or spiritual problem, no matter how dire they may seem.

In this light, the magical approach promotes a deep trust in the "unknown reality" of our "iceberg self" that we may never fully understand in purely rational terms (like simultaneous time, life after death, or reincarnation). But the fact remains that the magical approach exists even if we don't believe in it, because Framework 1 couldn't exist without it.

Therefore, learning to use the magical approach helps to develop your personal connection with the "God of You" through an intuitive, natural trust that the universe is designed for your best fulfillment and healing. It promotes a kind of natural optimism that there are solutions to any problem if you simply *let go of those beliefs that limit your choices and block your impulses*. It engages your spontaneous inner being which *always* has your best interests in mind.

However, and this is key: the magical approach is *not* limited to naïve, childish forms of magic—simple wish fulfillment where you think about something and it instantly manifests. Again, thoughts play an important role, but are not 100% causal. Seth's magical approach is not based on the idea that you stick a pin in a doll to create an illness in an enemy, or incant a spell to heal a friend. That approach is based on the belief that someone else can create your own reality for you, or you can create someone else's. As we have seen throughout, the mechanics of reality creation don't work that way.

The magical approach is a kind of *transpersonal* magic based upon deep intuitions, trust, and allowance that a higher power—the "God of You"—always has your back and will naturally help you solve *any* challenge you face. As such, the ultimate goal is to blend the magical approach and the rational approach, for they are complementary *when used properly*. In other words, taken to extremes the rational *or* the magical approach can lead to problems. Therefore, you must seek a balance between these two important modalities.

In this light, the natural approach is a variation of an earlier concept—Seth's high intellect—whose ideal is to blend intellect *and* intuition, reason *and* inner senses (see Chapter 9). Seth pointed out that the magical and rational approaches *must be combined* in order to get the best results. For example, people sometimes wrote to Jane and Rob about their wish to have more money, and yet, by simply quitting their jobs and waiting for the universe to magically provide them a windfall, they ended up ignoring impulses to find a new job, or volunteer in their community. By ignoring the rational approach to money, they blocked impulses that severely limited the effectiveness of the magical approach. In other words, just thinking or affirming that you're rich without acting upon your rational impulses will *not* create this reality for you.

Thus, the point *is not to adopt the "magic" of the magical approach by itself!* Seth emphasized it initially to help shift our overreliance on rational-only approaches based on cultural time, but it was never intended to replace or usurp it. They must work together for the best results. In this way, you can learn to access the full power of the potentials of Framework 2 *in conscious harmony* with the "God of You." You will cease to work against your own spontaneous nature and develop a greater sense of ease, comfort, and effortlessness in *anything* you do.

As such, it is more accurate to call this the *natural approach*, because the ideal is to combine the rational *and* magical, reason *and* inner senses, order *and* spontaneity. In this way, you can willfully tap into Framework 2 and the "God of You" to solve any problem, challenges, or health issues you face. But you must be willing to make an unequivocal change from the old way of doing things for the natural approach to work effectively.

The natural approach *combines* the intuitive practices of the traditional worldview (body, mind, soul, and spirit always work together), and the rational practices of the modern worldview (scientific method provides clear results) to synthesize a new, postmodern approach to reality creation. Seth is not talking about regressing to religious dogma and superstition, but integrating the knowledge of Spirit known by the traditions as well as the strengths of modern science to *create a brand new approach based upon their best practices.*[154]

KEY IDEAS: The magical approach activates your spontaneous, deep intuitive abilities along with your rational, reason-based abilities. Together, they form a natural approach to willfully allow helpfulness from Framework 2 and the "God of You."

Is the Seth Material a Religion or a Science?

We mentioned earlier that it's important to avoid any "Seth in a vacuum" or "pure Seth" approaches because they ultimately lead to forms of fundamentalism that marginalize other teachings, people, and methods. Even though we've seen that the Seth Material sets a "gold standard" in terms of clarity and depth, it is *not* a complete or finished body of work. For instance, the Eastern spiritual traditions have an extensive knowledge of the subtle energy centers known as *chakras*. There is no mention of them in the Seth Material. This omission may be due to Jane Roberts's lack of exposure to those traditions, preconceived notions that led her to block them, or Seth's desire to not focus on them.

And as we saw, Seth cautioned that neither he nor anyone was to be considered an infallible source. Therefore, the Seth material should never be considered the final say on all things (see Introduction). Neither Seth nor Jane and Rob were interested in starting a new religion, though Jane intuited that his ideas were indeed "the new way" in *The Way Toward Health.*[155]

The Seth Material is more of an art-science than a religion in the sense it seeks to falsify old assumptions that do not hold up to new objective evidence. At the same time, it aligns in many ways with the world's oldest spiritual traditions. For example, when we include our deep intuitions and subjectivity (inner senses), we achieve the kinds of altered states known to the ancient mystics that open the doors to the "unknown" reality of Framework 2.

Acknowledging the rational approach as a key element of the Seth material will naturally temper attempts to create new religious dogmas. This is the ethos that permeates Seth's dream-art sciences (high intellect) and informed Jane's American Vision. As such, it is neither a religion *nor* a science by traditional or modern definitions, but a postmodern attempt at the integration of the best of both.

Therefore, the Seth Material *foreshadows* the potentials of a postmodern approach to reality creation, one that includes objective *and* subjective ways of knowing. It functions as a herald at the bridge between current forms of religion and science as the new worldview struggles to be born.

As you apply the Seth Material in your everyday life, keep in mind that it exists in relation to *all* the other spiritual and scientific systems that preceded it. It is not intended to marginalize or usurp them, only to provide an updated approach to *how* you create your own reality based on a redefinition of their best practices.

Further, because the Seth Material presents such a fresh and undistorted "map" of All That Is, after careful study and direct experience it will begin to function as a kind of "Rosetta Stone of consciousness." In other words, once understood, it can also help you to unlock the secrets of those traditional religions (and sciences) that are losing their original transformative potentials because of distortions over time. For instance, according to Lama Govinda, a Zen Master:

> When religion grows in age, faith turns into dogma, and experience is replaced by book-knowledge, virtue by adherence to rules, devotion by ritual, meditation by metaphysical speculation. The time is then ripe for a rediscovery of truth and a fresh attempt to give it expression in life.[156]

With this in mind, you can use the Seth Material to mine the gems of the world's great mystical traditions because they *all* outline similar Frameworks of consciousness ("Levels of Reality") and multidimensional identity ("Levels of Selfhood"). This is *not* a map of their dogmas, ceremonies, costumes, places of birth, and other external features that calcify over time, but of the internal nature of the multiverse discovered by their pioneering founders. Thus, the following chart is only meant to ballpark key similarities as a point of departure for further exploration and refinement.[157]

Graphic layout courtesy of Brad Reynolds

Finally, all authentic spiritual traditions provide a set of transformative practices—yoga or praxis—in which to explore the mechanics of reality creation within All That Is. All the scientific traditions include a set of paradigms—methods or experiments—in which to explore the mechanics of reality creation (though they are limited mostly to Framework 1). Therefore, as you learn the natural approach—one that includes the best practices of the magical *and* rational approaches—you will see how the Seth Material actually complements them. The foundational exercises outlined in this book are designed to help get you started.

KEY IDEAS: The Seth Material is neither a religion nor a science by traditional or modern definitions. It is a postmodern attempt to integrate the best of both, one that includes objective (rational) and subjective (magical) ways of knowing.

What is the Secret of Reality Creation?

If it can be contained in a simple sentence, it's "you create your own reality," as coined by Seth in his classic *The Nature of Personal Reality* (1974). However, it's recently been popular to talk about "the secret" of how to get what you want through the "law of attraction." This "law" is defined as the means through which reality is created, based on what you focus your thoughts on. While this is somewhat true, as we've seen throughout, there's a much wider framework for reality creation that needs to be understood.

If you skipped ahead and peeked at this chapter before reading the other chapters, you may have done so to learn this: quick-fix approaches don't work in the long run, because they don't sustain authentic transformation. While you can read this chapter first, it won't mean as much if you haven't begun to fully explore your self, your world, and how we all get along (see Chapters 1-14). These "big three" *always* work together to create your own reality. To deny any one is to deny a crucial dimension of being, which artificially divides you from your sense of connection with All That Is, and limits your choices.

The law of attraction is *not* one of Seth's natural laws (see Chapter 11), which are broader and apply to all Frameworks of consciousness. Though it *does* play an important role, the law of attraction is only local to Framework 1, just like the law of gravity, speed of light, and strong and weak nuclear forces.

Seth did briefly refer to "laws of attraction" (note the plural) in a physical, biological, and psychological context, though he never fleshed them out further.[158]

The popular version of the law of attraction says that, in a nutshell, "like attracts like." However, when we look at quantum physics, scientists tell us that "opposites attract and like repels." For example, if you have two magnets and touch the two negative or positive poles together, they repel each other. But when you try to touch a positive to a negative pole, they attract and join together. So while calling it a "law" sounds scientific, the physics are clearly contradictory.

In terms of physics, the law of attraction is more like *sympathetic resonance*. For instance, if you take all the dampers off a piano's strings, and loudly hit low C's in the left-hand bass, when you damp those left-hand strings you'll hear *all* the harmonics in other strings sounding a chord *without* having been struck. The acoustic energy has simply been *transferred* because those same tones were *already vibrating as harmonics* on the left-hand bass strings.

Therefore, the law of attraction is actually a kind of *energetic transference* that makes our innate tone/beliefs/behaviors resonate more strongly in the presence of others vibrating in similar fashion. As such, it is based upon our own ability to *amplify them from within.*

All of this points out that the law of attraction could more accurately be called the "law of resonance" because *we're not really attracting anything outside of us;* we're simply tuning up, harmonizing, and amplifying our own natural tune. When played at a sufficiently *positive* volume, we will find other people, places, and potentials playing a similar tune, and that synergy often leads to unexpected breaks, insights, healing, and fulfillment.

When our tune has sufficient *negative* volume, we find others who synergize in negative ways. So this "law of resonance" *works both ways.* Our intention, beliefs, and behavior in relation to social and cultural factors conspire to co-create positive or negative outcomes. In either case, once we really get jamming, we're actually *transferring,* resonating, and helping others to jump-start their own cosmic symphonies *in harmony with our own.*

It's always our choice whether we wish to play a negative or positive tune. That's the double-edged design inherent in the "law of resonance." This is why it's so important to fully acknowledge and address our limiting beliefs. The more we "face up to the abilities of consciousness,"[159] the more we wake up and confront those shadow elements that act as roadblocks and detours from realizing our deepest desires.

As such, what Seth told us about the natural approach wasn't really a secret because the real secret always lies *within* each of us to discover and learn to use properly.

KEY IDEAS: The secret of reality creation is always within you. You must define it for yourself.

What is Seth's Version of the Secret?

Clearly Seth taught a version of "the secret," but how to best define it? Here is a distillation of Seth's key ideas on *how* you create your own reality through the simultaneous interaction of your self, your world, and how we all get along—the three irreducible dimensions of physical reality creation.

- **Your Self**: You are a multidimensional spiritual being, an "iceberg self," creating a physical experience, one of many; you have an innate soul intent—family of consciousness—that fuels your purpose in life; you get what you concentrate upon; you create your own worldview through the filters of your beliefs and physical, mental, and inner senses.
- **Your World**: You exist within multiple Frameworks of consciousness as an Aspect of All That Is; even though history appears as consecutive events in Framework 1, under the surface in Framework 2, all events are nested together; you share your world with others, together we are learning to become conscious co-creators.
- **How We All Get Along**: You are here to develop your abilities fully; the point of power is in the present; thou shalt not violate; the end never justifies the means; trust that you live in a safe universe and are of good intent; take action as a practicing idealist; take a natural approach to reality creation.

"The secret" to effortless reality creation, then, is to *learn how to focus specific actions* necessary to achieve success, however you define it, that fully integrate the above three dimensions of be-ing.

Put another way, "the secret" to success is through strongly focused desires properly aligned with your innate soul intent to create what you need. As you progress, you will discover that your entity always provides what you *need*, though not always what you *want*. As the Rolling Stones sang, "You can't always get what you want, but if you try some time, you just might find you get what you *need*."[160] Once properly tuned up, your strings of success will play beautifully, *guaranteed*.

In larger terms, keep in mind that there will always be psychic politics that generate conflict *to some extent* because 6.5 billion people are simultaneously co-creating their realities through different worldview *stages* and *types* of intention. These represent immense probability fields in which different expressions of competition *and* cooperation will always ebb and flow. Add the shadow and negative aspects of the human psyche and you begin to see why so much conflict still remains at present, and how some always will.

As such, use this knowledge to temper any unreasonable expectations you may have that "in the future *all* people will . . ." live in perfect peace, harmony, etc. Value fulfillment (divine love) ensures that collective reality co-creation will always include elements of competition *and* cooperation. So it depends on which elements and ideals *you* choose to concentrate upon.

Seth emphasized that the most powerful global change always manifests one person at a time, from the bottom up, not the top down. As Gandhi said, "Be the change you wish to see in the world." This is the *exact* approach taught throughout the Seth Material. And so, it always falls back on you to create the reality you wish to see in your world to make it a better place for yourself and others to share.

KEY IDEAS: You create your own reality through a simultaneous combination of Your Self, Your World, and How We All Get Along.

Which You? Which Worldview?

It can be a long, strange trip down the Yellow Brick Road as you begin to explore Seth's "unknown reality." But again, just like the main characters in *The Wizard of Oz*, everything that you really need has been inside of you all along, though you may not have known it.

In the same way, you have *all* the tools you'll ever need to solve any challenge or climb any mountain you truly desire *with-*

in you right now. It's just a question of which you and which worldview you decide to create. Therefore, it's always up to you to choose the kind of world you wish to live in, and the kind of ideals you wish to practice each day. As you continue on your journey, consider how the following core beliefs may be used to create your own new worldview:

- **You are Divine**, born in a state of eternal, natural grace which you have never left and never will.
- **Your life has innate intent** and is among an infinite number of expressions of the Divine. Your dreams, inspirations, and intuitions represent your direct, subjective connection with the Divine, which can also be thought of as Source, Spirit, Consciousness, or All That Is.
- **All life is sacred**, all elements are intimately connected with each other, regardless of size or distance, in cooperation, invested fully in the pursuit of individual and collective value fulfillment.
- **Your physical death is not the end of your life**. You as Consciousness experience many times and places in many dimensions. Space-time is not an absolute, but a construct. We influence the past as well as the future from the present.
- **Consciousness is Primal Cause**. Consciousness creates All That Is. Our universe is a multiverse of nested fields of consciousness, most of which are not perceivable by the five senses or their extensions (telescopes, microscopes) alone.
- **Human evolution includes worldviews** that unfold hierarchically in stages of increased complexity. Each stage creates new challenges that can only be solved by more sophisticated approaches or risk regression, arrested development, and, ultimately, extinction. There are traditional, modern, and emerging postmodern worldviews.
- **Channeling is part of your divine heritage.** For over 3,000 years people have spoken in inspired states and delivered useful information geared toward cultural needs. The Seth material, channeled by Jane Roberts, explores

information of high integrity, depth, and practical application.

▪ **Develop your abilities to their fullest** through the daily cultivation of curiosity, constructive skepticism, awe, loving kindness, mindfulness, grace, compassion, spontaneity, creativity, humor, and deep appreciation for the endless wonders of All That Is.

▪ **You create your own reality** through your thoughts, beliefs, emotions, impulses, expectations, moral intuition, dreams, physical-mental-inner senses, behavior, and the "God of You." Learn to take full responsibility for everything in your life because nothing ever "happens to you" that you don't create. In this light, there are never any real victims, just players on the stage of life.

As such, your life is a miracle—the Greatest Story *Never* Told—because you have yet to finish creating it! You stand on the cusp a new worldview. Dig your heels in and bask in the true power of your spontaneous being. Anything is possible. Learn to take advantage of the infinite possibilities in every moment and live your life fully. Take action, however you define it. Do your part to make the world a better place for yourself and others to share, and the rest will surely follow.

KEY IDEAS: Each moment of each day you have a choice to create the reality your heart desires, the kind of world you wish to live in, and the kind of ideals you wish to practice.

Epilogue

Where Do I Go From Here?

While it's ultimately up to you, the most important things to take away from this book are Seth's "map of consciousness" and introductory exercises. You could read forever about other dimensions, altered states and so on, but at some point you must verify what is and isn't true for yourself. Therefore, you will want the most accurate map available as you explore the nature of your consciousness and develop your own abilities. In this light, use upon the following three *types* of exercises as a foundation:

1. **Psy-time** (gateway to meditative/altered states, out-of-body projections, etc.)
2. **Belief work** (gateway to your subconscious self, hidden preferences and shadow elements)
3. **Dream work** (gateway to your dreaming self and entity)

Always remember the basic rule of reality creation—*you get what you concentrate upon*—so you'll concentrate upon these core practices as you go forward. Though they are called out separately to emphasize their importance, they work together in complementary fashion. So it's important to make all three daily habits, just like breakfast, lunch, and dinner.

How Long Will It Take to Benefit From Practicing the Seth Material?

Some people progress through the material and practices very quickly, while others take more time. Since there may be a lot of new information to assimilate, be kind to yourself and set your expectations appropriately. Keep it fun, and remember Seth's sense of humor and irreverence. He was fond of saying, "If it isn't fun [then] stop doing it!"[161] The journey of self-realization, while challenging at times, is really as simple or difficult as you choose to make it. It takes time to get used to the idea that you are your own ultimate authority and co-creator with All That Is!

In this light, the single most important thing, especially if you are new to these ideas, is to *gradually* establish a daily regimen within the above areas until they become automatic. This is where most people fall short—they give the practices a half-hearted try, get little or no results, and give up after only a few weeks or months. Remember, this is not a quick-fix system! It takes time to develop your inner abilities and widen your awareness, so *be persistent and patient*. Keep an open heart and mind, playfully experiment, tailor things to suit your own needs and circumstances, and the rest will follow.

Should I Do This Alone or Within a Group?

You can be a "lone wolf" and explore Seth's concepts in isolated fashion, or you may prefer to share your experiences within a group to get feedback and insights from those who have already tested the waters. There are a variety of local and Internet groups now available, and many people who volunteer their time who have decades of experience and insight to share.

Additionally, while it is normal to pursue long periods of concentrated effort, say several months at a time, it is also recommended that you take a break and allow yourself to assimilate your experiences. You will intuitively know when it's time to stop exploring a particular direction, because you will either get bored, or hit a dead end when you find yourself running on a hamster wheel (just get off!).

In the long run, trust that you will *always* discover what works best for you.

What is the Best Order in Which to Read the Seth Books?

There is no single best way. Some people read the books in order (rational approach), and some read randomly based on their intuition (magical approach). It can be fun to ask your inner self to magically select some beneficial material, and then randomly open a Seth book and begin to read. For those who like more order, at least while you're beginning, here's one way to try:

1. *The Seth Material* (Jane Roberts's summation of the first 510 sessions, a great introduction to many of Seth's core ideas. Easier to read than Seth books.)
2. *Seth Speaks* (Begins with session 511, provides excellent practices.)
3. *The Nature of Personal Reality* (Provides excellent practices.)
4. *The Education of Oversoul Seven* (A playful fictional story that illustrates many of Seth's core ideas; an easy read.)

And Finally...

Seth said that we are each on personal journeys, but we will always share the road with others. At the end of the day we each must face up to the abilities of consciousness, and do our best to develop our natural gifts and share them with others. You can do that this life, or you can do it in another one, so why not rise to the challenge *now*?

The Seth Material is designed to naturally transform your life and help you face your challenges with courage, grace, and compassion in order to realize your deepest desires. It provides a radically different view of the nature of reality, the origins of our multiverse, your true multidimensional nature, and most importantly, it explains *how* your life has a unique purpose and meaning.

Never forget: you are here for a reason! *You* chose to be born in this time, to your particular family, and to explore your current challenges (individually and collectively). As such, you also *have the power to change any element of your experience that isn't in alignment with your purpose and intent*. Many Seth readers are happy to just know that, but are naturally drawn to take things even further. As you explore the Seth books more deeply, you will master the nuances of *how* to consistently apply the mechanics of reality creation to any situation.

Since the Seth Material as a whole has only been available less than decade, because much of the early and deleted material was published well after Jane passed away in 1984, we have just begun to unpack its deeper secrets and probe the deeper areas of consciousness that await our discovery in any collective sense. Our evolutionary journey continues and the new worldview struggles to go global. Make whatever contribution suits your purpose and intent. As always, be kind to yourself and others, and enjoy the ride!

Endnotes

Introduction

[1] Jane Roberts, *Seth Speaks*, Amber-Allen, San Rafael, CA, 1994, p. 2.

[2] Philosopher Godfrey Leibniz (1646-1716) coined the term "Philosophia Perennis." Aldous Huxley made it famous in *The Perennial Philosophy* (1945), and religious scholar Huston Smith showed its continued relevance to modern and postmodern worldviews in *Forgotten Truth* (1992).

[3] Aldous Huxley, *The Perennial Philosophy*, Harper & Row, New York, NY, 1945, p. vii.

[4] Norman Friedman, Personal correspondence, May 1999.

[5] Arthur Hastings, Charles Tart, editor, *Body, Mind, and Spirit: Exploring the Parapsychology of Spirituality*, Chapter 12, Channeling and Spiritual Teachings, Hampton Roads, Charlottesville, VA, 1997, p. 199.

[6] Jon Klimo, *Channeling: Investigations on Receiving Information from Paranormal Sources*, Preface, North Atlantic Books, Berkeley, CA, 1998, p. 103.

[7] Klimo, Ibid, 1998, p. 2.

[8] Michael Brown, *The Channeling Zone: American Spirituality in an Anxious Age*, Harvard University Press, Cambridge, MA, 1997, p. viii.

[9] Arthur Hastings, *With the Tongues of Men and Angels: A Study of Channeling*, Holt, Rinehart, and Winston, Orlando, FL, 1991, p. 4.

[10] Hastings, Ibid, 1991, p. 78.

[11] For more information, see Paul Helfrich, *The Channeling Phenomenon: A Multimethodological Assessment*, Journal of Integral Theory and Practice, 4(3), Integral Institute, Boulder, CO, 2009, pp. 141-161.

[12] For more information, see Jane Roberts, *The "Unknown" Reality, Vol. 2*, 1996, p. 338.

[13] For more information, see Jane Roberts, *The Early Sessions: Book 9 of The Seth Material*, New Awareness Network, Manhasset, NY, 2002, pp. 187, 443.

[14] Jane Roberts, *The Early Sessions: Book 3 of The Seth Material*, New Awareness Network, Manhasset, NY, 1997, p. 172.

[15] For more information, see Jon Klimo, *Channeling: Investigations on Receiving Information from Paranormal Sources* (1998). It is the current standard of academic research on dozens of channelers since the time of Jane Roberts.

[16] For more information, see Paul Helfrich, *A Seth, Elias Comparative Overview*, Wildfire Media, Castaic, CA, 2000.

[17] Gebser used the terms *archaic, magic, mythic, mental,* and *integral* to describe his general stage-structures of cultural evolution (worldviews) in *The Ever-Present Origin* (1985). For simplicity's sake, we will use the terms *traditional, modern,* and *postmodern* throughout. Therefore, *traditional* represents the <u>sum</u> of *archaic, magic,* and *mythic* structures, *modern* represents *mental,* and *postmodern* represents *integral.*

[18] Stephen R. Covey, *The 8ᵗʰ Habit: From Effectiveness to Greatness*, Free Press, Simon & Schuster, New York, NY, 2004, p. 103.

[19] For more information, see Jane Roberts, *The Early Sessions: Book 2 of The Seth Material*, New Awareness Network, Manhasset, NY, 1997, p. 314.

Part 1: Discover Your True Self

Chapter 1: You Are More Than Your Body!

[20] For more information, see Jane Roberts, *The Nature of Personal Reality*, Amber-Allen, San Rafael, CA, 1994, pp. 20-21.

[21] For more information, see Ken Wilber, *The Eye of Spirit: An Integral Vision for a World Gone Slightly Mad*, Shambhala, Boston, MA, 1997.

[22] For more information, see Jane Roberts, *The Seth Material*, New Awareness Network, Manhasset, NY, 2001, pp. 280-281.

[23] Jane Roberts, *Psychic Politics*, Moment Point Press, Portsmouth, NH, 2000, p. 290.

[24] For more information, see Jane Roberts, *The "Unknown" Reality, Vol. 2*, Amber-Allen, San Rafael, CA, 1996, pp. 542-608.

Chapter 2: You Create Your Own Reality

[25] Jane's "idea constructions" weren't a new concept, but rather a contemporary translation of the perennial wisdom into a 1960s American cultural setting. For example, Idealist philosophers in the West from Plato (ca. 427-347 BCE) to Plotinus (ca. 204-270 CE) to Hegel (1770-1831), Schopenhauer (1788-1860), and others saw the physical world as a construction by a *hidden source domain*. Plato's cave is a famous metaphor that compares the limits of human perception to viewing shadows on a wall, while the "Source Light" exists "outside" the cave.

[26] For more information, see *Seth, Dreams, and Projections of Consciousness*, New Awareness Network, Manhasset, NY, 1998, pp. 44-47. Though Jane referred to this manuscript in various early books, an abridged version was published posthumously.

[27] For more information, see Jane Roberts, *The Early Sessions: Book 2 of the Seth Material*, New Awareness Network, Manhasset, NY, 1997, pp. 192-193.

[28] Rob Butts compared Seth's CUs to the principles in quantum theory. Quantum fields are the basic "units" used by modern physicists to describe all particles and waves in the physical world.

[29] For more information, see Jane Roberts, *Seth Speaks*, Amber-Allen, San Rafael, CA, 1994, pp. 63-68.

[30] For more details on the physics of Seth, see Norman Friedman's *Bridging Science and Spirit: Common Elements in David Bohm's Physics, The Perennial Philosophy and Seth*, Woodbridge Group, Eugene, OR, 1990.

[31] A gestalt is whole that is greater than the sum of its component parts. That is, it can never be reduced to those component parts. *Dictionary.com Unabridged (v 1.1)*, Retrieved February 08, 2009 from http://dictionary.reference.com/browse/gestalt.

[32] For more information, see Bruce Lipton's *The Biology of Belief: Unleashing the Power of Consciousness, Matter and Miracles*, Hay House, Carlsbad, CA, 2008.

[33] There are many books on belief work that have been inspired by Seth. Lynda Dahl has authored: *Ten Thousand Whispers* (1995), *Beyond the Winning Streak* (1993), *Wizards of Consciousness* (1997), and *The Book of Fallacies* (2001). Additionally, three workbooks by Nancy Ashley are highly recommended: *Create Your Own Reality* (1984); *Create Your Own Happiness* (1988); *Create Your Own Dreams* (1990). They were published by Prentice Hall, New York, NY. Though out of print, they can be found at used books stores and online.

[34] For more information, see Jane Roberts, *The Nature of Personal Reality*, Amber-Allen, San Rafael, CA, 1994, pp. 306-310.

[35] Jane Roberts, *The Nature of Personal Reality*, Amber-Allen, San Rafael, CA, 1994, p. 292.

[36] For more information, see Jane Roberts, *The Early Sessions: Book 4 of the Seth Material*, New Awareness Network, Manhasset, NY, 1998, pp. 8-16.

[37] For more information, see Jane Roberts, *The Nature of Personal Reality*, Amber-Allen, San Rafael, CA, 1994, pp. 292-306.

[38] Susan M. Watkins, *Conversations With Seth: The Story of Jane Roberts's ESP Class*, Moment Point Press, Portsmouth, NH, 1999, p. 89.

[39] For more information, see Roberts, Ibid, 1994, pp. 49-53.

Chapter 3: Lover, Gender, and Sex

[40] For more information, see Jane Roberts, *The Early Sessions: Book 2 of the Seth Material*, New Awareness Network, Manhasset, New York, 1997, pp. 14, 253, *Dreams, "Evolution," and Value Fulfillment, Vol. 1*, Amber-Allen, San Rafael, CA, 1997, p. 138, and *The Individual and the Nature of Mass Events*, Amber-Allen, San Rafael, CA, 1995, p. 259.

[41] For more information, see Jane Roberts, *The "Unknown" Reality, Vol. 2*, Amber-Allen, San Rafael, CA, 1996, p. 342.

[42] For more information, see Jane Roberts, *The Nature of the Psyche*, Amber-Allen, San Rafael, CA, 1995, p. 80.

[43] *Wikipedia: Innate Bisexuality*, Retrieved February 5, 2009, from http://en.wikipedia.org/wiki/Innate_bisexuality.

[44] For more information, see Jane Roberts, *Seth Speaks*, Amber-Allen, San Rafael, CA, 1994, pp.189-190.

[45] By 1973, homosexuality was no longer considered pathology by the American Psychiatric Association, though there were old school holdouts. It wasn't until 1994, when the *Diagnostic and Statistical Manual of Mental Disorders-IV* was published that homosexual preference was fully accepted. The scientific debate continues about whether heterosexual, gay, and lesbian behaviors result from cultural influences, biology (genes and DNA), or both.

[46] For more information, see Jane Roberts, *The Nature of the Psyche*, Amber-Allen, San Rafael, CA, 1995, p. 62.

[47] For more information, see Jane Roberts, *The Nature of Personal Reality*, Amber-Allen, San Rafael, CA, 1994, pp. 198-205.

[47] Jane Roberts, *The Nature of Personal Reality*, Amber-Allen, San Rafael, CA, 1994, p. 410.

[47] From 1 Corinthians 13:4-8.

Chapter 4: The Unlimited Power of Dreams

[48] Jane Roberts, *The Nature of Personal Reality*, Amber-Allen, San Rafael, CA, 1994, p. 410.

[49] From 1 Corinthians 13:4-8.

[50] For more information, see Jane Roberts, *Seth, Dreams, and Projections of Consciousness*, New Awareness Network, Manhasset, NY, 1998, pp. 367-378.

[51] For more information, see Jane Roberts, *Seth Speaks*, Amber-Allen, San Rafael, CA, 1994, pp. 97-104.

[52] For more information, see Susan M. Watkins, *Conversations With Seth: The Story of Jane Roberts's ESP Class*, Moment Point Press, Portsmouth, NH, 1999, p. 299.

[53] There are many books on this phenomenon. Though only recently rediscovered in the West, lucid dreams and projections have been known to Eastern religious traditions dating back sixteen thousand years to the Tibetan Bön tradition.

[54] For more information, see Jane Roberts, *Seth, Dreams, and Projections of Consciousness*, New Awareness Network, Manhasset, NY, 1998, pp. 315-329.

[55] For more information, see Jane Roberts, *The Early Sessions: Book 6 of The Seth Material*, New Awareness Network, Manhasset, NY, 1999, p. 209.

[56] For a great beginner's guide by one of Jane's students, see Rick Stack's *Out-of-Body Adventures: 30 Days to the Most Exciting Experience of Your Life*, Contemporary Books, Chicago, IL, 1988.

Chapter 5: Birth, Death, & Reincarnation

[57] For more information, see Jane Roberts, *The Early Sessions, Book 1 of The Seth Material*, New Awareness Network, Manhasset, NY, 1997, p. 163.

[58] For more information, see Roberts, *Seth Speaks*, Amber-Allen, San Rafael, CA, 1994, pp. 423-424.

[59] Roberts, Ibid, 1994, pp. 125-126.

[60] For more information, see *Chapter 27: "The Time is Now," Lydia says Goodbye and Hello, and Seven Remembers*.

[61] For more information, see Jane Roberts, *Seth Speaks*, Amber-Allen, San Rafael, CA, 1994, p. 307.

[62] For more information, see Jane Roberts, *The Seth Material*, New Awareness Network, Manhasset, NY, 2001, p. 253.

[63] For more information, see Jane Roberts, *Dreams, "Evolution," and Value Fulfillment, Vol. 2*, Amber-Allen, San Rafael, CA, 1997, Chapter 12.

[64] This is an updated translation of a famous "koan" by the Indian philosopher Shankara (788-820 CE).

Part 2: Discover Your Place in the World

Chapter 6: "Before the Beginning"

[65] Jane Roberts, *Dreams, "Evolution," and Value Fulfillment, Vol.1*, Amber-Allen, San Rafael, CA, 1997, p. 112.

[66] Seth never used the term "dreamtime." It comes from the Australian Aboriginal Creation Myth, which bears striking similarities with Seth's Creation Myth. It is used here because of its clarity to express the power and function of the dreaming selves who created our physical universe "before the beginning."

[67] For more information, see Jane Roberts, Ibid, 1997, p. 222.

[68] Jane Roberts, *The Individual and the Nature of Mass Events*, Amber-Allen, San Rafael, CA, 1995, p. 112.

[69] Jane Roberts, *Dreams, "Evolution," and Value Fulfillment, Vol. 1*, Amber-Allen, San Rafael, CA, 1997, p. 219.

[70] For more information, Seth's creation myth was presented in Chapters 1-5 of *Dreams, "Evolution," and Value Fulfillment, Vol. 1* (1997).

[71] Cut dialogue from Fit the Fifth, Douglas Adams, *The Original Hitchhiker Radio Scripts*, edited by Geoffrey Perkins, Harmony Books, New York, NY.

Chapter 7: Frameworks of Consciousness

[72] Seth introduced Frameworks 1 and 2 in *The Individual and the Nature of Mass Events* (1995). Though he provided a rich outline of Framework 2, very little material was given on Frameworks 3 and 4. For more information on Frameworks 3 and 4, see Jane Roberts, *The God of Jane*, Moment Point Press, Portsmouth, NH, 2000, p. 129, and Jane Roberts, *The Personal Sessions, Book Four of the Deleted Seth Material*, New Awareness Network, Manhasset, NY, 2003, pp. 36-48.

[73] See Brent Marchant's *Get the Picture: Conscious Creation Goes to the Movies*, Moment Point Press, Portsmouth, NH, 2007 for an excellent introduction to how Seth's ideas are expressed in films. He shows how various storylines and characters reflect familiar life challenges and self-generated obstacles, and how they may be overcome as we learn to apply these ideas to our everyday lives.

[74] For more information, Jane Roberts, *The Individual and the Nature of Mass Events*, Amber-Allen, San Rafael, CA, 1995, p. 115.

[75] For more information, see Jane Roberts, *The Individual and the Nature of Mass Events*, Amber-Allen, San Rafael, CA, 1995, pp. 77-78.

[76] For more information, see Roberts, Ibid, 1997, pp. 372-458.

[77] Jane Roberts, *Seth Speaks*, Amber-Allen, San Rafael, CA, 1994, p. 271.

[78] Dream research remains in its infancy in the West. To date, researchers have mapped five main brain states, though there may be others that current equipment cannot yet detect:

1. **Beta** ~ 14-100 cycles per second, normal alert waking state. Higher range associated with anxiety, dis-ease, fight or flight conditions.
    » **Gamma**—a subset of Beta, 40 cycles per second, but range from 24 to 70 cycles per second. Associated with an alert waking state, these have been found in meditative and lucid dreaming (REM) states. (These are included as a subset because they are associated with a sense of clarity

and wakefulness though you may be in a sleep, meditative, or trance state.)

2. **Alpha** ~ 8-13.9 cycles per second, just below the normal state of alertness. Associated with light relaxation, daydreaming, and self-reflection. A non-drowsy, yet relaxed, tranquil state of inward awareness that occurs before sleep. Beginning access to subconscious mind.

3. **Theta** ~ 4-7.9 cycles per second, deep relaxation, reverie, lucid dreaming, mental imagery, meditation, increased memory and focus, deep-rooted memories, and inspiration. Characterized mainly by light sleep, rapid eye movement (REM) dreams, and hallucinations. Hypnogogic imagery, deep meditation, access to subconscious mind.

4. **Delta** ~ .1-3.9 cycles per second, the deepest, most rejuvenating stage of dreamless, non-REM sleep and deep meditation. It also produces stress reduction, which can promote healing of the body. Human growth hormones released and loss of body awareness.

[79] Though Seth doesn't mention this directly, it is where "past life regressions" access reincarnational information.

[80] For more information, see Jane Roberts, *Seth Speaks*, Amber-Allen, San Rafael, CA, 1994, pp. 266-291, and Susan M. Watkins, *Conversations With Seth: The Story of Jane Roberts's ESP Class*, Moment Point Press, Portsmouth, NH, 1999, pp. 62-63, 216-218.

[81] For more information, see Watkins, Ibid, 1999, pp. 428-429.

Chapter 8: The Christ Drama

[82] For more information, see Jane Roberts, *Seth Speaks*, Amber-Allen, San Rafael, CA, 1994, pp. 237-247.

[83] For more information, see Roberts, Ibid, 1994, pp. 323-347, 366-369, 406-408.

[84] *Stanford Encyclopedia of Philosophy*, Retrieved March 18, 2009 from http://plato.stanford.edu/entries/prophecy/.

Chapter 9: Lost Civilizations, A Dream City, & UFOs, Oh My!

[85] The Stone Age consisted of Paleolithic, Mesolithic and Neolithic periods and began around 2.5 million BCE.

[86] According to Greek philosopher Plato (428-328 BCE), the mythic island of Atlantis was a naval power that ruled parts of Western Europe and Africa around 9600 BCE, and sank into the ocean after a cataclysm.

[87] For more information, see Jane Roberts, *Seth Speaks*, Amber-Allen, San Rafael, CA, 1994, pp. 212-236.

[88] For more information, see Jane Roberts, *The "Unknown" Reality, Vol. 2*, Amber-Allen, San Rafael, CA, 1996, pp. 635-644.

[89] For more information, see Susan M. Watkins, *Conversations With Seth: The Story of Jane Roberts's ESP Class*, Moment Point Press, Portsmouth, NH, 1999, pp. 197-201.

[90] For state of the art information on lucid and group dreaming that foreshadow Seth's dream-art sciences, see Robert Waggoner's book *Lucid Dreaming: Gateway to the Inner Self*, Moment Point Press, Walpole, NH, 2008. Also, there is excellent work being done by Ken Wilber's Integral Institute that acknowledges the basic principles of

integrating consciousness and altered states to explore valid sciences through the use of physical, mental, *and* inner senses.

[91] For more information, see Jane Roberts, *The "Unknown" Reality, Vol. 1*, Amber-Allen, San Rafael, CA, 1996, pp. 181-214.

[92] For more information, see Jane Roberts, *The Early Sessions, Book 2 of the Seth Material*, New Awareness Network, Manhasset, NY, 1997, p. 22, Jane Roberts, *The Early Sessions, Book 1 of the Seth Material*, New Awareness Network, Manhasset, NY, 1997, pp. 99-100.

Also, note that Seth used the term "plane" in his early material. Later he used the terms "reality" and "Frameworks of consciousness" as well.

[93] For more information, see Jane Roberts, *The Personal Sessions, Book Two of the Deleted Seth Material*, New Awareness Network, Manhasset, NY, 2003, pp. 52-66.

Chapter 10: Our Animal Heritage

[94] For purposes of introduction, Seth's definition of "animals" is very broad. Often he means mammals, but occasionally includes non-mammals.

[95] For more information, see Jane Roberts, *The Early Sessions: Book 9 of the Seth Material*, New Awareness Network, Manhasset, NY, 2002, p. 20.

[96] For more information, see Jane Roberts, *The Nature of Personal Reality*, Amber-Allen, San Rafael, CA, 1994, pp. 229-237.

[97] For more information, see Jane Roberts, *Dialogues of the Soul and Mortal Self in Time*, Prentice Hall, Englewood Cliffs, NJ, 1975, pp. 76-91.

[98] For more information, see Jane Roberts, *The Nature of Personal Reality*, Amber-Allen, San Rafael, CA, 1994, p. 244.

[99] For more information, Jane Roberts, *Dreams, "Evolution," and Value Fulfillment, Vol. 1*, Amber-Allen, San Rafael, CA, 1997, pp. 103-106.

[100] For more information, see Jane Roberts, *The "Unknown" Reality, Vol. 1*, Amber-Allen, San Rafael, CA, 1996, p. 39.

[101] James M. Robinson, editor, Translated by Thomas O. Lamdin, *The Nag Hammadi Library, The Gospel of St. Thomas*, Harper & Row, New York, NY, 1988, p.135.

[102] Seth spoke his final words in 1984, and since then great strides have been made in the emerging science of Integral Ecology. While it doesn't yet utilize the kinds of Dream-Art Sciences that Seth foreshadowed, it *does* acknowledge animal consciousness and interiority that goes "all the way down" to QFs. For more information, see Sean Esbjorn-Hargens and Michael Zimmerman's *Integral Ecology: Uniting Multiple Perspectives of the Natural World*, Integral Books/Shambhala, Boston, MA, 2009.

[103] For more information, see Jane Roberts, *The "Unknown" Reality, Vol. 1*, Amber-Allen, San Rafael, CA, 1996, p. 98, and Jane Roberts, *The "Unknown" Reality, Vol. 2*, Amber-Allen, San Rafael, CA, 1996, pp. 678-679.

[104] For more information, see Jane Roberts, *The "Unknown" Reality, Vol. 1*, Amber-Allen, San Rafael, CA, 1996, p. 110.

[105] For more information, see Jane Roberts, *The Way Toward Health*, Amber-Allen, San Rafael, CA, 1997, pp. 22-24.

Part 3: Discover How We Can Live in Harmony

Chapter 11: Sethics

[106] For more information, see Jane Roberts, *The Individual and the Nature of Mass Events*, Amber-Allen, San Rafael, CA, 1995, p. 261.

[107] For more information, see Jane Roberts, *Seth Speaks*, Amber-Allen, San Rafael, CA, p. 319. Though Seth said he would give them later, he never did. However, he explains how the law value fulfillment works in *Dreams, "Evolution," and Value fulfillment, Vol. 1 & Vol. 2* (1986).

[108] For more information, see Jane Roberts, *The Early Sessions: Book 2 of The Seth Material*, New Awareness Network, Manhasset, NY, 1997, pp 14-15, 71-77, 133-135.

[109] For more information, see Jane Roberts, *Dreams, "Evolution," and Value Fulfillment, Vol. 1*, Amber-Allen, San Rafael, CA, 1997, p. 170.

[110] For more information, see Jane Roberts, *The Early Sessions: Book 2 of The Seth Material*, New Awareness Network, Manhasset, NY, 1997, p 14.

[111] "Sethics" was coined by J. C. Mackin on the Sethnet e-mail list circa 1999. Though he didn't articulate a moral theory based on the Seth Material, he asked many excellent questions that no one could fully answer. The name has since stuck, and has provoked many discussions.

[112] For more information, see *Sex, Ecology, Spirituality: The Spirit of Evolution*, Shambhala, Boston, MA, 1995, pp. 640n-643n.

[113] For more information, see Jane Roberts, *The Nature of Personal Reality*, Amber-Allen Publishing, San Rafael, CA, 1994, pp. 137-145.

[114] For more information, see Roberts, Ibid, 1994, pp. 149-153.

[115] For more information, see Roberts, Ibid, 1994, pp. 154-157.

[116] For more information, see Jane Roberts, *The Early Sessions: Book 8 of the Seth Material*, New Awareness Network, Manhasset, NY, 2000, pp. 202-203.

[117] Jane Roberts, *The Nature of Personal Reality*, Amber-Allen Publishing, San Rafael, CA, 1994, p. 143.

Chapter 12: Why Do Bad Things "Happen to" Good People?

[118] For more information, see Roberts, Ibid, 1994, pp. 211-224.

[119] For more information, see Roberts, Ibid, 1994, pp. 367-374.

[120] For more information, see Roberts, Ibid, 1994, pp. 347-366.

[121] Jane Roberts, *The Way Toward Health*, Amber-Allen, San Rafael, CA, 1997, pp. 258-270.

[122] For more information, see Roberts, Ibid, 1997, pp. 275-276.

[123] For more information, see Jane Roberts, *Seth Speaks*, Amber-Allen, San Rafael, CA, 1994, p. 354.

[124] For more information, see Jane Roberts, *The Afterdeath Journal of an American Philosopher: The World View of William James*, Prentice Hall, Englewood Cliffs, NJ, 1978, p. 21.

Chapter 13: The Practicing Idealist

[125] Centers for Disease Control and Prevention (2009), Retrieved May 20, 2009 from http://www.cdc.gov/flu/about/qa/disease.htm.

[126] *The Project Gutenberg EBook of Leviathan*, by Thomas Hobbes, Retrieved May 20, 2009 from http://www.gutenberg.org/dirs/etext02/lvthn10.txt.

[127] Jane Roberts, *The Nature of Personal Reality*, Amber-Allen, San Rafael, CA, 1994, pp. 31-32.

[128] For more information, see Jane Roberts, *The Personal Sessions, Book Three of the Deleted Seth Material*, New Awareness Network, Manhasset, NY, 2004, p. 154.

[129] For more information, see Jane Roberts, *The Nature of Personal Reality*, Amber-Allen, San Rafael, CA, 1994, pp. 307-314, and Susan M. Watkins, *Conversations With Seth: The Story of Jane Roberts's ESP Class*, Moment Point Press, Portsmouth, NH, 1999, pp. 234-236.

[130] Freedomhouse, Retrieved May 22, 2009 from http://www.freedomhouse.org/template.cfm?page=368&year=2007.

[131] Jane Roberts, *The Individual and the Nature of Mass Events*, Amber-Allen, San Rafael, CA, 1995, p. 217.

[132] For more information, see Susan M. Watkins, *Conversations With Seth: The Story of Jane Roberts's ESP Class*, Moment Point Press, Portsmouth, NH, 1999, p. 227.

[133] Jane Roberts, *The Individual and the Nature of Mass Events*, Amber-Allen, San Rafael, CA, 1995, p. 303.

[134] For more information, see Roberts, Ibid, 1995, pp. 177-190.

[135] For more information, see Roberts, Ibid, 1995, pp. 192-206.

[136] For more information, see Roberts, Ibid, 1995, pp. 219-223.

[137] For more information, see Jane Roberts, *Dreams, "Evolution," and Value Fulfillment, Vol. 2*, Amber-Allen, San Rafael, CA, 1997, p. 360.

[138] For more information, see Jane Roberts, *The Individual and the Nature of Mass Events*, Amber-Allen, San Rafael, CA, 1995, pp. 296-297.

[139] For more information, see Roberts, Ibid, 1995, pp. 239-252.

[140] For more information, see Roberts, Ibid, 1995, p. 303.

Chapter 14: The Birth of Aspect Psychology and a New World-view

[141] For more information, see Jane Roberts, *Adventures in Consciousness*, SethNet Publishing, Eugene, OR, 1997, p. 210.

[142] For more information, see Jane Roberts, *The "Unknown" Reality, Vol. 2*, Amber-Allen, San Rafael, CA, 1996, pp. 406-408.

[143] For more information, see Roberts, Ibid, 1996, pp. 418-423.

[144] For more information, see Jane Roberts, *The Afterdeath Journal of an American Philosopher: The World View of William James*, Prentice Hall, Englewood Cliffs, NJ, 1978, pp. 58-67.

[145] New Advent, Retrieved May 31, 2009 from http://www.newadvent.org/library/docs_jp02tc.htm.

[146] Jane Roberts, *Psychic Politics*, Moment Point Press, Portsmouth, NH, 2000, pp. 6-7.

[147] For more information, see Roberts, Ibid, 2000, pp. 211-212, 220-221.

[148] Jane Roberts, *The God of Jane*, Moment Point Press, Portsmouth, NH, 2000, p. xi.

[149] Roberts, Ibid, 2000, p. 62.

[150] For more information, see Roberts, Ibid, 2000, pp. 53-66.

[151] For more information, see Roberts, Ibid, 2000, pp. 229-240.

[152] Susan M. Watkins, *Speaking of Jane Roberts*, Moment Point Press, Portsmouth, NH, 2001, p. 178.

[153] Watkins, Ibid, 2001, p. 167.

Chapter 15: The Secret Revealed

[154] For more information, see Jane Roberts, *The Magical Approach*, Amber-Allen, New World Library, San Rafael, CA, 1995, pp. 5-119.

[155] Jane Roberts, *The Way Toward Health*, Amber-Allen, San Rafael, CA, 1997, p. 85.

[156] Lotus Zen Temple, Retrieved June 15, 2009 from http://www.lotustemple.us/.

[157] This chart is based upon Huston Smith's *Forgotten Truth: The Common Vision of the World's Religions*, HarperCollins, New York, NY, 1992, and Ken Wilber, *A Theory of Everything: An Integral Vision for Business, Politics, Science, and Spirituality*, Shambhala, Boston, MA, 2000, p. 68.

[158] Jane Roberts, *The Early Sessions: Book 4 of The Seth Material*, New Awareness Network, Manhasset, NY, 1998, p. 331.

[159] Jane Roberts, *The Individual and the Nature of Mass Events*, Amber-Allen, San Rafael, CA, 1995, p. ix.

[160] Mick Jagger and Keith Richards, *You Can't Always Get What You Want*, Decca Records/ABKCO Records, London, 1969.

[161] Susan M. Watkins, *Conversations With Seth: The Story of Jane Roberts's ESP Class*, Moment Point Press, Portsmouth, NH, 1999, p. 372.

Glossary of Terms & Concepts

2075—The approximate date mentioned by Seth in which a religious reformation is to occur based upon the return of what he describes as "the Christ entity." This is one of the few predictions in the Seth Material. (*See also Christ Drama*)

Akashic Records—see Alpha States, Worldviews.

All That Is—Seth's term for what is traditionally referred to as God.

Alpha States—A spectrum of altered states used to consciously access "hidden," subconscious information.

Altered States—The channeling phenomenon that produced the Seth books is part of a larger spectrum of altered states that connect us with our own inner knowing—peak experiences, meditation, lucid dreaming, out-of-body projections, shamanic drug-induced, dreaming, deep sleep, and so on. These states have been consistently experienced throughout recorded history. You can learn to use the Seth Material to access these states, as shaman, yogis, and spiritual adepts have done for thousands of years.

American Vision—Jane Roberts's vision of a future in which no single person, group, family, corporation, government, religion, or ideology holds exclusive rights to The Truth or The Way. It's a decentralized, democratic vision driven by an innate moral intuition that promotes the individual, unalienable right to define Truth for ourselves, based upon our direct, individual connection to the "God of You" and All That Is.

Apparition—A type of secondary construction used to explain related phenomena like out-of-body projections, poltergeists, and so on. (*See also Constructions*)

Artificial Guilt—A rigid, dogmatic, and inflexible sense of false contrition based on a set of "thou shalts" that leads to all sorts of imbalances, dysfunctional behaviors, pathologies, and dis-eases. It is not to be confused with our innate, healthy sense of violation produced by natural guilt. (*See also Natural Guilt*)

Aspect Psychology—Invented by Jane Roberts to synthesize Seth's ideas on multidimensional identity (Aspect Selves). Her theory helps to explain how the waking self (outer ego) may interact with a variety of phenomena like Seth, automatic writing, projections of consciousness, worldviews, and more. It also provides a new way to model mental health in relation to altered states and psychological dis-eases that may occur over the course of human development.

Aspects—Distinct selves that can be accessed through altered states. They include other lifetimes, probable selves, and entities like Seth and Seth II.

Atlantis—A probable past, present, *and* future city within Framework 2. It functions as a future attractor—an impetus for development—in Framework 1 to create a mythical, precognitive yearning for the kind of civilization we hope ours to be. It mixes in a blend of elements from various civilizations in our past. (*See also Lumania, Framework 2*)

"Before the Beginning"—A paradoxical metaphor used in Seth's creation myth to show that there is no absolute beginning or end to our universe, and that Creation occurs in every instant. Therefore, you have always existed in some form, even before the Big Bang. (*See also Families of Consciousness, Sleepwalkers*)

Belief Systems—The thousands of beliefs that cluster around your conscious mind like planets around the sun. Identifying and addressing them will help you make successful changes in your life. Types of beliefs include core, limiting, invisible, subsidiary/corollary, directional, conflicting, joint, body, negative, active/passive, and private. (*See also Conscious Mind*)

Bisexuality—Your entity is innately bisexual: there is a "male" within each female and a "female" within every male.

Therefore, gender is not hardwired toward an exclusive sexual preference (gay, lesbian, or heterosexual). Coming to terms with the innate male and female qualities within you, will help you know your deepest self.

Blueprints for Reality—These define the laws in Framework 1 (like gravity, the speed of light, strong and weak nuclear forces) that promote the most favorable structures capable for value fulfillment. They are dynamic, and exist at every level: physical, biological, psychological, and spiritual. They originate in Framework 2. (*See also Frameworks of Consciousness, Root Assumptions*)

Bridge Personality—The temporary psychological "bridge" that allowed Seth to come through when Jane engaged a dissociative state. Seth's native identity could never be fully expressed in any single session because this bridge personality was a hybrid—neither purely Jane nor purely Seth.

Camouflage—The physical universe (Framework 1) is created in each moment by a nonphysical source reality (Framework 2) that consists of the idea constructions adopted by your entity in order to experience physical reality. (*See also Constructions*)

Channeling—A dissociative, altered state in which an Aspect Self (Seth, nonphysical person, probable self) communicates through a living person. This phenomenon has been documented for over 3,000 years and has occurred in a variety of social roles including fortune-tellers, oracles, seers, soothsayers, savants, visionaries, priests, gurus, prophets, saints, mystics, light workers, initiates, teachers, adepts, or masters. Jane Roberts and Rob Butts found the term misleading, but it has become part of the mainstream vocabulary.

Christ Drama—The Christ drama involved three main personalities—John the Baptist, Jesus Christ, and St. Paul—who were physically manifest Aspects of the Christ entity. Because Paul's role in creating the Church was left unfulfilled, he is due to return to lead a religious reformation that will decentralize the Church's authority and provide methods for the common person to directly communicate with their own entity. This is to be accomplished by approximately 2075.

Clock Time/Assembly-line Time—An artificial, manmade creation that is the result of the outer ego's fear that it is at the mercy of the elements, and needs tools to better predict and control its environment. This has forced the species into an array of artificial habits that are not in sync with the natural rhythms of the planet and environment. Clock time provides a false sense of stability where none is really needed, since time is inherently flexible. (*See also Magical Approach, Natural Time*)

Codicils—Eleven addendums that outline alternate hypotheses for private and public experience that would create new kinds of sciences, religions, governments, and educational and economic systems. They are not intended to usurp the moral foundations of Western society, but are offered as a mid-course correction like amendments to the US constitution.

Concept Patterns—A metaphor to describe the multidimensional blueprints of any idea. They serve as potentials for action that aren't limited by the boundaries of a "thing." During session breaks, Jane Roberts often sensed entire blocks of material just waiting for her from Seth to translate into spoken language.

Conscious Creation—Another way to say, "You create your own reality"—the phrase coined by Jane Roberts in *The Nature of Personal Reality* (1974).

Conscious Mind—Seth distinguished three primary qualities of the conscious mind—the outer ego, the subconscious, and the inner ego. Each is fully conscious, aware, and sentient based upon its own unique order of perception. Seth consistently refutes the idea that anything is *un*conscious. Your outer ego uses outer senses and reason, your subconscious uses outer and inner senses, and your inner ego uses inner senses to jointly create your own reality. (*See also Constructions*)

Consciousness Units (CUs)—A metaphor for emanations of pure Source Energy—the foundational Primal Cause within All That Is. They are ubiquitous, faster than light, nested "units" of aware-ized energy imbued with a propensity for creating gestalts of action, energy, and matter. Their unique characteristics include dreaming, inner sensing, and natural laws.

Constructions (Primary, Secondary)—Your outer ego in the physical field (Framework 1) is a primary construction created and maintained by your inner ego. Your outer ego, in turn, creates secondary constructions through its perception in the physical field. So the "you" who creates 100 percent of your reality includes the outer and inner ego. (*See also Space Continuum, Idea Constructions*)

Coordinate Points—These "black/white holes" are key functions in the physics of how you create your own reality. They facilitate the translation of Framework 2 source energy (EEs) into physical constructions (QFs) in Framework 1. There are three kinds: absolute, main, and subordinate.

Counterparts—Overlapping "reincarnational selves" within the same entity that share similar periods of history. Reincarnation is more than single series of consecutive lives, but instead a "cluster" of simultaneous multiple incarnations from your entity's perspective. Seth hints that there can be temporary counterpart relationships between people that do not share the same entity. (*See also Reincarnational Selves, Simultaneous Time*)

Dis-ease—Seth's term to show that physical, emotional, psychological, and spiritual illness is self-created. It can serve a variety of fulfilling purposes, some of which are restorative to a more balanced state, some initiate the death experience, and some provide a set of self-imposed constraints in which to experience reality creation (for example, birth "defects").

Dream Bodies—You have three main "bodies" or forms available during sleep and dream states:

1. The **first form** is used in regular dreams, lucid dreams and projections. You can levitate and perceive the past, present, and future on a limited basis.
2. The **second form** has expanded perception. You use this form to participate in group dreams.
3. The **third form** is "a true projection form," in which you can perceive past, present, and future in *other* dimensions as well as this one. You can also experience formlessness—a type of nondual consciousness.

Dream City—Seth encouraged ESP members to build an inner city within the dream state as a destination for group dreamers to jointly explore. As always, Seth made it a playful endeavor, one that promoted creativity, curiosity, spontaneity, and continued dream work.

Dream-Art Science—Emerging disciplines that integrate multiple ways of knowing that include your five senses, reason, and inner senses. Seth provided three exemplars:

- **Dream-art scientist** ~ a generic scientist
- **True mental physicist** ~ a physicist
- **Complete physician** ~ a healer

Dreaming Self—An Aspect of your subconscious mind that uses three dream bodies during sleep states. (*See also Projection Forms*)

Electromagnetic Energy Units (EEs)—Faster-than-light particles within Framework 2 earmarked for physical manifestation that "slow down" to form all matter, guided by the conscious mind and the pineal gland in the brain. Millions compose each atom. EEs are made up of the even "smaller," more fundamental, consciousness units (CUs).

Energy Personality Essence—Seth described himself as an "energy personality essence" who had finished his cycle of manifestation. It means that same thing as "entity." (*See also Entity*)

Entity—Another term for what is traditionally called the soul. It exists "beyond" gender and sexual preference. Other general terms used by Seth to describe the same psychological structure include psyche, inner self, inner ego, source self, and energy personality essence.

Entity Names—A moniker used by Seth for each person's multidimensional identity. He referred to Jane as "Ruburt" and Rob as "Joseph," and also used entity names with ESP class members.

Families of Consciousness—A metaphor to explain how our entities express nine complementary forms of innate intention to form the global collective within Framework 2. Each entity and every one of its physical lifetimes are imbued with variations of nine basic forms of innate intention. These inform your general purpose in every lifetime. (*See also "Before the Beginning" and Sleepwalkers*)

1. **Sumafi** ~ Teachers
2. **Milumet** ~ Mystics
3. **Gramada** ~ Innovators
4. **Vold** ~ Reformers
5. **Ilda** ~ Exchangers

6. **Sumari** ~ Artists
7. **Tumold** ~ Healers
8. **Zuli** ~ Body/Imagers
9. **Borledim** ~ Parents/Nurturers

Feeling-Tones—Every Aspect of All That Is has its own inner tone of consciousness. Just as a clarinet, violin, and electric guitar each have their own tone, we each have our own unique tone. Learning to consciously resonate with your feeling-tone helps you to directly communicate with your entity.

Focus Personality—A term used in Jane Roberts's Aspect Psychology to describe the outer ego or waking personality.

Fragment Personality—See Personality Fragment.

Framework 1—The physical universe, home of your body/mind, space, consecutive time, and the tip of your "iceberg self." Every object and all processes are idea constructions made of QFs, which form the thin outer physical "crust" of our reality. Local laws of cause and effect operate here in full force.

Framework 2—Source Energy as CUs/EEs originates here and gets earmarked for transformation into QFs by your entity. It operates as a spacious present in which space and time are simultaneous. Your entity's inner ego operates here to maintain physical life. The dream state and altered states serve as the "connective tissue" between Frameworks 1 and 2. Framework 2 is traditionally thought of as "heaven" and Plato's "world of ideals." The dead "awaken" here first. Some laws of cause and effect operate here to help them transition according to their belief systems. (*See also Strands of Consciousness*)

Framework 3—The main period of after-death transition occurs here. The dead move into this area to access all of their reincarnational selves and counterparts. They can explore probable realities by traveling through Framework 2, and into those probabilities connected with earth realities. This is where Seth and Ruburt [Jane's entity] initially interacted to engage a Seth session in Framework 1.

Framework 4—The source for other nonphysical realities that have little to do with space, time, or anything familiar within Framework 1. Your entity makes the decision to engage a "reincarnational cycle" here. This is also a "gateway" to Seth II, Life

Clouds and other more "inward" Aspects of All That Is that "seed" all four Frameworks.

Frameworks of Consciousness—A metaphor to explain how All That Is consists of a multiverse of complementary physical and nonphysical domains.

God of Jane—Jane Roberts's democratic way to personalize your entity as your direct connection to All That Is. The "God of You" levels the playing field, eliminates spiritual middle-men, and reinforces the belief that no single individual can ever claim to speak in Absolute terms for God to the exclusion of all others.

High Intellect—The superb blend of deep intuitions and reason that produces new cognitive abilities. This approach integrates multiple ways of knowing based upon your physical, mental, and inner senses.

Idea Constructions—All ideas originate in nonphysical Frameworks of consciousness that get transformed by your entity into physical constructions of matter and energy. Jane Roberts also wrote an essay in an altered state called *The Physical Universe As Idea Construction* (1963). This was Seth's first attempt to consciously contact her. (*See also Camouflage, Constructions*)

Impulses—An important avenue of direct communication from your entity designed to lead to your deepest fulfillment. However, impulses can be repressed, dissociated, or blocked which can have disastrous results and lead to addictive, abusive, and violent behavior on individual and collective scales. The goal is to learn to accurately discern and follow your authentic impulses.

Inner Ego—see Entity.

Inner Self—see Entity.

Inner Senses—Deep intuitions (commonly called the "sixth sense") that complement your five physical senses and reason. Used primarily by the entity at full strength, the outer ego can learn to manipulate these to engage a spectrum of altered states. There are three main groups: conceptual, empathic, and time-based. (*See also Appendix 1, Altered States*)

1. Inner Vibrational Touch (empathic)
2. Psychological Time (time-based)
3. Perception of the Past, Present, and Future (time-based)
4. The Conceptual Sense (conceptual)

5. Cognition of Knowledgeable Essence (empathic)
6. Innate Working Knowledge of the Basic Vitality of the Universe (conceptual)
7. Expansion or Contraction of the Tissue Capsule (empathic)
8. Disentanglement from Camouflage (conceptual)
9. Diffusion by the Energy Personality [Essence] (time-based)

Karma—See Reincarnation.

Laws of the Inner Universe—see Natural Laws.

Life Cloud—A metaphor used in Seth's creation myth to explain how Framework 1 was "initially" seeded. These are powerful progenitor "clusters of consciousness" that explore probabilities for maximum value fulfillment and contain ever-changing sources of creativity. When we dream, sleep, or think, we add to the experience of a Life Cloud.

Lucid Dreams—A type of dream state in which your outer ego becomes awake in a dream body. They can be used as a source of recreation, therapy, invention, or exploration. They also prepare you for the after-death experience, because you will exist in a form of your dream body. (*See also Out-of-Body Projections*)

Lumania—The second of three technically advanced civilizations "before the time of Atlantis." They also engineered an elaborate series of underground cities, and in this sense were the original "cavemen." Lumanian art was superior to ours because of its elaborate use of technology and their highly developed psychic skills.

Magical Approach—An approach to the art of creative living that emphasizes your intuitions, feelings, and subjective abilities. It promotes a deeper connection to the biorhythms of the natural world and the natural time of sunrises/sunsets, tides, and seasons. (*See also Natural Approach*)

Master Events—The collective Source Energy within Framework 2 that fuels all events throughout history in Framework 1. For example, the Creation of the universe and Christ drama were master events. (*See also "Before the beginning," Christ Drama*)

Moment Point—The present moment, the now.

Natural Aggression—A natural psychological mechanism whose intent is to communicate feelings of transgression in order to avoid further violence. In larger terms, a flower bursting forth from its bud, a butterfly emerging from its cocoon, or a human birth all involve a natural aggression which is the creative impetus toward action, growth, and fulfillment. It is not to be confused with artificial or pseudo-aggression and the related violent outbursts of blocked impulses.

Natural Approach—The combination of the intuitive practices of the traditional worldview (body, mind, soul, and spirit always work together), and the rational practices of the modern worldview (scientific method provides clear results) to synthesize a new, postmodern approach to reality creation. Seth is not talking about regressing to religious dogma and superstition, but integrating the knowledge of Spirit known by the spiritual traditions, and the strengths of modern science, to create a brand new approach based upon their best practices. (*See also High Intellect*)

Natural Compassion—An emotion derived from our animal heritage's innate biological sense of well-being. It underlies our ability to empathize or walk a mile in another's shoes. The emotions of natural compassion and natural guilt also produced an innate sense of violation that fueled ethical behaviors (innate justice) in our dawn ancestors. (*See also Natural Guilt, Violation*)

Natural Grace—A transparent, joyful acquiescence that is an essential part of all existence. Our bodies grow naturally and easily from the time of birth, not expecting resistance but taking their miraculous development for granted, with a great, gracious, creatively aggressive abandon. We are all born into a state of grace. Therefore, it is impossible for us to ever leave it. We share this "original blessing" with the animals and all other living things. We cannot "fall out of" grace, nor can it ever be taken from us.

Natural Guilt—Our innate moral intuition that holds the corporeal sense of justness, mutual understanding, and integrity that leads to maximum value fulfillment between all living creatures. It is our innate knowing that there is never a need to kill or destroy more than we need for physical sustenance. When we violate this integrity, we experience an inner knowing that the next time a similar situation occurs that we need not repeat a previous action. Natural guilt does not require penance or punishment, just a knowing that we crossed a line and should not repeat the behavior. (*See also Artificial Guilt*)

Natural Hypnosis—The acquiescence of the subconscious to conscious belief as the subconscious accepts those orders given to it by the outer ego. We constantly serve as our own subject and hypnotist, giving ourselves suggestions that constantly reinforce our belief systems. "You get what you concentrate on." (*See also Belief Systems*)

Natural Laws—These are not the scientific laws like gravity or the speed of light, but based upon the inner laws of the universe that are intended to guide all Aspects of All That Is to their maximum fulfillment. It stresses cooperation over competition, and safety, love, and compassion as traits intended for individual and collective well-being.

1. **value fulfillment**
2. **energy transformation**
3. **spontaneity**
4. **durability**
5. **creation**
6. **consciousness**
7. **capacity for infinite mobility**
8. **changeability and transmutation**
9. **cooperation**
10. **quality depth**

Natural Time—Guides the seasons, planetary, plant, and animal cycles and actions. Following the rhythms of natural time allows us to be in touch with our planetary, seasonal rhythms, all of which reflect the manifestation of inner rhythms that are geared to promote the deepest value fulfillment in all species. (*See also Clock Time/Assembly-line Time, Natural Approach*)

Nuclear Self—An expanded version of Seth's subconscious mind found in Jane Roberts's Aspect Psychology that reached far deeper than anything earlier psychologists like James, Freud, or Jung had discovered. It creates the physical body but also manages all probable bodies and events from birth to death for each lifetime. (*See also Subconscious*)

Officially Accepted Reality—As cultures evolve over time, a center of gravity or collective worldview emerges to embrace all the belief systems considered normal and abnormal, good and bad, healthy and pathological, etc. Historically, in Framework 1 terms, this center of gravity has evolved from traditional to modern to postmodern. Each period of history, then, consists of belief systems that form the consensus reality of the culture. (*See also Unofficial Information*)

Outer Ego—If we use an iceberg analogy to represent the conscious mind, then the outer ego represents the surface or physical portion that "protrudes" into Framework 1, drawing upon the source energy of the inner ego through the inner senses. This Aspect relies upon the outer senses and reason to manipulate in physical reality. It forms your sense of individuality, your center of gravity of various personality traits, discerns conditions in the physical world and makes decisions accordingly. (*See also Conscious Mind*)

Out-of-Body Projections—You have three dream bodies that you employ during various dream states (first, second, and third form). You may experience your dream body separating from your physical body (first form). Each subsequent body moves further "inward"—away from physical constructions—and engages more use of your inner senses. (*See also Inner Senses, Lucid Dreams*)

Perennial Philosophy—Philosopher Godfrey Leibniz (1646-1716) coined the term "Philosophia Perennis." Aldous Huxley made it famous in *The Perennial Philosophy* (1945), and religious scholar Huston Smith showed its continued relevance to postmodern worldviews in *Forgotten Truth* (1992). It expresses the common themes found in all the world's mystical traditions.

1. Framework 1 is not the only reality, because there is a nonphysical "source field" which is not usually perceived by the physical senses.
2. As long as we never experience our source we live in a world of separation, illusion, and impermanence (idea constructions).
3. We can, however, learn to directly experience our source, within and without, through the use of our inner senses.

Personagram—The term used in Jane Roberts's Aspect Psychology to describe what Seth called a bridge personality. (*See also Bridge Personality*)

Personality Fragment—A type of secondary construction used to explain related phenomena like out-of-body projections, poltergeists, and so on. It can also apply to counterparts. (*See also Constructions, Counterparts*)

Plane—A term used early on to describe a Framework of consciousness. (*See also Frameworks 1, 2, 3, 4*)

Practicing Idealist—A person who seeks to make the world a better place through the actualization of their own ideals. They understand that the difference between idealism and fanaticism is that the end never justifies the means. It means "thou shalt not kill in the pursuit of your ideals."

Primary Constructions—see Constructions.

Primary Pyramid Gestalt—Another term for All That Is, Seth's term for what is traditionally referred to as God. Seth also used the terms Primary Energy Gestalt, and Pyramid Energy Gestalt.

Probable Realities—Each life you live creates a "wrapper" or psychological boundary around a pool of probable events and selves so that your entity can explore all your potentials and abilities. You may learn to interact with them through use of your inner senses.

Probable Selves—Each lifetime creates probable selves that split off into parallel universes. In this sense, your entity is a multidimensional "cluster" of personality potentials.

Projection Forms—see Dream Bodies.

Pseudo Forms—A type of secondary construction used to explain related phenomena like out-of-body projections, poltergeists, and so on. (*See also Constructions*)

Psychic Manifesto—A poem by Jane Roberts in which she declared her independence from the limited definitions of the soul and God by traditional religions and modern science.

Quantum Fields (QFs)—The basic building blocks of all physical matter and energy, the basic stuff of Framework 1.

Rational Approach—Based upon clock and assembly-line time, it promotes an over-reliance on reason alone, of over-thinking and endlessly analyzing a problem to seek its solution.

This in turn often reinforces its manifestation and blocks more natural solutions based upon natural time and the magical approach. (*See also Magical Approach, Natural Approach*)

Reincarnation—Your entity is a source self that manifests multiple simultaneous lifetimes. Since your entity is also immersed in simultaneous time—Frameworks 2, 3, 4, and inward—there is no finished past or preordained future, no absolute cause and effect, no consecutive reincarnations, and no karma in the traditional sense.

Reincarnational Selves—When your entity engages a cycle of manifestation, it creates individual selves throughout a matrix of past, present, and future histories. Therefore, you exist as one reincarnational self in relation to all the others. When they overlap in historic periods, they are called counterparts. (*See also Counterparts*)

Root Assumptions—What we conventionally believe to be universal laws or scientific laws, but are actually only local to Framework 1 constructions, for example, the law of gravity or speed of light. (*See also Blueprints for Reality*)

Secondary Constructions—see Constructions.

Sethics—A made-up word used to explore how your innate moral intuition consists of natural compassion, grace, guilt, and sense of violation.

Seth Material—The name given to the thirty books by Jane Roberts that were dictated by a transpersonal source named Seth, and transcribed and edited by Robert Butts. It is the second most visited collection and the only metaphysical body of work archived at Yale University's Sterling Memorial Library in New Haven, Connecticut.

Seth—An "energy personality essence" who has finished his cycle of physical lifetimes (Seth also used the word *entity* to describe the same structure). In terms of Aspect Psychology, Jane Roberts likened Seth to a "psychic telegram" from her entity, one that came with a complete, though temporary, personality structure called a "bridge personality." Seth is really a composite of elements, a temporary construction that takes on the form of recognizable human characteristics. These include emotions, facial expressions, gestures, sense of humor, and even an accent, all to communicate within our cultural framework.

Seth II—A wider, more inward personality channeled by Jane Roberts. It is asexual, exists beyond our definitions of male and female, and yet provides the "blueprints for reality" that make genders possible. Seth II spoke slower and had a more distant vocal tone because "it" didn't use emotions or belief systems in its native dimension. Seth II functions as a kind of future Seth made of multitudinous selves, many of which have never been physical. (*See also Blueprints for Reality*)

Simultaneous Time—A paradoxical metaphor used to describe how your entity exists within multiple space-time frameworks to manifest multiple lifetimes. This forms a "spacious present" in which nine basic dimensions are available within any moment point (Present/PRESENT):

Past/PAST	Present/PAST	Future/PAST
Past/PRESENT	**Present/PRESENT**	Future/PRESENT
Past/FUTURE	Present/FUTURE	Future/FUTURE

Sleepwalkers—Part of Seth's creation myth that described our progenitor entities as families of consciousness who functioned within a "dreamtime" to create Framework 1. In that sense, they function as the "designers" of physical reality. They in turn were created "before the beginning" by the thoughts and dreams of All That Is. (*See also "Before the Beginning," Families of Consciousness*)

Source Self—A term used in Jane Roberts's Aspect Psychology to describe the functions of your entity. (*See also Entity*)

Space Continuum—Each primary construction creates its own unique space continuum of secondary constructions. In Seth's example, if five people were present at a Seth session, and Jane put her glass of iced-coffee on the table, there would actually be five glasses, one for each secondary construction created by each person. The notion that an individual glass exists independently of a perceiver, "out there somewhere," is inaccurate. (*See also Constructions*)

Spacious Present—See "Unknown" Reality, Simultaneous Time.

Speakers—Aspects of our entities whose purpose is to provide helpful inner knowledge for the development of all civilizations. They function as inner translators of master events and teachers throughout every period of history. In terms of religious iconography, nonphysical Speakers have been known as "guardian angels."

Spontaneous Self—Another term for inner self, soul, or entity, which is the source of all impulses meant to promote your deepest fulfillment. (*See also Entity*)

Strands of Consciousness—Framework 2 functions like a vast telecommunications network in which hidden portions of your entity are in instant contact with all others. Every thought, action, and desire ripples instantaneously throughout, seeking the best outcomes for all involved. They send out filaments of intent and desire that seek out similar strands based on inner "laws of attraction and repulsion" to manifest mutually beneficial events. In this way, everything and everyone are interconnected. (*See also Framework 2*)

Subconscious—If we use an iceberg analogy to represent your entity, then the subconscious is the buffer zone between the air (outer ego) and water (inner ego) that provides a psychological gateway between the outer and inner egos. Its primary job is to process vast amounts of physical data like digestion, cellular activity, breathing, heart rate, etc. (*See also Nuclear Self*)

Sumari—A trance language expressed as poetry, singing, pantomime, and math. Sounding like a Romance language, its purpose is to structure inner experience in such a way as to resist being translated into stereotypical belief systems. Also, it is one of the nine families of innate intention that Seth, Jane, and Rob belonged to. (*See also Families of Consciousness*)

Thought-forms—A type of secondary construction used to explain related phenomena like out-of-body projections, poltergeists, and so on. (*See also Constructions*)

Time Overlays—As master events get translated from Framework 2 into the events of history in Framework 1, time overlays function like overlapping chapters in a book. They are not limited to consecutive time. Since all pasts, presents, and futures are intimately connected in the vast communications meshwork of Framework 2, a future self may influence the past self, and vice versa, when fueled by a master event. This is how fresh action can emerge in the past, present, or future. (*See also Master Events*)

True Dreams from the Gates of Horn—A type of therapeutic dreaming that's not targeted to a specific dis-ease, but is used to mine helpful information from your subconscious. Traceable to the Egyptians, Greeks, and Romans, they can be used to recognize invisible beliefs, and harmonize and energize your being.

UFOs—An acronym that stands for *unidentified flying objects*, usually associated with alien visitation from other planets, dimensions, or times (past, future).

"Unknown" Reality—Framework 1 is the known reality of space and time, cause and effect. Frameworks 2-4 form the "unknown" reality that exists within a spacious present without space or time. It is home to your entity, and also the name of a Seth book. (*See also Simultaneous Time*)

Unofficial Information—As you gain familiarity with subconscious imagery in altered and dream states, you become aware of alternate and probable realities that may bleed through into waking state. For instance, in the midst of mundane activities, you may begin to experience clairvoyant imagery, clairaudient sounds, and even telepathic communications.

Value Fulfillment—A natural law emphasized throughout the Seth Material—an innate quality of Consciousness that promotes the maximum development for each individual in relation to All That Is. It provides the impetus toward all creative action in physical and nonphysical terms. In this way, individual growth, creativity, and happiness are innately nurtured by every Aspect of All That Is in a joint cooperative effort for the maximum benefit of one and all. This is one way that Seth expresses *divine love*, one that transcends yet includes human love. (*See also Natural Laws*)

Violation—The emotions of natural compassion and natural guilt produced an innate sense of violation that fueled ethical behaviors (innate justice) in our dawn ancestors. Therefore, a lie, a sex act, a scientific expedition may or may not be a violation, because it depends on the context of each situation. While normal aggressive thoughts are not a violation, committing a violent act to your own or someone else's body or spirit is. As such, killing anyone even in self-defense is a violation whether it seems justified or not. (*See also Natural Compassion, Natural Guilt*)

Worldviews—The sum total of all intention, behavior, cultural values, and social systems from which any individual or civilization creates their reality, living or dead, in waking or dreaming states. There are three main cultural worldviews whose belief systems influence global reality co-creation: traditional, modern, and postmodern. Worldviews may also be accessed in altered states. (*See also Belief Systems*)

Appendix 1: The Nine Inner Senses

Here are the inner senses in the order originally given in *The Early Sessions: Book 1 of the Seth Material* (1997). For an excellent summary, see *The Seth Material* (2001), Chapter 19, pp. 275-288.

1. **Inner Vibrational Touch** (empathic)—Used to merge with any object or thing in your sensory field, a kind of expanded super-touch-sensing. This leads to an expansion of experience, greater understanding, and compassion. Empathy is a superficial outer materialization of this inner sense.

2. **Psychological Time** (time-based)—Used as a mental gateway, in alpha state, to the inner world, inner ego, and other selves. All communications through the inner senses exist in psychological time. It's also used in the dream state and is the starting point to learn more about the other inner senses.

3. **Perception of the Past, Present, and Future** (time-based)—Used to simultaneously perceive temporal aspects of any concept pattern or inner blueprint. It allows you to see through the apparent barrier of time, seeing things as they really are. This is used in precognitive experiences and by the inner ego to directly experience concept patterns, freeing them from the limits of cause and effect.

4. **The Conceptual Sense** (conceptual)—Used for comprehending the deeper essential nature of any concept or idea. It involves experiencing a concept completely, to the extent of *being* a concept completely. We cannot truly understand or appreciate

any other thing unless we can become that thing. Otherwise we only receive an approximation translated through the filters of our physical senses.

5. **Cognition of Knowledgeable Essence** (empathic)—A deeper, more abstract form of inner vibrational touch. It does not involve the cognition of a concept. If, for example, we wanted to understand a relative or friend, this inner sense would enable us to literally enter into our friend and share and perceive their essential feelings. This sense in no way involves invasion. It does not imply that one inner ego can control another. It involves direct, instantaneous cognition of the essence of being.

6. **Innate Working Knowledge of the Basic Vitality of the Universe** (conceptual)—Similar to instinct, only much deeper. It's the spontaneous inner knowing of how things work, the innate knowledge that makes manipulation of energy from one form to another possible. It is used constantly by the inner ego to create and maintain space-time frameworks. It directs our physical growth, forms the cells of our physical bodies, and is the source of all revelatory knowledge, inspiration, and invention.

7. **Expansion or Contraction of the Tissue Capsule** (empathic)—Used to manipulate our energy field boundary—the tissue capsule—and allows us to change scale and merge with micro to macro aspects of self and the universe. It is used in projections of consciousness and lucid dreaming.

8. **Disentanglement from Camouflage** (conceptual)—Used to temporarily break up physical constructions, for example, suspending the laws of physics via levitation, teleportation, or shapeshifting.

9. **Diffusion by the Energy Personality [Essence]** (time-based)—Used by the inner ego to initiate the birth of one of its personalities in physical life.

Appendix 2: A Jane Roberts Bibliography

Seth-dictated books by Jane Roberts
(In order of original publication)

1. Jane Roberts, *Seth Speaks*, Amber-Allen, San Rafael, CA, 1994.
2. Jane Roberts, *The Nature of Personal Reality*, Amber-Allen, San Rafael, CA, 1994.
3. Jane Roberts, *The "Unknown" Reality, Vol. 1*, Amber-Allen, San Rafael, CA, 1996.
4. Jane Roberts, *The "Unknown" Reality, Vol. 2*, Amber-Allen, San Rafael, CA, 1996.
5. Jane Roberts, *The Nature of the Psyche*, Amber-Allen, San Rafael, CA, 1995.
6. Jane Roberts, *The Individual and the Nature of Mass Events*, Amber-Allen, San Rafael, CA, 1995.
7. Jane Roberts, *Dreams, "Evolution," and Value Fulfillment, Vol. 1*, Amber-Allen, San Rafael, CA, 1997.
8. Jane Roberts, *Dreams, "Evolution," and Value Fulfillment, Vol. 2*, Amber-Allen, San Rafael, CA, 1997.
9. Jane Roberts, *The Magical Approach*, Amber-Allen, New World Library, San Rafael, CA, 1995.
10. Jane Roberts, *The Way Toward Health*, Amber-Allen, San Rafael, CA, 1997.
11. Jane Roberts, *The Early Sessions, Book 1 of The Seth Material*, New Awareness Network, Manhasset, NY, 1997.
12. Jane Roberts, *The Early Sessions, Book 2 of The Seth Material*, New Awareness Network, Manhasset, NY, 1997.

13. Jane Roberts, *The Early Sessions, Book 3 of The Seth Material*, New Awareness Network, Manhasset, NY, 1998.
14. Jane Roberts, *The Early Sessions, Book 4 of The Seth Material*, New Awareness Network, Manhasset, NY, 1998.
15. Jane Roberts, *The Early Sessions, Book 5 of The Seth Material*, New Awareness Network, Manhasset, NY, 1999.
16. Jane Roberts, *The Early Sessions, Book 6 of The Seth Material*, New Awareness Network, Manhasset, NY, 1999.
17. Jane Roberts, *The Early Sessions, Book 7 of The Seth Material*, New Awareness Network, Manhasset, NY, 1999.
18. Jane Roberts, *The Early Sessions, Book 8 of The Seth Material*, New Awareness Network, Manhasset, NY, 2000.
19. Jane Roberts, *The Early Sessions, Book 9 of The Seth Material*, New Awareness Network, Manhasset, NY, 2002.
20. Jane Roberts, *The Personal Sessions, Book One of the Deleted Seth Material*, New Awareness Network, Manhasset, NY, 2003.
21. Jane Roberts, *The Personal Sessions, Book Two of the Deleted Seth Material*, New Awareness Network, Manhasset, NY, 2003.
22. Jane Roberts, *The Personal Sessions, Book Three of the Deleted Seth Material*, New Awareness Network, Manhasset, NY, 2004.
23. Jane Roberts, *The Personal Sessions, Book Four of the Deleted Seth Material*, New Awareness Network, Manhasset, NY, 2004.
24. Jane Roberts, *The Personal Sessions, Book Five of the Deleted Seth Material*, New Awareness Network, Manhasset, NY, 2005.
25. Jane Roberts, *The Personal Sessions, Book Six of the Deleted Seth Material*, New Awareness Network, Manhasset, NY, 2005.
26. Jane Roberts, *The Personal Sessions, Book Seven of the Deleted Seth Material*, New Awareness Network, Manhasset, NY, 2006.
27. Jane Roberts, *The Early Class Sessions, Book 1*, New Awareness Network, Manhasset, NY, 2008.
28. Jane Roberts, *The Early Class Sessions, Book 2*, New Awareness Network, Manhasset, NY, 2008.

29. Jane Roberts, *The Early Class Sessions, Book 3*, New Awareness Network, Manhasset, NY, 2010.
30. Jane Roberts, *The Early Class Sessions, Book 4*, New Awareness Network, Manhasset, NY, 2010.

Seth-related books by Jane Roberts
(In order of original publication)

31. Jane Roberts, *How to Develop Your ESP Power: The First Published Encounter With Seth*, Lifetime Books, Hollywood, FL, 1997. (Also called *The Coming of Seth*)
32. Jane Roberts, *The Seth Material*, New Awareness Network, Manhasset, NY, 2001.
33-35. Jane Roberts, *The Oversoul Seven Trilogy*, Amber-Allen, San Rafael, CA, 1995. (Originally published as three separate books 1973, 1979, 1984)
36. Jane Roberts, *Adventures in Consciousness*, Moment Point Press, Portsmouth, NH, 2005.
37. Jane Roberts, *Dialogues of the Soul and Mortal Self in Time*, New Awareness Network, Manhasset, NY, 2001.
38. Jane Roberts, *Psychic Politics (An Aspect Psychology Book)*, Moment Point Press, Portsmouth, NH, 2000.
39. Jane Roberts, *The World View of Paul Cézanne: A Psychic Interpretation*, New Awareness Network, Manhasset, NY, 2003.
40. Jane Roberts, *The Afterdeath Journal of an American Philosopher: The World View of William James*, New Awareness Network, Manhasset, NY, 2001.
41. Jane Roberts, *Emir's Education in the Proper Use of Magical Powers*, Hampton Roads, Newburyport, MA, 2000.
42. Jane Roberts, *The God of Jane: A Psychic Manifesto (An Aspect Psychology Book)*, Moment Point Press, Portsmouth, NH, 2000.
43. Jane Roberts, *If We Live Again, Or, Public Magic and Private Love*, New Awareness Network, Manhasset, NY, 2001.
44. Jane Roberts, *Seth, Dreams and Projections of Consciousness*, New Awareness Network, Manhasset, NY, 1998.
45. Jane Roberts, Abridged by Richard Roberts, *A Seth Reader*, Vernal Equinox Press, San Anselmo, CA, 1993.

46. Jane Roberts, *The World View of Rembrandt*, New Awareness Network, Manhasset, NY, 2006.

Seth-related books by Susan M. Watkins
(In order of original publication)

47. Susan M. Watkins, *Conversations With Seth, Book 1: 25th Anniversary Edition*, Moment Point Press, Portsmouth, NH, 2005.
48. Susan M. Watkins, *Conversations With Seth, Book 2: 25th Anniversary Edition*, Moment Point Press, Portsmouth, NH, 2006.
49. Susan M. Watkins, *Speaking of Jane Roberts: Remembering the Author of the Seth Material*, Moment Point Press, Portsmouth, NH, 2001.

The Seth Audio Collection ~ ESP Class Sessions
(Published by New Awareness Network, Manhasset, NY.)

1. *Your Unlimited Power*
2. *Tuning into Probable Realities*
3. *Love and Hate - Understanding Your Emotions*
4. *Abandoning Yourself to Your Spontaneous Being*
5. *Dream Reality and Out of Body Experiences*
6. *Reincarnation, Simultaneous Time and the Multidimensional Self*
7. *The Safe Universe*
8-39. *Various Topics from ESP Class*

Appendix 3: Seth-related Resources

Publishers of Seth-related Books

Amber-Allen Publishing: www.amberallen.com
New Awareness Network: www.sethcenter.com
Moment Point Press: www.momentpoint.com
Hampton Roads: www.hamptonroadspub.com
New World Library: www.newworldlibrary.com

Conferences and Workshops

California Seth Conference: www.californiasethconference.com
Colorado Seth Conference: www.coloradosethconference.com
Maine Seth Conference: www.mainesethconference.com
New Awareness Network: www.sethcenter.com
NewWorldView: www.newworldview.com
Seth Network International: www.sethnet.org

Books on the Channeling Phenomenon

Michael Brown, *The Channeling Zone: American Spirituality in an Anxious Age*, Harvard University Press, Boston, MA, 1997.

Arthur Hastings, *With the Tongues of Men and Angels: A Study of Channeling*, Holt Rinehart and Winston, Orlando, FL, 1991.

Jon Klimo, Foreword by Charles Tart, *Channeling: Investigations on Receiving Information from Paranormal Sources*, North Atlantic Books, Berkeley, CA, 1998.

Sanaya Roman, *Opening to Channel: How to Connect with Your Guide*, HJ Kramer, Novato, CA, 1993.

Index

D

Darwin, Charles, 114, 131,
199, 216, 241
Darwinian Beliefs, 216-217
Death, 86, 210-213, See also
Transition
Discernment, 7
Dis-ease, 53, 63, 71, 74, 75,
84, 86, 143, 169, 200,
210, 212, 215, 216, 217,
218, 219, 221, 249, 283g
Divine Love, 55-61-, 66,
111, 114, 142, 186-187,
192-194, 206, 211, 261,
*See also Value Fulfill-
ment*
Dream Bodies, 76-77, 88,
92, 116, 133, 160, 212,
283g
Dream City, 152, 160, 162,
283g
Dream-Art Science, 161,
284g
complete physician, 163,
284g
dream-art scientist, 162,
284g
true mental physicist, 163,
284g
Dreaming Self, 57-58, 69,
71, 76, 80, 87, 101, 284g

E

EEs, See Electromagnetic
Energy Units
Einstein, 14, 30, 97, 166
Electromagnetic Energy
Units, 37-40, 47, 68, 80,
87, 89, 97, 99, 108-109,
113-114, 120-124, 138,
162-164, 186, 205, 284g
Elias, 13
Energy Personality Essence,
10, 284g
Entity, 5, 6, 10-13, 20-22,
29, 33-39, 41, 47-52, 56-
60, 65, 68, 74, 76, 78-81,
84-101, 119-123, 125,
127, 132, 136-143, 145-
147, 157, 162-164, 171-
172, 193-195, 202, 204,
210-211, 230-235, 239,
244-245, 251-252, 260,
264, 284g
Entity Names, 20, 56, 284g,
See also Joseph, Ruburt
Ethics, 201, *See also Sethics*
Evil, 91, 95, 115-116, 118,
140, 168, 188-189, 194-
196, 198-202, 231

F

Families of Consciousness,
27-28, 101, 113, 284g
Fanaticism, 184, 223-224,
228
Feeling-Tones, 8, 22, 25-26,
36, 69, 129, 133-134, 193,
285g
Focus Personality, 234, 285g
Fragments, See Personality
Fragments
Framework 1, 108-115, 119-
131, 136, 139, 142, 153-
154, 158-176, 184-188,
192, 195-196, 203, 208,

About the Author

PAUL M. HELFRICH, Ph.D., has explored the Seth Material for more than thirty years. He has been a regular attendee of Seth conferences and related gatherings since 1996, and was the admin for the Sethnet email list from 1998-2009. He has been a regular presenter at East and West coast Seth conferences, including Seaside, OR (1998), Elmira, NY (1999), S2K, San Diego, CA/New Haven, CT (2001), Colorado Seth Conference (2006-2009), California Seth Conference (2010) and LA Seth Conference (2009-10).

He has authored essays, presented workshops, and lectured nationally on the Seth Material, the channeling phenomenon, and Integral Psychology.

His *Mindscapes* music CD (2003) is also available on *iTunes*, *Rhapsody*, and *CDBaby*.

A percentage of his royalties from this book are being donated to:

- *Institute of Noetic Sciences* (www.ions.org)
- *Integral Institute* (www.integralinstitute.org)
- *Anthroposophical Society* (www.anthroposophy.org)

Join Me Online:

www.facebook.com
www.paulhelfrich.com

NEWWORLDVIEW

Provider of educational media and programs that artfully help you realize your unique purpose in life—the source of your greatest fulfillment.

www.newworldview.com

6096680R0

Made in the USA
Charleston, SC
13 September 2010